NATIVE AMERICAN HIGHER EDUCATION IN THE UNITED STATES

NATIVE AMERICAN HIGHER EDUCATION IN THE UNITED STATES

CARY MICHAEL CARNEY

TRANSACTION PUBLISHERS
NEW BRUNSWICK (U.S.A.) AND LONDON (U.K.)

This book is printed on acid-free paper that meets the American National Standard for Permanence of Paper for Printed Library Materials.

Library of Congress Catalog Number: 99-14822
ISBN: 1-56000-417-7
Printed in the United States of America

Library of Congress Cataloging-in-Publication Data

Carney, Cary Michael.
   Native American higher education in the United States / Cary Michael Carney.
      p. cm.
   Includes bibliographical references (p.   ) and index.
   ISBN 1-56000-417-7 (alk. paper)
   1. Indians of North America—Education (Higher)—United States. I. Title.
E97.C34   1999
378.1'982''97—dc21   99-14822
                                                    CIP

For my parents,
Robert V. and Billie Jean Carney

Contents

Acknowledgements

Whoever first coined the term "independent research" either had never done any, or was a master of the oxymoron. A more keenly felt collective peering over one's shoulder cannot be imagined. I wish to express my sincerest appreciation to Dr. Dave Webster of Oklahoma State University for his constructive guidance, excellent editing, and infectious friendship. My sincere appreciation also extends to Drs. L. Nan Restine, Lynn Arney, and L. G. Moses of OSU, whose guidance, assistance, and support were also invaluable. I also wish to thank Dr. Martin Burlingame, Theda Schutt, Brenda Brown, and the rest of the faculty and staff of the OSU Department of Educational Administration and Higher Education, as well as those of Edmund Low Library at Oklahoma State University, McFarlin Library at the University of Tulsa, the Oklahoma State Historical Society, the library at the University of Minnesota at Minneapolis, and the library of Dartmouth College.

Not that the list of those deserving acknowledgment for their support and encouragement ends there. Deserving of special mention are Drs. Adrienne Hyle, Molly Tovar, Mary Jane Warde, and Tom Stone of Oklahoma State University. Particular gratitude goes out to long-suffering friends Dana Christman and Matt Runs-Above, and to that most excellent and incisive companion of endless trips back and forth across Oklahoma, Celia Stall-Meadows. Impromptu visits to Bacone yielded unexpectedly plentiful assistance, not to mention new friends, in the persons of Dr. Marlene Smith, Professors John Williams, Mary Lou Ziegenfuss, Ann Marie Shackelford, and Librarian Frances Donelson.

Finally, I would like to thank my parents and my wife, Pam, for encouragement, love, and understanding throughout this whole process. And, last but not least, special thanks to Jeff and Gail Huber, proprietors of the best unofficial rest stop of the Oklahoma highway system. I am surprised the collective sigh of relief at the completion was not audible across the land.

Preface

Many phases of Native American education have been given extensive and adequate historical treatment. Works are plentiful on the boarding school program, the mission school efforts, and other select aspects of Native American education. Higher education for Indians, however, has received little attention. Select articles, passages, and occasional chapters touch on it, but usually only regarding selected topics or as an adjunct to education in general. There is no thorough and comprehensive history of Native American higher education in the United States. It is hoped this study will satisfy such a need.

The subject of this study is the historical development of higher education for the Native American community, specifically within the continental United States, from the age of discovery to the present. Although, strictly speaking, the colonial period predates the United States, the society and culture of the nation as well as several of its more prominent universities stem from that period. Consequently, the colonial period is included due to its important contribution to subsequent developments.

The history of Native American higher education is seen as comprising three eras: The colonial period, featuring several efforts at Indian missions in the colonial colleges; the federal period, when Native American higher education was largely ignored except for sporadic (and frequently interrupted) tribal and private efforts; and the self-determination period, highlighted by the recent founding of tribally controlled colleges.

It is reasonable at this point to raise the question of why a study on Native American higher education. In those libraries with more extensive Native American material, such volumes can run well into the thousands, Within these are major works by DeJong, Debo, Deloria, Prucha, Szasz, Tierney, and many others that treat various aspects of Native American culture, history, and relations with the federal government and white society with penetrating insight, laced with passion and detailed analysis.

As a result, many phases of Native American education have been given extensive and adequate historical treatment. Material is plentiful on the boarding school program, the mission school efforts, and other select aspects of Native American education.

Higher education for Native Americans, however, has received little attention as a topic in its own right. Material on it, even by these authors of such standing and significance in telling the Native American story, tends to be found in select articles, passages, and occasional chapters within larger works or subjects.

Most such material exists as an adjunct to a discussion of Native American general education or relations with white society. Some selected higher education topics, such as the colonial college efforts or the experience relative to specific colleges, have been treated independently. However, it is apparent that the overall story of Native American higher education has yet to be told concisely or comprehensively. It is hoped that this study, albeit clearly a first effort, will help fill such a gap. It is further hoped that it will prompt others to strive to advance knowledge and analysis in this area, to improve on what is presented here.

Mike Carney
Independence Community College
Independence, Kansas
September 24, 1998

1

Introduction

*[The purposes of Harvard College are] The aduancement
of all good literature, artes, and sciences.
The aduancement and education of youth in all manner of
good literature, Artes, and Sciences.
All other necessary provisions that may conduce to the
education of the English and Indian youth of this Country
in knowledge; and godliness.*

—Harvard College charter, 1650

*[William and Mary College has among its purposes] that
the Church of Virginia may be furnished with a seminary of
ministers of the Gospel, and that the youth may be piously
educated in good Letters and Manners, and that the
Christian faith may be propagated amongst the Western
indians, to the Glory of Almighty God.*

—William and Mary College charter, 1693

*[Dartmouth College would exist] for the education and
instruction of youths of the Indian tribes in this Land in
reading, wrighting, and all parts of Learning which shall
appear necessary and expedient for civilizing and Chris-
tianizing Children of Pagans as well as in all liberal Arts
and Sciences; and also of English Youth and any others.*

—Dartmouth College charter, 1769

With these statements, three of the original nine U. S. colleges founded
during the American colonial period embraced the education of the indigenous Native American population as central to their purposes. A
fourth, the College of New Jersey (Princeton) did not formally name
Indian education as a stated purpose, but did admit a few Indian students during the same period.

These original nine schools (Harvard, William and Mary, Yale, Pennsylvania [Philadelphia], Princeton, Columbia [King's], Brown [Rhode

Island], Rutgers [Queen's], and Dartmouth) represent the beginning of what would grow to be one of the largest, most diverse, and arguably the best system of higher education of any nation in existence. With such an apparent substantial level of interest and involvement in American Indian higher education during this early period, one might expect to find that Native American higher education had likewise subsequently grown and expanded to similarly impressive heights.

However, the record does not support such an inference. In spite of these professed goals and the construction of specific buildings to house the Indian colleges on the campuses of William and Mary and of Harvard, the number of Indian students to attend and to graduate from these early colleges during and subsequent to the colonial period is not particularly impressive. Harvard had only five Indian students with one graduating in the 1650–1693 era during which its Indian college existed, and only one more Indian student by 1776 (Smith, 1950; Weinberg, 1977).

William and Mary's record of Indian education is less clear due to the loss of records in a 1705 fire (Szasz, 1988). Several students likely attended, but the majority were preparatory, not college. The only years with evidence of Indian enrollment are 1705–1721, and show little activity. The Brafferton Building to house its Indian college was built in 1723, thirty years after the founding of the college, and no Indian students enrolled and were housed there until 1743, a full twenty years later (Wright, 1988). Only five or six Indian students attended William and Mary after the building of Brafferton until the Indian college was closed in 1776 (Wright and Tierney, 1991), for a total of sixteen students overall (Belgrade, 1992), with none taking the baccalaureate degree.

Dartmouth, the colonial college that has the strongest "Indian college" tradition attached to its founding (Axtell, 1981; Szasz, 1974), had only twenty-five Indian students with three graduating prior to 1800 (Belgrade, 1992), and thirty-three more with eight graduating prior to 1893 (Wright and Tierney, 1991). In fact, right up until the present day, from 1769 until 1973, Dartmouth records only 187 Indian students, with twenty-five graduating (Weinberg, 1977).

Some summary descriptive statistics can reveal how dismal the colonial record is regarding Indian higher education. Prior to the American Revolution (1800 in the case of Dartmouth), these three institutions professed to be devoted to providing higher education to Native Americans for a combined total of 240 academic years. During that time, their official records account for a total of forty-seven Indian students in attendance, with only four graduates. As will soon be discussed in far greater detail, virtually every instance of professed devotion to Indian higher education by the colleges during the colonial period was actually an exercise in fund raising or in access to funds requiring an Indian mission.

As unimpressive as the colonial period was regarding higher education for Indians, it would prove to be a high point for interest in and effort toward Native American higher education, not to be equalled until the 1960s. With the birth of the new nation, the administration of most aspects of Indian life, including education, passed to the U. S. federal government. And just as quickly, if apparently as something of an afterthought, the focus shifted from higher education to a consistently low level of vocational training (Wright and Tierney, 1991). In fact, this shift in focus may have been partly in response to the limited results of colonial attempts at Indian education (Wright and Tierney, 1991).

From the Revolutionary War until the 1960s, higher education for Native Americans languished, largely ignored during this extended period when the focus of Indian education was on relatively low level agricultural, industrial, and domestic training combined with religious instruction. For roughly the first hundred years, until the 1870s, Indian education was carried out mostly by various religious missions, often with funds made available by the federal government as provided by various treaty provisions (Layman, 1942). Thereafter, the government established what would become a reasonably extensive system of boarding schools, day schools, and reservation schools (Prucha, 1984). Little, if any, change in the curriculum was forthcoming, other than possibly a shift from favoring the religious training toward that of the vocational areas (Adams, 1995).

During the nineteenth century, this nation experienced an explosion of college founding, as state, regional, and local boosterism, combined with the later land grant legislation, prompted many communities to seek to establish local colleges, seen as necessary for economic and civic growth, not to mention pride (Potts, 1977; Rudolph, 1962; 1990). This same period saw the advent of numerous specialty colleges. A number of women's colleges were founded, particularly before the concept of co-educational campuses took hold. And, after the Civil War, a number of separate and not-terribly-equal colleges for blacks were founded, including several that would overcome the burden of racism and prove academically respected and prestigious in their own right.

However, the founding and development of institutions of higher education for Indians appears to have been not so much denied, as simply overlooked. Little such activity, successful or otherwise, seems to have occurred. A number of colleges grew out of lower-level Indian schools, academies, or seminaries. But in most such cases, concern for the attraction of sufficient numbers of students caused the founders to establish their colleges for and open enrollment to all, not just Indians. Given the very low minority levels of Indians in the population, particularly those prepared to enter college, such moves had the effect of instantly making the new college a part of the country's educational mainstream, not a traditionally or culturally Native American institution. In such cases, the Indian student population quickly found itself in a minority position, often by a substantial margin, if not quickly and totally absent. At the turn of the twentieth century, only two colleges were operating that exclusively served Native Americans (Beck, 1995), and they were both quite small.

From the founding of the nation to the "New Deal" administration of Franklin Roosevelt, nearly the only attention paid to Native American higher education beyond these two schools was the occasional provision of funds for scholarships or loans to support individual Indian students in the Eastern colleges. Some funds were provided by religious groups, some by the federal government, including as part of occasional treaty provisions, and some by specific tribes themselves, particularly the Cherokee and Choctaw. But such funding programs bore little resemblance to the individual financial support programs of today. Nothing in the way of support systems, counseling, or recruitment programs existed to seek out and assist what today we would call "at-risk" students.

A major turning point was the Indian Reorganization Act of 1934. The result of a series of reforms toward the appreciation and preservation of Indian cultures in place of a century and a half of federal attempts at elimination and assimilation, the act provided for the reestablishment of tribal governments as a move toward Indian self-government (Deloria, 1993). Regarding higher education, it established a loan fund for Indian college students. In this respect, it was different from what had gone before in degree only. The loan fund was for $250,000 (Szasz, 1974), a piddling amount by today's governmental standards, but quite likely equal to the sum of all that had gone before, all the way back to the first $500 appropriated by the Continental Congress in 1775 to support Indian students at Dartmouth (LaCounte, 1987).

Although the $250,000 college fund associated with the 1934 Indian Reorganization Act marked the turning point in support of Native American higher education, it was not until the post-World War II period that the nation saw a significant increase of Native Americans in higher education, just as it did in college access and attendance for the general public. Various tribes then began supporting higher education, twenty-four by the late fifties, including the establishment of scholarship funds, either with tribal money or by earmarking available federal funds (Szasz, 1974).

Regarding today's Native American presence in U. S. higher education, the *Chronicle of Higher Education* (Sept. 2, 1996) cites a total national enrollment figure of 14,278,790 and a Native American figure of 127,372, representing 0.9 percent of the total. In spite of this apparent parity, Native Americans are arguably the historically least well served of our minorities regarding higher education (Tierney, 1992). An initial awareness of this situation was forthcoming with a Bureau of Indian Affairs (BIA) advanced education survey of 1932 (Szasz, 1974). It found, nationwide, a total of only fifty-two Indians with college degrees, while 385 Indians were then in college and only five schools offered Indian scholarships.

Subsequent investigation found little change through the 1960s. As late as 1963 few Native Americans tried college and were often ill-prepared regarding basic knowledge, cultural barriers, personal support systems, and the development of proper study habits (Szasz, 1974). In 1961, there were only sixty-six Native Americans who graduated from college nationwide. By 1968, this number had tripled, a significant change but still a small figure (Szasz, 1974).

Native Americans remain in a catch-up position regarding higher education at the present time. A majority (55 percent) are in two-year schools, while overall 39 percent of college students are in such two-year schools. Completion figures also lag somewhat behind. 15.5 percent of all college students were awarded degrees in 1996 compared to 10.5 percent of the Native American students (*Chronicle of Higher Education*, 1996, September 2). Of the degrees awarded to Native Americans, 40 percent are associate degrees, compared to 30 percent for blacks and Hispanics, and 20 percent for whites and Asians (Pavel and Colby, 1992). Overall, the proportion of Native Americans with degrees is slightly less than half that of the general population (*Chronicle of Higher Education*, 1996, September 2; Fries, 1987).

In addition to its own significance, the Indian Reorganization Act represented a turning point leading to a number of educational acts and efforts, during and since the 1960s, of a far more self-deterministic nature. Beginning in 1968, the establishment of thirty tribally controlled colleges (four of which have since closed) marks what appears to be a major new era of Native American higher education. These institutions have been encouraged and funded by the Navajo Community College Act of 1971, the Indian Education Act of 1972, the Indian Self-Determination Act of 1975, and the Tribally Controlled Community College Act of 1978, among others.

Today, Native Americans are served by thirty-two traditionally Native American colleges. Three are private, including Bacone, the oldest by quite a margin, and two small Bible colleges. Three more are federally controlled, having developed out of schools in the earlier federal boarding school system. As such, they have long traditions as Indian schools, such as the Haskell Institute, formerly known as the U. S. Indian Industrial Training School since 1884 (*Haskell Indian Nations University Catalog*, 1997). However, their functioning as institutions of higher education extends only from their charters as colleges (Haskell in 1970; Southwestern Indian Polytechnic Institute in 1971; and the Institute of American Indian Art in 1962). The remaining twenty-six are newly established tribally controlled colleges, the first being Navajo Community College, founded in 1968 (*Navajo Community College Catalog*, 1997).

Besides these schools purposefully or traditionally serving Native Americans, there are twenty-five mainstream colleges and universities that offer a range of special cultural, support, or academic programs for Native Americans (*Native Education Directory*, 1993). Included in these is the University of Arizona which, in the fall of 1997, offered the first Ph. D. program in American Indian studies (*Chronicle of Higher Education*, 1996, December 20).

Most of the thirty-two Native American colleges are two-year institutions. Only six offer bachelor's degrees—Sinte Gleska University, Haskell, Nazarene Indian Bible College, American Indian College, Oglala Lakota College, and Salish Kootenai College. Of these, only two, Sinte Gleska and Oglala Lakota, offer master's degrees. The bulk of these degrees are in education and social work/human services, a typical pattern for the initial development of degrees and disciplines within a new population segment of higher education.

An initial interpretation of this preponderance of two-year schools could be that Indian colleges are somewhat stunted and vocational-oriented. However, it seems more reasonable to see this pattern as related to the newness of the schools since only one existed as a college prior to 1962 and only three prior to 1970. Historically, a pattern often seen in the development of higher education institutions is the initial establishment of a normal school, teacher's college, or, since the advent of the junior college in the early twentieth century, a two-year program. In cases of success, this is frequently followed by expansion to four-year and ultimately graduate offerings. If such is the case, the Native American schools are actually progressing normally, even quite well (Stein, 1992), suffering only from a delay of some 200 years over that of the higher education system of the rest of the country. That delay is the focus of this study.

Research Objectives

The purpose of this research is to explore the historical record to ascertain what transpired in Native American higher education from its colonial beginnings to the present day. A wealth of material exists on Native American life and the relationships between Native American and white society since the discovery and colonization of the Americas by the Europeans. Within this body of literature, select aspects of Native American life have been given extensive treatment, including education. Works are plentiful on the mission school efforts, the boarding school program, and other select topics within Native American education. However, Native American higher education has apparently received little attention as a subject in its own right. Certainly there has been nothing in the way of treatment of the history of Native American higher education in a unified sense.

Computer searches of terms such as colleges, universities, or higher education combined with Native American, American Indian, or Indian yield little, and nothing of a comprehensive nature. What literature on the topic exists is found only piecemeal in select articles, chapters, or passages. These usually only cover selected specific occurrences or institutions, or are included as an adjunct to education in general. It is apparent there is no thorough and comprehensive history of Native American higher education in the United States. It is hoped this study will be a first step in satisfying such a need and will prompt others to strive to improve on what is offered here.

In investigating the historical record of Native American higher education in the United States, there are several relevant questions to be addressed. First, what explanation can be found to account for the loss of interest in Native American higher education after the relatively strong beginnings and levels of interest in the colonial period? Second, what factors prevented the Indian population from benefitting from our national predilection to found colleges in general, and specialty colleges in particular, during the late nineteenth century? Third, what factors are present now, over a century after the push to establish other specialty colleges, which support the establishment of the tribal colleges?

Of a structural nature, much, if not most of the literature on the general history of U.S. Indian education divides it into three epochs. Typically, they are the era of evangelical control from 1568 to 1870, federal control from 1870 to circa 1964, and Indian control from 1964 on (Thompson, 1978). Here a similar but different three-epoch structure will be employed, different because of variations that arise from the tendency in the past to not treat higher education separately from education in general.

The first designated epoch in this history of U. S. Indian higher education will be the colonial period. In a strict sense, of course, the United States did not yet exist at that time. However, the culture and society that would become the U. S. certainly did, as did the colleges that would provide the foundation of its higher education system. The colonial treatment of Native American higher education is sufficiently distinctive and important to its later development to stand alone.

The second epoch is that of federal control, from the Revolutionary War to the decade of the 1960s. While much of Indian education was administered by various religious organizations and occasionally even by the tribes themselves for the first hundred years of this period, it was done so with the tacit approval and cooperation of the government, usually with some funding involvement on its part. The control was in the hands of the federal government, regardless of the extent to which it saw fit to exercise, delegate, or abdicate the responsibility.

The third is that of Indian control, beginning with the 1960s. The principal feature of this period is the establishment of the tribally controlled colleges. This marks the first time that the Indians have had local control over their own education, a historical fact of life for virtually every other segment of our society (Gustafson and Knowlton, 1993), but a new and long-delayed experience for them.

Definition of Terms and Concepts

Two terms in particular need to be well defined for the purposes of this study. The first is "higher education." This study is intended to focus specifically on the formation of higher education institutions that traditionally or purposefully serve a predominately Native American population. Other aspects of Native American higher education, such as mainstream schools that offer special programs or financial support for American Indians, will enter into the discussion, but they are peripheral to the issue of interest.

Similarly, technical schools will not be covered, although the vocational nature of the curriculum of some community colleges and past boarding schools may play a role in discussing changing educational objectives. Kindergarten through twelfth-grade education is likewise of no concern here other than of an indirect nature, usually in reference to Native American preparation for college-level education, or to a historical pattern of some K-12 (approximate) boarding schools which evolved into colleges.

The other term needing particular attention is "Native American." Also used interchangeably elsewhere and within this study are "American Indian" and "Indian" when speaking of the Americas only. Use of such a common term or terms nevertheless acknowledges a wide range of differences among tribes and individual people.

Native Americans within the United States population are in a substantial minority position in absolute terms. The 1990 U. S. census gives the general population as 248,710,000. Native Americans represent only 1,959,000 or 0.8 percent of that total (U. S. Bureau of the Census, 1991). More recent estimates give the general population at 262,755,000 and Indians at 2,200,000 (Foster, 1997; *Chronicle of Higher Education*, 1996), still 0.8 percent of the total.

Remarkably, this comparatively small figure represents a rebound of the Native American population. In 1900, the U. S. Indian population reached a low of 237,000. Since that time, it grew slowly until the thirties, and has increased substantially since 1960, nearly doubling in the 1970s. As a percentage of the general population, Indians represented 0.4 percent in 1970, 0.6 percent in 1980, and the above 0.8 percent of 1990 (U. S. Bureau of the Census, 1991).

In part, this growth may be attributed to a flexible definition of who is an Indian. It is anything but a simple question, and one that is decided at several differing and often conflicting or problematic levels. The federal government has been active in denoting who is or is not an Indian for over 100 years. Such official recognition is usually the basis for the funding of various programs, including higher education. Virtually no other racial or ethnic group is in the position of relying on the government for their definition (Bennett, 1990).

The tribes themselves are also very active in defining one's "Indian-ness," and are varied in their approaches, sometimes in disagreement with the government. Some have established policies that seek to maintain the ethnicity of the Indian, being concerned about population trends and studies that make predictions such as only 34 percent of Indians will be "full-blood" by 2000, dropping to 0.3 percent by 2080 (Foster, 1997). Smaller tribes in particular are prone to require one-quarter or even one-half blood (the Miccosukees of Florida) to qualify for membership in an effort to maintain their ethnic distinctiveness. Others, responding to shrinking population figures, relax their requirements to retain or attract tribal members, such as the Apache choosing to drop their minimum from one-eighth to one-sixteenth blood in November 1996 (Foster, 1997).

At the extreme of that policy, the largest tribes often have the least restrictive requirements for membership. Four tribes (Cherokee, Navajo, Chippewa, Sioux) contain 40 percent of the nation's Indians (U.S. Department of Commerce, 1992). The largest tribe, Cherokee with 308,000 members, has a minimal blood requirement, basically requiring only documented descent from a person listed on any past tribal rolls. Since federal funding is often on a per capita basis for a variety of programs and entitlements, many tribes are more than willing to admit those who are only minimally Indian. This pattern was no doubt exacerbated by the tendency in the 1980s for it to be fashionable to claim Indian status.

Such varying requirements for tribal membership also allow a third level of decision making as to who is an Indian, that of individual choice. No doubt a great many people could meet the minimal blood and descent requirements who have simply not made themselves aware of it, or who do not bother to perform the necessary documentation and effort required to enroll on tribal rolls.

Besides the question of which individuals are Indian, the issues of designating to which tribe does one belong and the varying recognition of tribes are similarly complicated. There are about 600 tribes overall in North America (O'Brien, 1989). In the words of Vine Deloria, Jr. (1970), Native Americans represent 1 percent of the population and 50 percent of the diversity.

The federal government effectively only recognizes tribes that have or have had a provable land base, an interesting position for the entity that devoted so many years to relieving tribes of their land. Varying levels of success for efforts toward recognition have shifted this figure over the years, from 481 in 1987 (LaCounte), to 502 in 1989 (O'Brien), and 542 in 1992 (U.S. Department of Commerce). The Department of Commerce (1992) gives population counts for the 542 federally recognized tribes, 366 of which have less than a thousand members each.

Besides the federally recognized tribes, there are some recognized by individual states, the largest probably being the Lumbees of North Carolina (*Dictionary of Indian Tribes of the Americas*, 1980). LaCounte gives seventeen of these in 1987, and O'Brien gives twenty-six in 1989. The remaining, unrecognized tribes may maintain a cultural identity but are not recognized for population or funding purposes (O'Brien, 1989).

2

The Colonial Period

Beginnings

At about 10:00 P.M. on the night of October 11, the Captain himself, looking west from the stern of his flagship, saw the light. It appeared to be "a little wax candle bobbing up and down" (Dunn and Kelley, 1989, p. 73). The crew had recently been on the verge of mutiny, although at the moment they were in good spirits. They had agreed to sail west for only three more days, no more, even though sea birds and bits of vegetation, as well as a carved stick, had been sighted. Knowing he was too eager to offer an end to the voyage and disappointed by two previous false landfalls, the Captain was wary of trusting his eyes. His valet also saw the light when it was pointed out, but others saw nothing (Dor-Ner and Scheller, 1991). Whatever the light might have been at that distance, if it really existed, has never been explained.

At 2:00 A.M., a cannon report from the *Pinta* signalled a landfall, estimated to be six miles away in the moonlight. With three hours until dawn, the decision was made to furl all but the mainsails, and to tack back and forth in the darkness (Dor-Ner and Scheller, 1991). While waiting for that dawn of October 12, 1492, none aboard could have understood the significance of their accomplishment or have conceived of the changes that would result. At first light, Columbus anchored and set off to land.

He unfurled the royal banner and flags of the Spanish monarchs, and charged those in his party "to bear witness that I was taking possession of this island for the King and Queen" (Fuson, 1987, p. 76). In this ceremony, he was following the protocols of the law of discovery. This very Eurocentric use of an earlier Roman practice held that the nation discovering a new land held title to that land (Falmouth Institute, 1992). The inhabitants made little difference, particularly if they were different from the Europeans (and not capable of mounting an effective resistance). Unknown to all concerned, the pattern of white encroachment pushing Native Americans off the land, which would last for centuries, had begun.

There were other witnesses to the event. Even before leaving the ships, Columbus had recorded that "we saw naked people" on the shore (Fuson, 1987, p. 75). While he promptly named these people "Indios," as natives of the Indies, a general term for islands of that latitude, he is presumed to have expected them to be subjects of the Grand Khan of China. We are not informed of when and to what extent he first began to suspect that he was dealing with previously unknown lands and peoples, but it may have been almost immediately. While he went to his grave unaware that he opened the way to two unknown (to Europeans) continents, and later sailed around the Caribbean looking for the passage to China's mainland, he also seemed to feel completely at liberty to claim the land for Spain and to speculate on future relationships with these natives.

Besides lacking clothes, the natives also obviously lacked technology. Columbus notes they were unarmed except for short wooden spears tipped with fish teeth and other natural sharp objects. When he showed one native his sword, the man grasped the blade, cutting himself (Dorner and Scheller, 1991). Columbus began to almost immediately speculate on future relations with the natives, obviously quickly taking what would become the familiar position that these people were savages, and just as quickly giving voice to the duality that would characterize the white treatment of the Indian thereafter. His log records that he hoped for a friendly relationship because he felt "they are a people who can be made free and converted to our Holy Faith more by love than by force. I think they can easily be made Christians." Yet a sense of condescension and threat permeates subsequent entries that "they ought to make good and skilled servants, for they repeat very quickly whatever we say to them," and "with 50 men you could subject everyone [on the island] and make them do what you wished" (Fuson, 1987, pp. 76–80).

Later echoes of this duality can be inferred in the U. S. Government's vacillation between programs of removal versus assimilation, the late nineteenth-century War versus Peace Policies, and the stewardship versus selfdetermination policies of the twentieth century (Prucha, 1984), but its initial expression would be the debate over whether the natives were noble savages, unspoiled, idyllic, romantic examples of mankind; or simply savages, brutish, lazy, and childlike (Bennett, 1990).

Distance affected the viewpoint held. Those who actually were in the new world, and later on the frontier, faced with the threat and occasional fact of disputes and conflict with the Indians, more frequently took the less charitable view. The noble savage image, itself a product of European imagination and egocentrism, was more evident among the stay-at-home Europeans and later among the population located on the U. S. East Coast (Hirschkind, 1983).

Both views contrasted the savage with civility. It is ironic that the European defenders of the natives, while seeing the noble savage as an ideal, uncorrupted model of humanity, sought to transform these people into ideal citizens according to the European-Christian model (Greer, 1993). Assessments of the natives, favorable or otherwise, were made from the perspective of European culture as the ideal, definitely the superior.

It very quickly became apparent that previously undiscovered lands and peoples were being dealt with and, while efforts for trade routes to China were still made, new unanticipated agendas pushed to the forefront. Easily the most prominent was the claiming of these new lands, and subsequent exploitation and extraction of wealth. But another, quickly apparent objective was the conversion and civilization of the natives (Prucha, 1984; Szasz, 1988).

Early reports by Columbus, Amerigo Vespucci, and others were spotty, widely spaced, and often conflicting. Initial reports were usually of timorous, gentle people, later of monstrous, bestial behavior, including reports of cannibalism. Columbus himself first reported a somewhat naive view of the natives as living in a state of primordial innocence. But on his second voyage, he found the garrison he left at La Navidad had been annihilated, giving rise to a much crueler version of the savages in his later reports (Dickason, 1984).

The infrequent, incomplete, and conflicting nature of the stream of reports to Europe led to a wealth of speculation and rumors. Stories circulated that the new lands were variously populated by men with faces in their chests, with dog's faces or heads, with great flat ears that could be used as blankets, and with only one leg and foot. Other tales spread of the natives as descendants of Ham, part-apes, or "wild men of the woods," hairy men very much akin to the later sasquatch-bigfoot-yeti-abominable snowmen legends (Dickason, 1984). Such public reaction to the sparse information bears a striking similarity to modern-day UFO-alien sightings.

It is unfortunate that we have no record of the reaction in the native community to these first sightings. With ships bigger than lodges, white sails that could be mistaken for clouds, and a wide-ranging variety of new and exotic clothing, weaponry, technology, facial hair, and fair hair and skin coloring, the potential for speculation and rumor among the natives far exceeds any impact in the opposite direction.

As reports became more frequent, the information became more mundane and accurate, although it did little to alter the view and subsequent treatment of the natives as savages. The information provided dwelled on aspects seen as negative in the eyes of the Europeans. That the natives ate seated on the ground was quite frequently reported (Adams, 1988; Dickason, 1984). Apparently, the lack of tables and chairs made quite an impression on the Europeans. Also, their use of few if any clothes, that they were polygamous, and had few or no sexual inhibitions in the eyes of the Europeans elicited frequent comment (Dickason, 1984).

When attempts were made to make more meaningful, substantive observations on native social and political structure and culture, the sense that the natives were hopelessly primitive and unsophisticated was still evident. Reports focused on their lack of externalized institutions such as written codes of law or a common religion; or that wars were waged as a means of survival, not over differing political ideologies (Bennett, 1990).

That power and wealth existed in society rather than individuals was particularly noted. A perceived lack of willingness by individuals to acquire and keep wealth, choosing instead to give it away in elaborate ceremonies (Adams, 1988; Bennett, 1990) struck the Europeans as childlike and naive. That their societies did not vest power in their chiefs, who could persuade but not command, made conquest and domination easy for the Europeans. A chief's influence was based on eloquence and generosity, resulting in him often being the poorest in the community. If a rival attracted followers, the option of splitting away was definitely available (Dickason, 1984), resulting in ineffectiveness when faced with the aggressive, efficient nation-states of Europe.

Quasi-scientific attempts were made to prove the natives were savages from these random observations. Lists of characteristics, civil versus savage, were compiled as support for the Eurocentric designation of the natives as savages. Pierre d'Avity, Seigneur de Montmartin, formulated something called "five degrees of brutality" (Dickason, 1984) on which to gauge the level of savageness of the natives. These were observations of (1) the non-use of reason; (2) reliance on hunting/gathering like animals instead of agriculture, as well as particulars of diet and food preparation (eating on the ground again); (3) a lack of morality, and presence of nudity; (4) the types of habitation used; and (5) a lack of (recognizable) government structures (Dickason, 1984, pp 65–68). He omitted dirtiness, cruelty (not surprisingly, given the nature of the current Spanish Inquisition), a lack of writing, cannibalism, and a lack of sexual mores. The last two were frequently reported, but may be included under 1, or 3, lack of reason or morality. Other observers cited the apparent lack of monogamous marriage, the lack of reliance on agriculture for subsistence, the lack of a work ethic, and the lack of private property as the basis for economic and social organization as objective, scientific justification for labeling the natives savages (Adams, 1988). Four hundred years later, Commissioner of Indian Affairs Thomas J. Morgan would still be citing, as objective proof that Indians required civilizing, that "a wild Indian requires a thousand acres to roam over, while an intelligent man will find a comfortable support for his family on a very small tract" (Adams, 1988, p. 17).

There were voices in favor of the natives, of not subjugating, displacing, or dominating them. But the debate on the subject was all but lost in the rush to acquire and exploit the new world. At the heart of this debate was the validity of Aristotle's doctrine of natural slavery (Ross, [1928] 1955). In his concept of subhumans and natural slavery, Aristotle had argued that "a portion of mankind was set aside by nature to be slaves for the service of others...and that, as slaves, this part of mankind did not have property rights" (Duchene, 1988; Hanke, 1969, p. 13). This argument, combined with the native's lack of a concept of private property, was used as a justification of the belief that Europe had a "divine right" to use the new world as it saw fit.

This topic was disputed in a confrontation of scholars and theologians at Valladolid in 1550–1551 (Hanke, 1969). While several argued that the Indians were inferior, thus falling under Aristotle's doctrine, others argued quite eloquently against it. The Dominican friar, Bartolome de Las Casas took the position that "mankind is one, and all men are alike in that which concerns their creation and all natural things, and no one is born enlightened" (Hanke, 1969, p. 11). He compared the "savage peoples" to "uncultivated soil," needing only attention, seeing this as the basis for the belief that the way to civilize them was to bring religion and education to them.

Francisco de Victoria, Spanish theologian, Dominican professor at the University of Salamanca, and one of the first and most important founders of international law (Hanke, 1969), took an even more enlightened view of the natives. He argued that

> Indians must be treated as owners and not disturbed in their possessions. The aboriginals in question were true owners, both from the public and private point of view. (Duchene, 1988, p. 103; de Victoria, [1696]1917)

After further review of the arguments and international law, he concluded that

> the aborigines undoubtedly have true dominion in both public and private matters, just like Christians, and that neither their princes nor private persons could be despoiled of their property on the ground of their not being the true owners. (Duchene, 1988, p. 116; de Victoria, 1696/1917)

Friar de Victoria was supported in this question by Hugo Grotius, Dutch jurist, statesman, and theologian. Grotius declared it impermissible to apply the ancient Roman practice of asserting jurisdiction over a territory simply because it was occupied by a people whose government was different from Rome's (Duchene, 1988; Grotius, 1901). Somewhat later, Roger Williams, the politician, theologian, and founder of the colony of Rhode Island, similarly argued early in favor of the view that the Native Americans had rights, including the right to be paid for land taken from them (Will, 1997). Friar de Victoria even managed to inject a very modern-sounding element of humor into the debate. He once remarked that if a canoe full of Indians had somehow reached Spain and "discovered" it, the fact would by no means justify Indian sovereignty over Spain (Hanke, 1969).

One may see in the positions of de Victoria and Grotius the first hint of a sense of cultural preservation as an important consideration. But the European explorers and colonists managed to overcome this scholarly and legal advice, choosing to adhere to the concept of racial superiority as an excuse to push the Indian from the land. Later the invention of anthropology, in its early stages, provided a conveniently formal, academic, scientific means of justification with its notion of race to classify and label various peoples. Initial and unsophisticated use of the concept created a sort of caste system of humanity (Duchene, 1988).

As with other social institutions, the Europeans saw the natives as lacking a means of education. The Indians had developed an educational process concerned with preparation for life, meeting the demands of society, and transmitting their culture from one generation to another (Otis, 1971). In this, it differed not at all from education around the world. However, it was primarily conducted by the family unit, the extended family, or tribal elders. Sometimes an apprenticeship system of attachment to those with expertise was used. Sometimes the natives employed folk "seminars," discussions, or lectures, free of coercion and bureaucratic rigidity, more than a little like the academy of Plato (Lutz, 1980). Overall, Native American education was so unstructured as to be nonexistent in European eyes. The level of Eurocentrism prevented them from seeing the similarity between Europe's church-oriented education system, primarily concerned with perpetuating European culture, and that of anyone else's, including the Native American's.

Some native cultures, as yet barely discerned by the Europeans, had more elaborate educational structures. The pre-Columbian Aztecs had the *calmecac*, an advanced collegiate or university-style institution for the education of religious and secular leaders (Lutz, 1980). The Mayans and Incas had also possessed similar centers for advanced leadership and religious training. But since such institutions obviously did not transmit European culture, in the narrow view of that time, they hardly qualified as educational in nature.

In education, as in all else, the Eurocentric position dictated what was to come. Early colonists, it cannot be denied, attached importance to native education. But it was education on European terms, assimilationist in concept and curriculum, predicated on the assumption that it was the duty of civilized man to bring enlightenment to the less civilized areas of the world (Robbins, 1974). Early efforts focused exclusively on conversion to and the civilizing influence of the Christian faith. Thus, the drive to deny and destroy Native American cultures, and rebuild them according to perceived Christian principles, began almost immediately (Dickason, 1984). For over four hundred years, the Indians would be the reluctant recipients of a contrived social, political, economic, and religious disruption visited upon them in the name of civilization and Christianity (Robbins, 1974).

Not surprisingly, since the Spanish were more active in the earliest days of contact with the new world, they made the first efforts to establish schools for the natives. The earliest of those efforts was an impressive one, given the immediacy of other concerns such as survival, conflicts with the natives, and simply exploring the new lands. In and around the future Mexico City, beginning in the 1520s, the Spanish conquistadors supported and encouraged the opening of several institutions intended as real colleges for the natives. Their lofty objective was to raise the entire Indian population to a European level of culture in a generation or two (Haring, 1947; Lutz, 1980). The most successful of these was Santa Cruz del Tlaltelolco, an Aztec-oriented university that opened in 1536 with sixty students (Haring, 1947). The students learned Latin and Christian theology, as well as rhetoric, logic, philosophy, and music, all elements of classical European education. The only concession to local culture was the inclusion of Mexican medicine in the curriculum (Haring, 1947).

This institution proved so successful that in 1548, after only twelve years, the school was turned over to the native alumni. Later they even taught Latin to the sons of Spaniards, and began developing a literature of Aztec culture and traditions. In terms of native control and cultural preservation, it may be considered a true precursor to today's tribally controlled colleges. The school lasted another twenty years in this manner (Haring, 1947; Lutz, 1980; Parkes, 1938).

However, in this guise it proved unpopular with the Spanish colonists, who did not wish to see Indians become their equals. After a few decades; due to the combination of the more exploitative goals of Spanish imperialism, this fading of popularity with the colonists, and the growing discomfort of the Spanish priests with such learned natives able to debate the fine points of Christian doctrine; the Spanish ceased to support the school, and it faded from history (Lutz, 1980; Parkes, 1938). To say the least, it was a remarkable start, but it was too soon.

Somewhat later, in 1568, the Jesuits founded a mission school for the Florida Indians. The school was located in Havana and was not, nor was it intended to be, a collegiate, higher-level institution (Oppelt, 1990; O'Brien, 1989; Thompson, 1978). In several respects, the shift from the collegiate Tlaltelolco to the mission school at Havana presaged the direction American Indian education would take. The focus shifted from religious and classical academic study to simple religious instruction. As will be seen, this very broadly is the pattern from the collegiate-level efforts of our colonial period to the vocational-religious training focus in the United States after the Revolutionary War.

Also, the decision to remove Florida Indian students to Cuba may similarly be seen as an early hint of the later U. S. policy right up until the 20th century of favoring removal of the students from the influence of home and tribe as a means of facilitating their acculturation into white society. This pattern of removal of students from their homes would begin early and prove quite durable. In his letters recorded in "The Jesuit Relations," Father LeJeune of Quebec, writing in 1634–1636, spoke of problems in interference by Indian parents and the need to remove the children from the home (Layman, 1942). He also felt the presence of their children in Quebec would cause the Hurons to treat the French well, effectively acknowledging that the children were to serve as hostages.

In a sense, John Eliot based his system of towns of "praying Indians" on similar removal from tribal influence. Beginning in 1637, he began working with captives from the Pequot War, learning their language. By 1646, he was preaching to the Indians in their native language. He developed a sort of commune approach to Indian education and conversion. He set up planned, self-governing towns of Indians, providing instruction in crafts, arts, agriculture, and domestic skills, as well as Christian ethics, letters, Latin, and Greek (Berry, 1969; Layman 1942). The first such town was Natick, where he quickly began to train promising Indian students to become teachers for other, future students. There he also coined his term of "praying Indians" for his converts.

Over some thirty years, Eliot established fourteen such towns, with a total population of 497, mostly in and around the Massachusetts colony (Layman, 1942; Smith, 1950). As successful as they were, given his objectives, they represented almost a third entity in early New England. Set off from and certainly not assimilated into white culture, they were ostracized by the Indian societies as well for having given up their own culture for that of the whites (Berry, 1969; Smith, 1950). They were far too small to represent a real inroad for white culture among the Indians, and likely added to the tensions later evident in King Philip's War and other conflicts.

Much later, in the 1870s when removal was the established overall federal Indian policy, with the advent of the U. S. boarding school system of Indian education, removal from the influences of home and tribe would continue to be central to the educational philosophy being employed (Adams, 1995; Pratt, 1964). Similarly, it would prove no more successful.

Henrico

Activity concerning education for the natives shifted to the English colonies in the early seventeenth century. Education, including higher education, for the Indians was often of concern to the colonists, although the focus was primarily on conversion to Christianity, usually combined with agricultural and vocational training (Prucha, 1984; Wright, 1988; Wright and Tierney, 1991), as evidenced by Eliot's program.

The first attempt to establish a college for Indians was made quite early indeed. Within the first decade of the Jamestown settlement in Virginia, plans for an Indian college were underway (Wright and Tierney, 1991; Wright, 1988). Unfortunately, this first attempt was not successful. Had it been so, it not only would have been the future nation's first Indian college, it would have been our first college overall, usurping Harvard's claim to that honor by fourteen or so years.

A great deal of interest of a social experimental nature existed in England on the subject of civilizing, converting, and educating the natives. In 1609, Robert Gray argued that

> It is not the nature of men, but the education of men, which makes them barbarous and uncivil...and then therefore change the education of men, and you shall see that their nature will be greatly rectified and corrected. (Wright, 1988, p. 3)

This basically is a continuation of the Eurocentric savage image— they live that way because they have not had the benefit of a classical education—and would later be espoused by such luminaries as Thomas Jefferson.

Much of the sentiment in England favored the more informal means of transporting the Indian youth to be reared in English homes (Szasz, 1988). However, the principal objective of providing such education for Indians was to enable them to then return to their own people as missionaries, so they could then teach and convert others (Wright, 1991; Szasz, 1988). The readily apparent inefficiency of transporting limited numbers to and from England led to a growing interest in establishing a college in the colonies for the Indians (Layman, 1942; Prucha, 1984; Szasz, 1988; Wright, 1988; Wright, 1991).

Both approaches were featured on an extended trip to England in 1616–1617 by a party headed by Sir Thomas Dale, governor of the Virginia colony. Included were John Rolfe, Pocahontas, their son, and ten or twelve young Indian women to be educated in England (Layman, 1942, p. 28). Pocahontas, as the first and best known of the early Jamestown Indian converts, served as the major attraction in and around London on this trip to raise funds for Native American education (Wright, 1988; Szasz, 1988). She was so well received that her death on shipboard on the return trip, if anything, had the effect of solidifying the effort (Szasz, 1988).

The avowed plan was to use the proceeds of the trip to construct Indian churches and schools, particularly a planned Indian college to be called Henrico. The name was chosen in honor of Prince Henry, the eldest son of King James I (Layman, 1942).

The trip was quite a success, receiving a substantial boost from the highest possible source. So impressed was King James with Pocahontas that on March 24, 1617, he instructed the archbishops of the Church of

England to collect and send funds to Jamestown for the erection of some churches and schools "for ye education of ye children of those Barbarians in Virginia," charging them to deliver the funds "to the treasurer of the plantation to be used for the godly purpose intended and no other" (Layman, 1942; Wright, 1988; Wright and Tierney, 1991). George Yeardley was named governor of Virginia in 1618, and was given orders "that a convenient place be chosen and set out for...a university...the said college for the children of the Infidels" (Wright, 1988). One thousand acres of land seized from the Indians (the seed of the subsequent revolt?) was platted and set aside for the college fifty miles upriver from Jamestown.

By May 26, 1619, Sir Edwin Sandys, treasurer of the Virginia Company, announced the fund had reached 1,500 pounds (Layman, 1942; Wright, 1988). Of this amount, 700 pounds was in stock in the Virginia Company due to the company having "borrowed" it (Layman, 1942; Wright, 1988). Basically, Sandys seemed to have seen an opportunity to use the money to promote the colony and attract immigrants while postponing the college.

There was some grumbling by knowledgeable donors, but donations continued to flow in, both cash and gifts. Over 1619–1620, the future college was given a communion set, a collection of books for the library, and 550 pounds anonymously from someone signed "Dust and Ashes" expressly to support Indian students (Layman, 1942, pp. 33–36). By 1620, the fund stood at 2,043 pounds plus some acquired property (Wright, 1988).

On February 7, 1620, "Dust and Ashes" wrote the company, expressing dismay at the delay of the college, and demanding that the fund be "speedily and faithfully applied to the use intended for it" (Layman, 1942, p. 36). The donor also promised another 450 pounds to be used to educate Indians in London, or for a free school in Virginia for both English and Indian children.

Sandys, in a report to company directors and stockholders, answered that the money had been invested in an ironworks, the profits of which were to be used to educate thirty Indian children. Governor Yeardley then told of difficulty in securing Indian children to be educated (Layman, 1942; Szasz, 1988). The anonymous donor was later found to be a Gabriel Barber, who was present at the report, but there is no further record of inquiry into the fund or its diversion to company economic schemes (Layman, 1942; Wright, 1988).

In spite of the obvious diverting of funds into the Virginia Company, donations still continued. On April 19, 1620, the estate of Nicholas Ferrar left 300 pounds for the education and support of ten Indians at Henrico. And on a passage from England, 135 pounds were collected on shipboard for the purpose of establishing a preparatory school at Charles City to feed into Henrico (Layman, 1942).

By 1622, the college lands were being worked by settlers, the Reverend Patrick Copeland had been named rector of the as-yet-unrealized college, and George Thorpe had been named deputy in charge of the college lands. Both were actively negotiating with the local Indian leaders, King Lasawpers and his brother, Chief Opechancanough, on the pressing problem of convincing the Indians to send their children to the college. There was even a house being constructed for Chief Opechancanough (Layman, 1942).

Then, on Good Friday, March 22, 1622, the chief led a major Indian uprising against the Virginia settlement, killing 347 including Thorpe and the tenants of the college lands (Layman, 1942; Wright, 1988; Wright and Tierney, 1991). The colony became focused on Indian extermination as its determined policy. Some interest did linger for the establishment of the college for friendly Indians. Also renewed proposals were made (but turned down by Sandys) to send Indian boys to England for education. But interest in both was minimal. With the loss of friendly relations with the natives, the college largely became a dead issue, and disappeared entirely with the revocation of the Virginia Company charter in 1624 (Layman, 1942; Szasz, 1988).

Harvard

The ineffectual experience at Henrico seems to have had no negative impact on the English public's interest in and support for Indian higher education. Plans for a similar college for the natives in New England were being discussed just prior to the founding of Harvard. In 1635, an undated document found in the study of the late Dr. John Stoughton, rector of St. Mary's, Aldermanbury, London, discussed such a similar proposed institution, for the now-familiar purpose of civilizing and converting the Indians. The best estimate for the date of the paper was 1634, just prior to his death (Layman, 1942; Morison, 1935).

There were three societies founded in Great Britain for the purposes of supporting missionary work and education among the Indians and the raising of funds to support those ends. The earliest of these, founded in 1649, was the President and Society for the Propagation of the Gospel Among the Indians in New England and Parts Adjacent (Layman, 1942). Among its early governors was Robert Boyle, the renowned chemist. At his death, he specified that his estate be used for "pious purposes." His executors used the bulk of his estate to purchase the Brafferton estate in Yorkshire, the profits and rents from which to be used thereafter to support Indian students in the colonial colleges.

From this "Boyle Fund," Harvard received an initial 200 pounds, plus forty-five pounds yearly for Indian education and missionary work. Later, William and Mary College received a sizable grant with which to build its Indian college, and fourteen pounds per year to support Indian students from this same fund (Layman, 1942; Szasz, 1988; Weinberg, 1977).

The other two societies were founded somewhat later. They were the Society in Scotland for Propagation of Christian Knowledge, founded in 1700; and the Society for Propagating the Gospel in Foreign Parts, 1701 (Layman, 1942).

When Harvard was founded in 1636, no mention was made of Indian education as one of its purposes. However, the ongoing public interest in it seems to have awakened such an interest at the college. In 1645, John Eliot sent two "hopeful young plants" to Harvard's President Dunster to be prepared for college (Layman, 1942, p. 70; Morison, 1935, pp. 313–314; Szasz, 1988). Dunster demurred, saying the boys were too young. Even so, Dunster professed to be interested in Indian education. A 1643 promotional tract by the college, "New England's First Fruits," exaggerated the levels of area Indian conversions and promised great strides in Indian education. It recommended that contributions be sent directly to President Dunster, effectively linking Harvard needs to those of Indians (Layman, 1942; Wright, 1988).

It was not until the 1649 founding of the Society for the Propagation of the Gospel in New England, followed shortly by the establishment of the Boyle Fund, that Harvard's interest in Indian education peaked. In 1650, its charter was rewritten to include the purpose of "the education of the English and Indian youth of this country in knowledge" (Morison, 1935; Weinberg, 1977; Wright, 1988; Wright, 1991; Wright and Tierney, 1991). Grants for the building of a hall to house its proposed Indian college were solicited and received in 1651 from both the society and the fund (Layman, 1942; Weinberg, 1977; Wright, 1988).

The Indian college building was not constructed until 1656. It had the capacity to house twenty students. However, it did not house its first Indian student until 1660 and, in the nearly forty years of its existence, it housed only four students total. It instead served to house English students, as well as the campus printing press. In 1693, the building was razed, with its bricks salvaged to be used for construction of another building (Belgrade, 1992; Szasz, 1988; Weinberg, 1977; Wright, 1988). In exchange for the bricks, Harvard promised that future Indian students "should enjoy their studies rent free in said building" (Layman, 1942, p. 75; Weinberg, 1977). This never came to pass.

Harvard records only six Indian students in all the prerevolutionary war period, including four during the 1656–1693 existence of its Indian College building. Besides being so few in number, they were also a particularly starcrossed group, with five of the six dying during or just after their attendance at Harvard.

The first was John Sassamon (Sarsamon), who was sent to Harvard by John Eliot and attended in 1653. He later served as an interpreter of the Indian King Philip. He was killed by King Philip on suspicion that he had divulged the war plans of the upcoming "King Philip's War" to the English (Layman, 1942; Oppelt, 1990; Smith, 1950).

In 1660, two Indian students came to Harvard, Caleb Cheeshahteaumuck and Joel Iacoomis (Hiacoomis). Cheeshahteaumuck became the first and only Indian to take a degree from Harvard in the colonial period, in 1665. He was fluent in four languages—Latin, Greek, English, and his own (Algonquian), and by all appearances quite an accomplished scholar. However, he died within a few months of graduating from "consumption" (Layman, 1942; Wright and Tierney, 1991).

His classmate, Iacoomis, like Sassamon, had the misfortune to be killed by other Indians. Returning from a trip to Martha's Vineyard to visit his family, his boat ran aground and Iacoomis was cast ashore near Nantucket. Unfriendly natives in that area reportedly killed him (Layman, 1942; Smith, 1950; Szasz, 1988).

The same year that Cheeshahteaumuck graduated, the next Indian student, John Wompowess (Wampus, Wompuss) arrived at Harvard. However, he stayed only one year (Layman, 1942; Smith, 1950; Szasz, 1988). Harvard's fifth Indian student, the fourth (and last) of its "Indian College" period, was known only as Eleazar, arriving in 1674 (Layman, 1942; Smith, 1950; Szasz, 1988). He died while in school.

The last colonial-period Indian student at Harvard was Benjamin Larnell (Lornel), in 1712 (Layman, 1942; Smith, 1950; Szasz, 1988; Weinberg, 1977). He is referred to as an Indian only in reference to his efforts to remain close to the campus and gain readmittance to the school after his dismissal due to some unnamed infraction (Smith, 1950). Apparently he was successful in gaining readmission since, like Eleazar, he died while still in school in 1714 (Weinberg, 1977).

William and Mary

The same year that Harvard tore down its Indian college building, 1693, saw the founding of William and Mary College. A 1691 draft of its proposed charter made no mention of Indian education. However, it soon became apparent that it would be profitable to do so as a means of qualifying for support from the Boyle Fund (Weinberg, 1977). Consequently, the 1693 charter included the reference "so that the Christian faith may be propagated amongst the Western Indians" (Layman, 1942; Szasz, 1988; Wright, 1988; Wright and Tierney, 1991). This was the first effort in support of Indian education in Virginia since the 1622 uprising that sealed the fate of Henrico (Layman, 1942).

William and Mary's relationship with the Boyle Fund was quite similar to that of Harvard. Indian students were to be funded at fourteen pounds per year, and the school received a grant to construct a building for its Indian school. This building was named the Brafferton and was not completed until 1723, thirty years after the founding of the college. It was for an Indian college that effectively did not exist (it had no students at that time) and would house none until 1643, twenty years later (Layman, 1942; Szasz, 1988; Wright, 1988; Wright and Tierney, 1991).

The William and Mary effort at Indian education was twofold. On campus there was the Brafferton for the Indian college itself, as well as a grammar school to prepare Indian children for future college work. This school was known variously as the Fort Christiana School, the Boyle School, or simply the Indian grammar school at William and Mary (Szasz, 1988).

Dr. James Blair, the college's first president, began what would be a very aggressive, if not necessarily fruitful, policy of recruiting students for the duration of the Indian college (Weinberg, 1977). Exact figures are difficult to arrive at due to the loss of records in a 1705 fire, but generally William and Mary provided schooling for more Indians than did any other higher education institution of that time (Szasz, 1988). However, the majority of the students were in the grammar school. College-level Indian students were few in number, as at Harvard.

The first verifiable evidence of Indian enrollment at the college level was in 1705, with none after 1721. There was never enough to keep one teacher completely busy (Wright, 1988). From 1721 to 1743, there were no Indian students, then only a few at a time until the Revolutionary War (Wright, 1988; Wright and Tierney, 1991). A total of sixteen Indian students attended William and Mary during the colonial era, none of whom took the baccalaureate degree (Belgrade, 1992).

After a slow start, William and Mary's Indian program and recruitment practices, as instigated by President Blair, involved a remarkable blend of progressive thought and foresight coupled with a notable lack of sensitivity. On July 23, 1700, Virginia Governor Nicholson reported to the Archbishop of Canterbury that the college was ready to accept students. He referred primarily to the grammar school, stating they would accept three or four children, providing all their needs and instruction. He also requested funding for an Indian adult to be hired to accompany the students to "talk to them in their own language so that they would not forget the speech of their fathers while they were among the English" (Layman, 1942, pp. 51–52). This was an impressive recognition of and concession to the needs of the students, particularly considering that virtually every other attempt by white society at Indian education for over four hundred years would consciously strive to deny the use of native language as a means of extinguishing rather than preserving their culture (Duchene, 1988; Ellis, 1996; Prucha, 1984).

Frequent commentary over the years expressed concern for the effectiveness of the Brafferton College and argued for possible directions it should take. In a letter of November 17, 1711, to the Council of Trade in London, Governor Alexander Spottswood stressed the inadequacy of the Boyle Fund regarding the provision of a quality education for Indian students. He requested supplemental funds to be raised, particularly through the Society for the Propagation of the Gospel (Layman, 1942).

Somewhat later, in 1724, Hugh Jones, a former faculty member, expressed dismay at the results of the William and Mary Indian education program. He described the problem as minimal results for maximum money expended, and pointed to a problem that would continue to trouble Indian education well into the future. He described his Indian students as having completed their education, only to relapse into their "own savage customs upon returning to their people; or continuing to live in Williamsburg but seldom raising themselves to a higher level, choosing an idle life or jobs as servants" (Layman, 1942, p. 59).

William Byrd, writing in his 1728 "Histories of the Dividing Line Betwixt Virginia and North Carolina," concurred with Jones's assessment. Both alluded to a problem that would continue to be commented upon but never fully recognized for 200 years—the futility of providing advanced education but no corresponding economic development within the Indian community, or effective integration into the white society and economy to provide an avenue for fulfillment of that education (Byrd, 1728; 1961). As a means of furthering an assimilationist policy, education on white terms certainly held promise. However, the assimilationist policy itself lacked follow-through, rendering it so truncated as to be nonexistent past the education phase.

Thomas Jefferson, in his *Notes on the State of Virginia* ([1781] 1904), referred to more effective possible use of the Boyle Fund. He suggested the establishment at William and Mary of a perpetual mission among the Indians, to not only instruct them in Christianity, but "to collect their traditions, laws, customs, languages, and other circumstances which might lead to a discovery of their relation with one another or descent from other nations" (vol. 8, p. 393). Had this plan been carried out, William and Mary would have had the first chair of anthropology on Native American studies in an American college, again a lost opportunity for an early and far-reaching effort at cultural preservation.

Juxtaposed with such ongoing concern and enlightened proposals for the Brafferton school are some remarkable admissions of unusual student recruitment practices, and indications of a lack of interest within the Indian community. In the same 1711 letter by Governor Spottswood, he admitted that it was the custom of the college administration to purchase Indian children captured in warfare to ensure that William and Mary might continue to benefit from the Boyle Fund (Layman, 1942; Weinberg, 1977), effectively paying a bounty for new students.

Spottswood also collaborated with the William and Mary administration by injecting the school into treaty provisions whenever possible. He led the negotiation of a treaty with the Tuscaroras who had attacked in North Carolina. The treaty required that a minimum of two children from each of eight chiefs of Tuscarora towns be sent to William and Mary as hostages to secure the treaty. The Tuscarora refused to comply with such a hostage provision, but it did seem to stimulate some interest on their part in white education. The following year, 1712, there were twenty new Indian boys in the William and Mary grammar school (Layman, 1942). Such provisions in treaties for students at William and Mary to serve as security, signs of good faith, or simply as an educational offering became a commonplace means of recruiting students for the school.

However, judging from surviving responses recorded in treaty negotiations, such recruitment was not well received and usually, if politely,
refused. At a large, multifaceted treaty negotiation between the Six
Nations of the Iroquois and the commissioners of Maryland and Virginia in Lancaster, Pennsylvania in 1744, a number of Indian leaders
quite eloquently expressed their views of English education. Foremost
among these was Conassatego, an Onondaga-Mengwe chief. He arrived in Lancaster accompanied by 230 warriors. In a land dispute between the Delaware and Pennsylvania, Conassatego sided with Pennsylvania (Drake, 1832).

Speaking to the commissioners on the morning of July 4, 1744,
Conassatego sounded like a concerned and somewhat leery parent, expressing disagreement with the English practice of removing students
from the influence of home and tribe:

> We must let you know we love our children too well to send them so great a way,
> and the Indians are not inclined to give their children learning. We allow it to be
> good. And we thank you for your invitation; but our customs differing from yours,
> you will be so good as to excuse us. (Ben Franklin, 1744, Van Doren, ed., 1938, p.
> 76; Wright and Tierney, 1991).

However, the commissioners pressed the issue, wanting six sons of
chiefs, one from each Iroquois nation, to attend William and Mary as a
sign of good faith. Conassatego again responded negatively, this time
emphatically arguing the irrelevance of white education to the Indians
and making a very acerbic counter-offer:

> We know that you highly esteem the kind of learning taught in those Colleges, and
> that the Maintenance of our young Men, while with you, would be very expensive
> to you. We are convinced that you mean to do us Good by your Proposal, and we
> thank you heartily. But you, who are wise must know that different Nations have
> different Conceptions of things and you will therefore not take it amiss, if our
> ideas of this kind of Education happen not to be the same as yours.
>
> We have had some experience of it. Several of our young People were formerly
> brought up at the Colleges of the Northern Provinces, where they were instructed
> in all your Sciences; but, when they came back they were bad Runners, ignorant of
> every means of living in the woods; unable to bear either cold or hunger; knew
> neither how to build a cabin, take a deer, or kill an enemy; spoke our language
> imperfectly; were therefore neither fit for Hunters, Warriors, nor Counsellors, they
> were totally good for nothing.
>
> We are, however, not the less obliged by your kind offer, though we decline
> accepting it; and, to show our grateful Sense of it, if the Gentlemen of Virginia will
> send us a dozen of their sons, we will take Care of their Education, instruct them in
> all we know, and make Men of them. (Langer, 1996; Otis, 1971, p. 23)

In spite of all these efforts and input, positive and less so, response was minimal, resulting in little change in funding and the total of sixteen students by the Revolutionary War. The outbreak of the American Revolution brought access to the Boyle Fund to an end, effectively closing the Brafferton Indian College (Layman, 1942; Szasz, 1988; Wright, 1988). The lists of students from 1776 include the names of Baubes, Gunn, and Sampson, the last Indians to receive their college education from the Boyle Fund (Oppelt, 1990; Layman, 1942).

When Jefferson, as governor, reorganized William and Mary in 1778, Brafferton was listed as a college, but with no mention of Indians (Szasz, 1988). At the Peace of 1783, William and Mary sued for the accumulated rents from the Boyle Fund during the war, but lost in court. Thereafter the Boyle Fund was used for negro education in the British West Indies (Oppelt, 1990; Layman, 1942).

Dartmouth

With Harvard and William and Mary, the first two of the original nine colonial colleges of the nascent United States had professed a commitment to Native American education. Thereafter, a hiatus occurred with the founding of the next six colleges, as none addressed Indian education as an objective, although the College of New Jersey (Princeton) did admit three Indian students. Their first, a Delaware in 1751, died while in school. The second, in 1759, was expelled. The third, in 1773, was forced out of school by the American Revolution due to a loss of funding, an indication of involvement of the Boyle Fund or some other English source (Wright and Tierney, 1991). It was not until the founding of Dartmouth in 1769 that another college expressed a specific Indian mission (Szasz, 1974).

The origins of Dartmouth's Indian mission lay in the experiences of its founder, Eleazar Wheelock, dating back to at least 1733. That was the year that the "Great Awakening" began in New England, the greatest religious revival in the history of the colonies. Wheelock was involved as a Puritan preacher and educator, and was particularly interested in the prospects of saving Indian souls (Layman, 1942). Like so many others of that time, his main purpose was the conversion of Indians to Christianity with education as a means to that end (Smith, 1950).

Wheelock started a boarding school for Indian youth called Moor's Charity School in 1754 (Wright, 1988). It was on property deeded to the school by Joshua More, and supported by a maze of small contributions and grants (Layman, 1942).

Wheelock's method was to remove the students from their native environment and surround them with the Puritan influence of English homes (Smith, 1950; Wheelock, 1765). Basically, he made extensive use of the outing method, similar to that applied later by the U. S. boarding school system. In the Charity school, his curriculum included Greek and Latin, as well as husbandry, apparently a dignified term for farm chores. He later received frequent complaints from students and parents alike about too much time being spent on farm labor and too little on academics (Layman, 1942; McCallum, 1969). In spite of changing hands, More's property was apparently still a working farm.

By 1763, Wheelock's interest was expanding to include the founding of a liberal arts college (Axtell, 1991). He envisioned it as providing the education for Indian missionaries and teachers who could then go back to work among their people (Wheelock, 1765; Wright, 1988). However, he very quickly found himself frustrated by the racist attitudes of colonial citizens. His local efforts at fund raising more often resulted in rebuffs and animosity than in money. One collection plate passed in Windsor, Connecticut, returned with only "a Bullet and flynt" (*Wheelock Papers*, 1763, p. 581). Another attempt resulted in a heated discussion in which the citizens of Middletown stated they saw no hope of converting Indians by anything but "Powder and Ball" (*Wheelock Papers*, 1767, p. 604.1). Such sentiments would prove durable, being echoed in the "only good Indian is a dead Indian" aphorism of more than a hundred years later (Brown, 1970).

Wheelock, like others before and since, came to the realization that better luck was to be found at sufficient distances for the Indian to be perceived as exotic rather than as a threat or obstacle. He resolved to raise funds in England and in this he was helped beyond his wildest dreams by a young Indian protege of his, Samson Occum (Axtell, 1991).

Samson Occum, a member of the Mohican (Mohegan) tribe, was born in 1723 and was converted the Christianity at age sixteen or seventeen (Szasz, 1994). Occum's subsequent schooling was less structured, but nonetheless every bit as effective as that of any who attended the formal institutions. He was easily the preeminent Indian scholar of our entire colonial era.

He studied with Wheelock in Wheelock's home for six years, 1743 to 1747, mastering the various subjects and disciplines of the then-typical English classical education. He was ordained in 1759, and became a teacher and minister among the Montauk Indians of Long Island (Axtell, 1981; Smith, 1950; Szasz, 1994).

Occum was well respected and influential among the Indians. He was involved in the closing of a long-standing conflict (since 1740) over land known as the "Mason Case." This was a dispute over land claims between the Mohegans and Connecticut. The settlement gave all but a 5,000-acre reservation to Connecticut. This result was quite a shock to Occum, and taught him the value of establishing and maintaining legal records:

> I am afraid the poor Indian will never stand a chance against the English in their land controversies because they are very poor, they have no money. Money is almightly now-a-days, and the Indians have no learning, no wit, no cunning, the English have it all. (Love, 1899, p. 123)

Occum later led the tribal coalition to move to Oneida, and took care there to legally register their lands (Love, 1899; Szasz, 1994).

In spite of his education and influence, Occum lived in relative poverty. He was afforded no opportunity to apply his abilities within the white society, and on Long Island had to engage in all manner of odd jobs to provide enough income for his support. He sharpened knives, farmed, made and repaired furniture, and generally lived a hand-to-mouth existence (Axtell, 1981).

Notwithstanding, Wheelock was greatly encouraged by his success in teaching Occum, who would, in fact, be Wheelock's most successful student. This encouragement made Wheelock all the more desirous of attempting Indian higher education on a larger scale (Layman, 1942; Smith, 1950).

In 1765, Wheelock prevailed upon Occum to undertake a fund-raising trip to England, both as a spokesman of the proposed college and an example, the most successful of Wheelock's experience with Indian education (Axtell, 1981; Layman, 1942). Occum agreed, and he, accompanied by the Reverend Nathaniel Whitaker, spent 1766 to 1768 in England and Scotland raising money (Layman, 1942).

The trip was a spectacular success. Occum, much like Pocahontas 150 years earlier, created a sensation. The list of contributors included King George III himself, who gave 200 pounds. The total raised was some 12,000 pounds, easily the largest sum to date for Indian education (Axtell, 1981; Layman, 1942; Smith, 1950; Wright, 1988). The fledgling college was so well funded, it actually caused the Boston and Massachusetts governments to cease their contributions (Layman, 1942; Wheelock, 1775).

However, Wheelock was experiencing disillusionment and discouragement about the efforts of his Indian students and the effectiveness of his Indian missionaries (Layman, 1942; McCallum, 1969; Wright, 1988). He was beginning to think more in terms of the education of whites who could then do mission work among the Indians (McClure and Parish, [1811]1972; Wheelock, 1775; Wright and Tierney, 1991).

This did not mean he lost his appreciation for the fund-raising value of appealing to the English interest in the Indians. While Occum and Whitaker were in England, Wheelock had arranged to sell the Moor's Charity School property and move it to New Hampshire, to the campus of his proposed college (Wheelock, 1775). In writing the charter for Dartmouth College, he had originally phrased it as "for English youth, and also youths of the Indian tribes." In the final 1769 draft, he reversed the emphasis to read

> for the education and instruction of youth of the Indian tribes in this land...and also of English youth and any others...(Layman, 1942; Wright,1988; Wright and Tierney, 1991)

The move to New Hampshire and start-up of the college was completed by 1770. There was very little Indian representation in the college. Even though his primary interest was now in Dartmouth, Wheelock continued the Charity school and some students did choose to enter the college.

The lack of Indian students was readily apparent. The English trustees of the donated funds were displeased, feeling the focus was now on English students. They demanded separate reports for the Charity school and refused to have anything to do with Dartmouth College (Chase, 1891; Layman, 1942). However, from a distance they were not able to effectively supervise Wheelock who was able to channel funds through or hide college expenses with the Charity school (McCallum, 1969). By 1774, that portion of the fund controlled by the English was exhausted (Layman, 1942; Wright, 1988).

Occum likewise was aware of and distressed by the lack of Indians in this Indian college (Wright, 1988). He complained to Wheelock that the English were crowding out the Indians, citing the example of a boy named Symons (Simms, Simmons) who was turned away because the school was full. Wheelock responded that his focus was on Indian education and he had "not taken a step nor struck a stone but with that view," maintaining he hoped to be able to "support a hundred Indians or *youths designed for Indian service* with a short time" (Layman, 1942, p. 88, italics added). He also acceded to Occum's pleading of the Symons case and enrolled the student, who became Dartmouth's first Indian graduate (Layman, 1942).

Occum felt betrayed in having been used to raise funds for a college now clearly not exclusively or primarily for Indians (Wright, 1988). He pressed his argument with Wheelock:

> Your having so many white scholars and so few or no Indian scholars, gives me great discouragement....Your present plan is not calculated to benefit the poor Indians. (Axtell, 1981, p. 108)

He maintained that the Indians had a valid claim to the funds, stating "we were told we were begging for poor miserable Indians" (Wright, 1988, p. 11).

Occum also realized he had been warned in England but had ignored it. He stated he had been told

> "You have been a fine tool to get money for them, and when you get home, they won't regard you. They'll set you adrift." I am ready to believe it now. (Wright, 1988, p. 11).

Chase, in his 1891 history of Dartmouth, was even more harsh in his condemnation of Wheelock's financial ploys, including his ultimate attempt to pass control of the fund on to his son:

> The charitable collection for Indian education is all expended. Dartmouth is without funds. It was intended that only the interest should be annually spent, but the fund itself is consumed. Though this was primarily designed for Indians, yet the only Indian [*sic*] that has graduated there was obliged to beg elsewhere towards supporting him the last year of his college residence....Such a mixture of apparent piety and eminent holiness, together with the love of riches, dominion, and family aggrandizement is seldom seen. (Chase, 1891, p. 559)

Occum's abilities, however, went beyond mere eloquence. His experience with the Connecticut land dispute, coupled with the reluctance of Scottish contributors to hand over their donations to the English, had enabled him to protect that portion of the fund, known thereafter as the Scottish fund (Lord, 1913). It was far more closely administered and protected for Indian use. Although it had to be applied to Dartmouth tuition and expenses, it was awarded through specific, identified Indian students.

Wheelock fought to gain control of this fund as well. Decades later, in 1817, in the close of the fight for its control, it was adjudicated exempt from the control and jurisdiction of the college trustees, although the four Indians then on the fund were dismissed until the controversy could be resolved (Lord, 1913).

Earlier, at his death, Wheelock had turned Dartmouth over to his son, John, and attempted to will the Scottish fund directly to Dartmouth (McCallum, 1969). This attempt was successfully defended against, after a very long court battle, and the fund was used well into the nineteenth century to finance Indian students (Lord, 1913). Doubtless, Wheelock was not so appreciative of this ultimate indication of his success with Samson Occum.

Dartmouth's record of Indian attendance is somewhat better than that of Harvard or William and Mary, not just in absolute numbers, but due to its existence as a colonial college for only a very short time before the American Revolution. In fact, it graduated no Indians prior to 1776. Prior to 1800, it had twenty-five Indian college students. Three of these graduated: Daniel Simms (Simmons, Symons) in 1777, a Narragansett Indian; Peter Pohquonnoppect in 1780, a Stockbridge; and Lewis Vincent in 1781, tribe unknown (Belgrade, 1992; Layman, 1942; Lord, 1913).

By 1893, the Scottish fund was exhausted, and Dartmouth had only had thirty-three more Indian students, with eight graduates (Axtell, 1981; Wright and Tierney, 1991). In fact, even up to the present day, Dartmouth has had relatively little Indian representation. Between 1769 and 1973, it has enrolled only 187 Indian students, with a total of twenty-five having graduated (Weinberg, 1977), this in spite of the fact that it has maintained a Native American program and retains some popularity among Indian students to the present day.

The "Indian College" tradition that still is attached to Dartmouth survives largely because it fails to distinguish between Wheelock's Moor's Indian Charity School and Dartmouth College itself. Wheelock did found and maintain this well-known boarding school for Indians in Connecticut for fifteen years. He did found Dartmouth in 1769, claiming Indian education as its primary focus. And he did move the Charity school to Dartmouth by 1770 to prepare boys for admission to Dartmouth (Axtell, 1981). Finally, Dartmouth did admit and graduate more Indians than the other colonial colleges. In fact, given the small student body populations of the time, their Indian representation was fairly reasonable. But the two schools were always separate, and had distinctly differing levels of Indian enrollment and involvement.

Overview

A recounting of their activities and records regarding Native American higher education in the colonial era is hardly complimentary to the former Jamestown colony, colonial Harvard, William and Mary, or Dartmouth. Most of their self-generated literature tends toward glorification and piety, but clearly much of a deceptive nature occurred (Morison, 1935; Wright, 1988). An initial exposure to this material can easily give the impression of an unrelieved litany of impropriety, if not outright fraud. However, there are elements and circumstances present that may serve to mitigate, if not excuse, their actions and mollify one's judgment of them.

First, there clearly was a significant level of diversion and misappropriation of funds intended for the purpose of Indian education (Morison, 1935; Wright and Tierney, 1991). However, these are not individuals who elected to embezzle the funds and line their own pockets. In the cases of Harvard, William and Mary, and Dartmouth, they were concerned with founding and ensuring the financial existence of colleges. Only in the case of the Virginia company does such a motivation appear questionable, and that may be because the uprising of 1622 cut off any possible further development of Henrico.

The founding of the colleges as their primary objective may be defended, and one suspects would be done so if these individuals could speak on their own behalf, by two lines of reasoning. First, to benefit the Indians or anyone else, the colleges must simply come into being and remain in existence. Such a practical motivation could well call for the use of any available source of donations, such as the English interest in the Indians, and the admission of any potential students, not just Indians. A college must have students to survive and it would make little financial sense to look to Indians only for support while ignoring the far larger English population.

Second, the securing of English donations intended for Indians, and then employing those funds in a more generalized manner could likely be defended by what is often termed being a necessary evil. The founders needed funds. In the course of establishing new settlements, little was available locally, and those in England were not interested in supporting the colonial efforts themselves. Only regarding the Indians was there sufficient interest to prompt an outpouring of donations. The founders saw themselves as taking advantage of this interest for the broader purpose of establishing their schools, while still maintaining that they were going to benefit the Indians, if not immediately, then eventually.

This defense may be seen as analogous to the present day where university decisions about what research to pursue are often made based not solely on interest, but on what grants may be forthcoming. Or even more clearly, in the case of major universities supporting major (and occasionally embarrassing) football programs, due to their impact on income, exposure, public relations, and alumni support. The benefit to the university is seen as the greatest good.

While reasonable persons may disagree on the acceptability of these defenses, the fact remains that no clearly venal individuals profited personally from these actions. The Virginia company was able to support their economic development, possibly to start their college in the future. Harvard's Dunster and William and Mary's Blair were able to support their floundering colleges. And Wheelock was able to found Dartmouth, all respectable objectives and all involving Indian funds for part of their support. That they had to or chose to do so in this manner instead of by more direct means set the stage for instances of deception, neglect, and self-righteousness (Wright, 1988).

Argument may also be taken with the low numbers of Indian students as being evidence of neglect by the colonial schools of their Indian missions. In absolute terms, certainly few Indians benefitted from the presence of our early colleges. Prior to the American Revolution (1800 for Dartmouth), only forty-seven Indian students are recorded, fifty if you include Princeton. Only one graduated prior to 1776, four by 1800.

Yet, one must place these figures in the context of their time. College education in the seventeenth and eighteenth centuries was extremely elitist, far more so than we are now accustomed to viewing it. It provided a classical education for the sons of wealthy gentlemen and little else. Not only did few Indians go to these colleges, few of the English did as well. Harvard's class of 1771 was its largest in its first 175 years. It was comprised of only sixty-three individuals (Rudolph, 1962; 1990). Indians were clearly in the minority, but not so absolutely so as these bare figures would seem to indicate.

Another important contributing factor to a less than exemplary record of service to Indian students would be resistance to white education within the Indian community (Wright, 1991; Wright and Tierney, 1991). Not that all Indians were resistant to the whites' education. A number of them were interested in it, sought it out, and seemed to believe it may hold the key to both their own future in their rapidly changing world, and to the future of relations between whites and Indians. Obviously, Samson Occum believed in it, both for himself and his people, and clearly took issue with Wheelock's failure to follow through on what Occum felt had been promised. Also the parents and students who complained to Wheelock about too much time spent at farm labor obviously held academics to be valuable.

However, it is probable that in these early years of contact with white culture, more Indians resisted white efforts at education than not. And not without reason. The behavior of the colonists and simply the nature of European education at that time provided several avenues of justification for such resistance. Conassatego had a point.

Resistance of this type has been present throughout the history of white-Indian relations, as sentiments within the Indian community have been split on white education. Some have seen it as necessary and valuable in dealing with the fact of and the need for making a place for oneself in the larger white society. Others, with more than a little justification, have seen it as a threat to the continued existence of the Indian culture and a contributing factor to the demise of a once cherished way of life.

In later years, some examples of such resistance, such as the hope that the whites would simply disappear associated with the Ghost Dance movements of 1870 and 1890 (Thornton, 1987), while honestly and clearly felt, called for a certain level of denial, if not suspension, of reality. However, during the earlier colonial years, resistance to the white culture could be seen as more rational and based on several lines of reasoning.

First, the education offered was not intended to be of practical benefit or use to the individual, not in the usual economic sense. The colonists offered education to the Indian as part of their concern for and desire to convert the Indians to Christianity. Doubtless, this tied the education to the issue of religion for most Indians. Little if any of the education dealt with the purpose of preparation for a viable career or vocation, certainly not in the sense that we know it today.

As if to emphasize this lack of economic impact of education, the white society remained closed to the Indian, educated or otherwise. No jobs, no opportunities, no acceptance in white society was forthcoming for those Indians who engaged in colonial education. Even the very accomplished Samson Occum found it necessary to support himself by menial labor.

There also seems to have been a certain level of reaction within the Indian community against those Indians who accepted the whites' education. Although it does not seem to have been a problem for Occum, the two Harvard Indian students murdered by their own tends to give rise to suspicions regarding the motives of these murders and whether the victims' involvement with the white culture played a role. Also, as previously mentioned, Eliot's system of towns of "Praying Indians" was clearly segregated, from Indian as well as white settlements.

The Indians, as evidenced by Conassatego's comments in 1744, also saw the white education as lacking relevance to their lifestyle. Besides focusing on a foreign religion, offering preparation for no available application or occupation, and making oneself a stranger to one culture while still not being welcomed in another, the white education did not address the real-world practical skills and knowledge known to be important and useful to the Indians. Such a perceived lack of relevance to or concern for Native American culture would easily conflict with any universal sense that education should serve to preserve and transmit culture.

To some extent, this argument against the classical European education as not pertinent to the needs of the Indian society might be interpreted as the beginnings not just of an urge toward Native American educational self-determination, but of a general social questioning of the relevance of education associated with the new nation. Our higher education history has been characterized by not only expansion of its accessibility, but by modification of the curriculum to more closely fit the needs and applications of the student population. It would not be until the efforts of Charles Eliot, during his remarkable forty-year tenure as Harvard's president, and others that we would see the development of the elective system (Rudolph, 1962; 1990). That such a flexible and responsive approach to education was not in existence at that time may be seen as having an impact on the willingness to see value in white education by the Indians of the colonial era.

A final contribution to Indian resistance to white education may have been a general feeling or hope that the whites would somehow withdraw. Much later, during the Ghost Dance movements, this would be a fervent, if unrealistic, hope of many Indians (Thornton, 1987). However it is far easier to envision the whites all piling back into their ships and returning to wherever they came from when they were still only somewhat tenuously established along the eastern shore than when they, their cities, and their railroads were spread from one coast to the other.

The treatment the Indians received from the European and colonial governments may have contributed to any such imperfectly formed hope that the native lifestyle could continue into the future. The interest of the English toward the Indian was primarily concerned with the spread of the gospel (Wright, 1988). In fact, the colonial governments were relatively disinterested in Indian education, leaving it and its objectives mostly to religious groups (Layman, 1942). Little of a subjugation or enslavement nature seemed to be involved, beyond the whites' appetite for land. True, the whites used education for this religious purpose and mostly neglected the Indian concerns, but the Indians were less than interested for the most part and probably were quite comfortable with often being left alone.

The Indians' experience with the European governments involved a certain level of being treated as sovereign equals. They became fairly adept at playing the English and French off each other. Although land disputes would arise and create conflict, the Indians were still primarily dealing with distant governments that had their own land base. This was to change drastically with the American Revolution.

For the Indians, the principal effect of the Revolutionary War was this shift from dealing with foreign governments to a localized one. What had been important or allowable for governments concerned with the maintenance of an overseas empire ceased to be so for a new government occupied with problems of survival and dominance in its own territory (Prucha, 1984; Smith, 1950). Suddenly,they were dealing with a single nation that needed a land base of its own, one that would be taken at the Indians' expense. At just the moment when an army of Samson Occums, schooled in the culture, laws, and procedures of the white world, would have been invaluable to the Indian, the interest in making such training available to Indians was to change drastically. No evidence of a conspiracy exists for the conscious dismantling of higher education for Indians to deny the Native American community such a cadre of advocates in the courts and halls of government of the nation, but the effect was the same.

The white society seemed to have a notably limited view of the value of education for the Indian beyond the issue of religious conversion. With the advent of the new nation, the focus of Native American education by the whites would shift. Where most efforts had been on conversion plus offering a classical higher education, of suspect relevance to the Indians, the new nation would continue the focus on religious training, but move to an extreme concern for very low level agricultural, domestic, and mechanical skills. Training for positions of leadership in society for Indian youth would be available more in spite of than because of the United States government.

Very early in the formative years of the new nation, Jefferson and Washington both would come out in favor of this change of focus. As justification, they would point to the very limited results of the colonial approach to Native American education (Wright and Tierney, 1991). Particular emphasis was placed on the fact of (widely) scattered examples of Indians who had attended the various colonial colleges, with not a single one having apparently made any mark on white (or Indian) society (Jacobs, 1969). That this was influenced by the poor survival rates of colonial era Indian students, that it ignored completely the excellent record and example of Samson Occum, or that it may be seen as more indicative of a lack of social, political, or economic assimilation necessary to enable such education to be profitably applied seems not to have been noticed.

As an explanation for the question of the loss of interest in Native American higher education following the American Revolution, a professed disappointment in the limited results of colonial efforts sounds minimal and insufficient. In the absence of any known argument to the contrary, it seems likely that the stated goal of removing the Indians until such time as they could be assimilated into white society amounted to little more than a rationalization for simply removing them. What assimilation through education as did exist during the subsequent federal period was carried out at such a low socioeconomic level (and so little supported by actual assimilation within the larger society) as to ensure no attraction or desire to participate within the Native American community. Basically, the much ballyhooed assimilationist policy, instead of being supported by an assimilationist educational policy, actually only existed in the area of education. No elaborate reinterpretation of history is required to see that if the nation truly desired to assimilate the Indians, a top-down approach with a comprehensive higher education system was called for. Higher education would have been useful to provide the training of the necessary leaders and role models within the Native American community for such a social shift.

Likewise, any disappointment in the results of colonial higher education regarding Native Americans would seem more logically to have resulted in an expanded effort at such education, not its abandonment. It seems reasonable to infer that the professed desire to assimilate was, at best, overstated, to be left to distant future generations to actually implement.

3

The Federal Period

Federal Policy

The American Revolution brought about radical changes in the relationship of the Indians with the white government. The British and French had dealt with the various tribes as sovereign nations on a government to government basis (Falmouth Institute, 1992). With the establishment of the United States, the tribes were now faced with a domestic government in need of Indian lands to establish and expand its own land base, and one with sufficient strength to enforce such claims.

This new government continued to treat with the tribes much as the European governments had done, but with some newly developed procedures and protocols designed to address the new situation. The first treaty between the new nation and the Indians was signed in 1778, with the Delaware (Falmouth Institute, 1992). This seemed to affirm the tradition of treating tribes as sovereign political entities and opened what is now called the treaty period of U. S.-Indian relations. Over nearly 100 years, from 1778 to 1871, 645 separate treaties were negotiated with the various tribes (Jackson and Galli, 1977).

By negotiating with the tribes, the federal government recognized the sovereign nature of the tribes. This sovereignty was implied by the language of the Constitution. The Constitution gives Congress the power "to regulate commerce with foreign nations, and among the several states, and with the Indian tribes" (Prucha, 1984; Constitution of the United States, 1787, Art. 1, Sec. 8, paragraph 3), thus setting the stage for sovereign nation status. It also mentions Indians twice, both referring to "Indians not taxed" (Constitution of the United States, 1787, Art. 1, Sec. 2, paragraph 3; 14th Amendment, July 9, 1868, Sec. 2, paragraph 1). This would seem to imply immunity from state and federal taxes, and some kind of political allegiance to one's own tribe (Deloria and Lytle, 1984), another implied basis for sovereignty. Much later, such an interpretation was apparently supported by the language of the Indian Citizenship Act of 1924. With this act, citizenship status was granted to all native-born Indians. The act further adds that this does not infringe on their rights as members of their tribes, recognizing a dual citizenship status (Deloria and Lytle, 1984).

After the adoption of the Constitution, it became established procedure by the Treaty of Greenville in 1795 for the executive office to negotiate and sign the treaties, then submit them to the Senate for ratification without consulting the Senate beforehand. Thus the United States used the same legal procedures with Indian tribes that it did with foreign nations, acknowledging a form of autonomous nationhood for the tribes (Prucha, 1984).

Confirmation of Indian sovereignty is found primarily in two Supreme Court cases. In *Cherokee Nation versus Georgia*, 1831, the Court held that a tribe is a distinct political entity, a state, capable of self-management and government, but not a foreign nation. The Court here established the concept of "dependent nations," internal to the United States. These nations had fewer rights. For example, the U. S. could claim their land, and the tribes could not treat with other nations (Falmouth Institute, 1992; *Cherokee Nation versus Georgia*, 1831).

By confirming the fewer rights of "dependent nation" status, the Court was confirming applicable portions of the Treaty of Ghent at the close of the War of 1812, and Congressional legislation limiting Indian trade rights. The Treaty of Ghent ended the British right to treat or trade with U. S. Indians directly, and in 1816 Congress had extended such limitations to cover all foreign nations regarding U. S. Indians (Prucha, 1984).

In *Worcester versus Georgia*, 1832, the Court held that the tribes and the United States, not the states, had jurisdiction over tribal lands (Falmouth Institute, 1992), implying the tribes were elevated over the states and equal with the U. S. in status. In writing his opinion, Chief Justice John Marshall clearly confirmed the sovereign status of Indian tribes:

> The constitution by declaring treaties already made, as well as those to be made, to be the supreme law of the land, has adopted and sanctioned the previous treaties with the Indian nations, and consequently admits their rank among those powers who are capable of making treaties. The words "treaty" and "nation" are words of our own language, selected in our diplomatic and legislative proceedings, by ourselves, having each a definite and well understood meaning. We have applied them to Indians, as we have applied them to the other nations of the earth. They are applied to all in the same sense. (*Worcester versus Georgia*, 1832,, p. 559; Prucha, 1984, p. 57)

The establishment of the "dependent nation" concept was basically the dawn of the paternalistic relationship of the federal government toward the Indian (Prucha, 1984). Thereafter, what became known as the "Indian problem" was seen as an internal and domestic issue, a "trust responsibility" of the federal government (Deyhle and Swisher, 1997). However, the tribe's recognized sovereignty and ability to negotiate with the federal government made the relationship unusual and often difficult to understand (Fink, 1997, June 29; Deloria, Jr., 1991).

The duality of this sovereign yet dependent status may be seen as a manifestation of the white tendency to take polarized and often conflicting views of the Indian, dating back to the earliest noble savage versus simply savage images of the era of original contact. Such dichotomies could continue to characterize the conflicting federal policies driving U. S.-Indian relations throughout our history (Robbins, 1974; U. S. Senate Commission on Civil Rights, 1973).

However, it often seemed as though conflicting perspectives of the Indian would lead to similar conclusions or actions. Thus, both Thomas Jefferson, very receptive to and kindly disposed toward the Indians, and Andrew Jackson, widely known and very proud of his reputation as an Indian fighter, would see removal as the best solution to the "Indian problem" in the early nineteenth century. And, late in that century, as the nation expanded to fill the available land, assimilation would replace removal as the primary policy (Weeks, 1990), and be espoused by Grant, one of the most Indian-friendly of presidents, and Theodore Roosevelt, whose views on Indians were anything but enlightened. The basis for conflicting policy seems to have been similarly conflicting visions of what would be the ultimate destiny for the Indians, whether extinction or assimilation (Adams, 1988).

Jefferson tended to believe, or fear, that extinction might be the case. He believed that Indians were vanishing, noting the shrinkage or disappearance of the tribes of the Powhattan Confederacy since 1607. He saw four reasons for this trend; a combination of small population, the influence of liquor, wars, and the loss of territory. His fourth reason, the loss of territory, he saw as causing the eastern tribes to be absorbed into the western tribes. He also saw this land issue as one of primary U. S. interest due to its land needs, and recognized it would lead to a tangle of legal and moral complications, military conquest, and legal sanctions (Thomas Jefferson, in Lipscomb, ed., 1781; 1904, vol. II). He justified this on the superior claims of civilization and the higher moral good, citing the biblical injunctions to till the earth, and the corresponding theory of Indian improper use of the land (Jefferson, in Lipscomb, ed., 1781; 1904, vol. II). While unspoken, this amounts to falling back on the view of the Indian as savage (uncivilized) and inferior.

At the founding of the nation, both Washington and Jefferson expressed confidence in the Indian's powers of "improvement" (Dippie, 1982). This "improvement" referred to the Indian's capacity to adapt to and adopt the white culture. Jefferson recognized the dilemma of the white need for and Indian possession of land. He saw the solution as one of Indians adopting white lifestyles, enabling them to live off considerably less land:

> While they are learning to do better on less land, our increasing numbers will be calling for more land, and thus a coincidence of interests will be produced between those who have lands to spare, and want other necessaries, and those who have such necessaries to spare, and want land. (Thomas Jefferson to Benjamin Hawkins, Feb. 18, 1803, in Lipscomb, ed., 1904, vol. X)

Jefferson predicted full assimilation of the Indian, including ethnically (Jefferson, in Lipscomb, ed., 1781; 1904, vol. II). His view of racial harmony presupposes that the Indian would be sufficiently attracted to the elements and trappings of white culture that they would experience a simultaneous interest in delivering their lands to the whites.

However, Jefferson's strategy for assimilating Indians into the mainstream of white American society had as one of its principal tactics the removal of Indians from the influence and frictions of the American frontier (Unrau and Miner, 1985). Besides the obvious fulfillment of long-term land needs of the nation, his proposed amendment to authorize the Louisiana Purchase proposed the removal of Indians beyond the Mississippi. He anticipated the use of some of that land to exchange for land previously occupied by Indians (Jefferson, in Lipscomb, ed., 1781; 1904, vol. II).

In spite of being so influential that he gave his name to the era, Jefferson was not able to fully persuade his contemporaries that Indians were or could be rational, intellectual equals (McNickle, 1970). And the War of 1812, with its fierce fighting and Indian alliances with the British, tarnished his view of racial harmony and Indian interest in assimilation (Dippie, 1982). Madison was similarly affected, changing from a benevolent to an adversarial view of the Indians, due to the associations and depredations of that war (Dippie, 1982).

It was not until 1825, at the end of his administration, that President Monroe made the first comprehensive proposal of a removal policy

(Debo, [1940]1968; Dippie, 1982; Mardock, 1971). He envisioned such removal as "voluntary," and advocated two policies. First, he wanted to preserve and civilize the Indian, addressing the issue of their possible disappearance but at a distance. Then, he advocated not allowing them to control more land than they could cultivate (DeRosier, 1970). However, it was left up to Andrew Jackson to actually implement a removal policy.

By Jackson's administration, the assimilationist policies had become very unpopular (Unrau and Miner, 1985). A few true believers persisted, pressing for more economic activity and trade with the Indians, more concentrated reservations to encourage industry, more missionary activity, and the establishment of model Indian communities (Unrau and Miner, 1985). In spite of being considered as more pro-Indian than the removalist policies, it should come as no surprise that Indians were less than enthusiastic about either choice. These assimilationist policies, like those of the colonial period, such as Eliot's towns, seem a peculiar form of assimilation in absentia. The assimilationists wanted the Indians to adopt white lifestyles, methods, and culture, but invariably desired them to do so elsewhere, separate and isolated from the very society into which they purportedly were being assimilated.

Jackson was the first president clearly unfriendly to the Indian cause. He had made his national reputation as an Indian fighter, being credited with the deaths of thousands of Creeks, Cherokees, Seminoles, and others. He was called "Sharp Knife" by the Indians (Brown, 1970), and had been quoted as likening Indians to wolves (Nabokov, 1993). Early on, he had argued against the practice of signing treaties with Indian tribes, labeling it a mistake to so recognize their political existence (Prucha, 1984).

Jackson was inflexible on the issue of removal (Dippie, 1982). He even argued that the prehistoric mound builders could serve as a justification for the whites displacing the Indians, just as the Indians had done so to this "earlier people" (Dippie, 1982). He did build political bridges to the assimilationists. Basically, he coalesced the two policies, presenting removal as a way to give time for the acculturation process to proceed (Weeks, 1990).

In his first message to Congress, in 1829, Jackson recommended that all Indians be removed westward beyond the Mississippi (Brown, 1970), stressing that it was for the Indian's "protection" (Fixico, 1986). On May 28, 1830, the Indian Removal Act made his proposal law (Brown, 1970; Debo, [1940]1968; Falmouth Institute, 1992). Shortly thereafter, the series of removals to Indian Territory of the southeastern Indians began, collectively known as the Trail of Tears. By 1840, this series of removals was complete (Weeks, 1990). Less well known, but every bit as disruptive of Indian societies, the Indians of the Midwest and Great Lakes regions were also removed to the west, eventually to present-day Oklahoma as well.

During the treaty period, the federal government basically had relatively little to do of a direct nature with Indian education, even though education was clearly seen as part of its assumed trust responsibility toward the Indian (Belgrade, 1992; Layman, 1942; Thompson, 1978; Wright, 1991). The government's primary activities concerning Indian education were in the areas of policy and funding.

A nearly unanimous policy shift with the founding of the United States was the concentration on vocational education rather than higher education for the Indians (Belgrade, 1992). Jefferson considered the Indian to be "in body and mind equal to the white man," regarding any differences as environmental (Jefferson, in Lipscomb, ed., 1904, vol. XIV, pp. 136–137). However, he and Washington were affected by the limited results of the colonial colleges, and chose to minimize higher education for Indians in favor of relatively low-level vocational training (Layman, 1942; Wright and Tierney, 1991).

In doing so, they and others set Indian education on a course that would endure for the entire period of federal control. It would severely affect the acceptance of white education by Native Americans, and limit the development of Native American higher education institutions. The persistent effort to provide vocational education to all but a select few Native Americans could be interpreted as having what would later be termed a Marxist quality (Churchill, 1983).

Although Native Americans often see such federally sponsored education as alienating them from the land, strictly speaking, that is a matter of cultural perspective and could be argued in reverse. The Native American perspective interprets being limited to the cultivation of a small tract, instead of free to roam and hunt vast expanses, as such alienation, and often seems to confuse Marxism with capitalism (Churchill, 1983). From a white perspective, such agricultural training is designed to make them all the more involved with and dependent on the land, the antithesis of Marxism.

Indian education, as provided by the federal government, may be argued as Marxist more in the sense that Zwerling (1976) argues that the focus on the "cooling out" function by junior colleges is Marxist.

Zwerling's contention is that, rather than offering an avenue to socio-economic mobility, junior colleges serve to deflate the aspirations of their students, steering them to settle for lower-level job preparation, thus ensuring a steady flow of lower echelon workers for society (Dougherty, 1987; Zwerling, 1976).

This certainly seems the case with the vocational focus of Native American education. The very low level training in agricultural, mechanical, and domestic skills seemed to consign the Native American to positions at the lowest level of white society. It is almost as if the remark of Columbus 300 years previous, about making Indians into servants, was employed to determine federal policy. Coupled with the fact that there was no acceptance, no integration into white society, even at those levels, it should have come as no surprise to anyone that many, if not most, Native Americans would not find white education acceptable or attractive.

In spite of the focus on lower-level occupational training instead of higher education, the basic policy professed as driving Native American education during the federal period was assimilationist. Lower level or not, the presumption was that the students were being trained for livelihoods found in white society. That such an educational policy was in direct conflict with the larger federal policy of removal driving basic white-Indian relations during the early life of the nation seemed not to have elicited comment. From a historical perspective, it may well be that such an assimilationist educational policy was a means of assuaging the assimilationist voices, while the government more actively pursued removal as its primary policy in dealing with Indians.

That Native Americans were not convinced of the value of white education was clearly demonstrated at a June 23, 1796 council held between government officials and the chiefs of the Creek nation. In response to a presentation of the advantages of establishing schools, Chief Cussetah Mico complained that Indian youths educated by whites were often troublesome and worthless to both Indian and white alike (Layman, 1942). His remarks clearly echo the sentiments of Conassatego in 1744. The government officials replied that the cause of difficulties was not the education but that the youths had associated with bad elements during their school period. They, in a rare offer by the government, made the suggestion that better results might be had if the schools were established in the Indian communities. However, although the Indians would later agree and seek their own schools, in this instance that proposal was not well received (Layman, 1942).

In spite of this isolated response, in a broader sense, the lack of local, tribal control of education may be seen as affecting Native American acceptance. Throughout both the colonial and federal periods, the control of Native American education offered by the whites was in the hands of someone other than the Indians, resulting in educational objectives set by outsiders. In the colonial period, the purpose was religious conversion. During the federal period, it was this peculiarly lower-echelon assimilation ("Tribal Colleges," Carnegie Foundation, 1989). Whereas, in virtually every known society, a central purpose of education is the stewardship and passing on of culture, white education as offered to the Indian dwelled on the dissolution of their culture. In the rush to replace it with white culture, Indian culture was ignored or denied, viewed as not worth knowing. In the process, much lore of Indian mythology, knowledge of the Indian management of fisheries, forests, deserts, and other economic settings, and a large segment of American history was lost (Nabokov, 1993). This effort was so pervasive and long-lasting that Indians reasonably feared they would completely lose their cultural identity if they received a "white man's education" (Otis, 1971).

A few voices were heard in opposition to such an overwhelming concentration on vocational education. The chief advocate of broadening the educational offerings to Native Americans was the Reverend Jedidiah Morse (Unrau and Miner, 1985). Morse was commissioned by Secretary of War Calhoun in 1820 to investigate new means of educating and civilizing the Indians (Prucha, 1984). He filed his report in 1822, calling for sweeping changes in Indian education. He proposed family-involved education, with vocational training to be accomplished by local practitioners (a quasi-outing system) located in close contact with white commerce. He proposed that churches and schools be administered by the Indians themselves. Finally, he advocated the founding of a central college for all Indians, to be located on Indian land, and publicly (and well) funded (Prucha, 1984; Unrau and Miner, 1985).

However, such a progressive plan fell on deaf ears. Despite its trust responsibility, during the entire federal period the government maintained no higher education institutions for Native Americans. Higher education provisions for Native Americans during the federal period were limited to a minimum level of funding provided for Indian students to attend the eastern colleges (Layman, 1942). With little in the way of preparation or encouragement, it is not surprising that only rarely were Indians enrolled in college during the nineteenth century (Weinberg, 1977).

Federal policymakers went so far as to question the advisability of even such a minimal level of higher education for Native Americans. In 1844, Secretary of War Wilkins argued that the nation should stop sending the few Indian students to college. He took the position that "a few too highly educated may succumb to selfish acquisition and oppression of the uneducated" (Prucha, 1984, p. 288). This is an ironic position to take on a people once judged to be savages because they were not acquisitive enough by a man who presumably had no argument with higher education for a select few of his own race.

Shortly thereafter, in 1847, Commissioner of Indian Affairs William Medill, in his annual report, basically repeated the argument of Washington and Jefferson against higher education for Native Americans as having had excessively limited results. Medill stated that sending a few away to college had failed to produce the beneficial results anticipated. Consequently, it was his intention to stop funding such students and use the funds to support lower- level boarding schools on Indian land (Prucha, 1984).

Federal activity in Native American higher education during the early years of the nation by such funding of students was at such a low level, one wonders that it could draw the above comments from Wilkins and Medill. Even before the founding of the nation, the Continental Congress of 1775 took steps to avoid having Indian students sent home for lack of funds, thus causing difficulties with Indian relations (Layman, 1942). The Congress first authorized $500 to be applied to the support of Indian students attending Dartmouth (Berry, 1969; Jackson and Galli, 1977; LaCounte, 1987; Layman, 1942). It then passed a resolution directed to Captain White Eyes, a Delaware, promising future support for Indian education as a means of securing good relations.

In 1779, this original appropriation to Dartmouth Indian students was increased by $925, enabling Dartmouth to be the only college to function continuously during the war (Layman, 1942). Then, on February 12, 1780, the Board of War recommended replenishing this Dartmouth fund with $5,000 with the avowed purpose of seeking, through such support of Indian education, the security of white settlements on the Connecticut River (Berry, 1969; Layman, 1942). In both cases, the support of Indian education was clearly intended to serve U. S. military or diplomatic purposes, not the educational, vocational, personal, or cultural enhancement of the students. Also, since the $5,000 appropriation was never fully allocated, it established what would become a common pattern of not following through on provisions made for Indian education (Layman, 1942).

In 1787, the Continental Congress enacted the Northwest Ordinance, which included a pledge to provide education for the Indian people (DeJong, 1993). This pledge would frequently be cited when educational provisions were included in treaties, provisions that again were all too often ignored rather than honored.

The single most important piece of legislation for Indian education in the treaty period, certainly the largest in terms of funding, was the Indian Civilization Act of 1819 (Jackson and Galli, 1977; Layman, 1942). It authorized the president to employ "persons of good moral character" to teach agriculture to the Indians, and authorized the establishment of what would come to be called "the civilization fund," $10,000 annually to support Indian education (Berry, 1969; Jackson and Galli, 1977; Layman, 1942; Oppelt, 1990; Thompson, 1978; Trennert, 1988; *Tribal Colleges*, Carnegie Foundation, 1989).

This "good moral character" phrase led the government to choose not to administer educational programs itself, but to release funds to various religious and missionary groups for that purpose. The result was the establishment of mission schools among the Indians, albeit with federal money (Layman, 1942; Trennert, 1988; Thompson, 1978; *Tribal Colleges*, Carnegie Foundation, 1989).

This, in turn, meant that the focus on religious instruction, now combined with agricultural training, was still a major part of the curriculum. No input was sought directly from Native Americans, and resistance by the Indians was still their primary response (*Tribal Colleges*, Carnegie Foundation, 1989).

Eventually, this subcontracted approach to federal control of Indian education proved problematic. The religious groups, besides dealing with resistance in the Native American community, found it difficult or impossible to operate schools due to the frequent warfare and dislocations resulting from the federal removal programs (Trennert, 1988). Also, a growing public debate over the separation of church and state led to pressure for the government to cease giving such funds to support what was perceived as religious programs. In 1870, this pressure led to a termination of this program by the federal government (Thompson, 1978).

Although the civilization fund represented the bulk of the federal funds provided for Native American education, the various treaties of the period contained more specific educational provisions, including many that were then supported by the civilization fund. These treaty provisions represented one way in which the Indians theoretically could express what they desired of an educational program. Unfortunately, our history regarding the meeting of treaty obligations leaves a great deal to be desired, and given the frequent resistance to white education by Native Americans, educational obligations were among the easiest provisions to fail to honor.

In the treaties themselves, common sections would typically include the declaration of peace, a description of affected territories, the same of Indian land relinquished, likewise of reservation lands established, and any forthcoming compensation for the Indian lands (Jackson and Galli, 1977). Of the 645 total treaties, only ninety-seven contained educational clauses (Belgrade, 1992; Thompson, 1978).

The first with such a provision was a 1794 treaty with the Oneida, Tuscarora, and Stockbridge Indians (Berry, 1969; DeJong, 1993; Layman, 1942). Its educational provision was minimal. It provided for the erection of a grist mill and a sawmill, including training in milling and sawing (Layman, 1942).

Prior to this treaty, the only educational concessions made to specific tribes were a 1791 promise to the Senecas to provide two teachers of husbandry and agriculture, and a 1792 similar promise to a band of unidentified hostiles on the Maumee River (Layman, 1942). However, neither of these was formally documented in treaties.

The second treaty with an educational provision was in 1803 with the Kaskaskia tribe. It agreed to a payment of $100 a year for seven years for the support of a Catholic priest to teach (Berry, 1969; Layman, 1942). Little imagination is required to envision more religious instruction than academic work occurring as a result.

Cherokee and Choctaw Educational Programs

The occasional negative comments and general lack of interest in white education notwithstanding, the value of education and its possible impact on relations with the whites were appreciated within the Indian community (Otis, 1971; Wright, 1991). That is why educational provisions were occasionally included in treaties, although rarely in a manner entirely acceptable to the tribes or effectively implemented.

The so-called five civilized tribes were notably active in rapidly adopting white social institutions, in particular the Cherokee and Choctaw nations (Debo, [1940]1968). They clearly perceived education as useful, and both established churches and developed school systems based on the American educational model (Berry, 1969; Otis, 1971).

Each nation had extensive school systems, numbering around 200 for the two combined (Wright, 1991; Wright and Tierney, 1991). At the base were neighborhood elementary schools, similar to the rural schools of the whites in adjoining states (Debo, [1940] 1968). They also had boarding schools, academies, and seminaries above the elementary level (Debo, [1940] 1968). The Choctaw had a school of higher education in the planning stages just prior to removal (Szasz and Ryan, 1988), but the removal to Indian Territory stopped it at that point.

The tribes experienced quite a bit of difficulty keeping their school systems operating, mostly due to actions of the federal government. When they were removed from the southeast to Indian Territory, the resulting economic losses effectively destroyed their educational system (Debo, [1934] 1961). To their credit, both nations immediately set about reestablishing their schools. In 1833, the Choctaws opened twelve schools (Szasz and Ryan, 1988), and had their system largely back to normal by 1842 (Layman, 1942). The Cherokee reopened a few schools in 1841, just after their arrival in Indian Territory. By 1852, they had 1,100 students in twenty-one schools and two academies (Berry, 1969; Debo, [1934]1961; Szasz and Ryan, 1988).

Then, during the Civil War, the tribes found themselves geographically isolated and nearly contained by the Confederacy. Although they hoped to avoid the conflict, all five of the civilized tribes found it necessary to sign various types of treaties of alliance with the South (Bode, 1957). A few minor battles occurred, and the Cherokees and Creeks experienced some divisions and internecine conflict as the fortunes of the Confederacy declined. However, little actual fighting occurred (Debo, [1934] 1961).

The federal government, wary of the actions of Native Americans in general during the Civil War, responded to these alliances by treating the tribes as hostile (Layman, 1942). This was particularly upsetting to the Choctaw, who had made it their proudest boast that they had never taken up arms against the United States (Debo, [1934] 1961). Federal annuities were suspended, causing the close of the Choctaw school system until after the war's end (Layman, 1942). Their Civil War association with the Confederacy was also subsequently used as a justification for the ceding of more Choctaw land to the United States (Debo, [1934] 1961).

Near the end of the nineteenth century, the federal government stepped in to take over the supervision of the Indian schools, leading to eventual deterioration (Otis, 1971; Prucha, 1984; Wright and Tierney, 1991). This resulted from the government's attempt, in what came to be known as the allotment period, to destroy the tribal structure and assimilate the native Americans as individuals. This scheme was extremely popular and well supported within the federal government, as indicated by President Theodore Roosevelt's remarks in his 1901 report to Congress:

> In my judgment, the time has arrived, and we should definitely make up our minds to recognize the Indian as an individual and not as a member of a tribe. The General Allotment Act is a mighty pulverizing engine to break up the tribal mass. (Williams and Meredith, 1980, p. 50)

This assault on the tribal foundation of Indian life assumed an inability to treat people as both individuals and as members of a group simultaneously. In this instance, it indicates a total lack of sensitivity, or even comprehension, of the importance of group or tribal association in the Indian culture.

The first step was the General Allotment Act, or Dawes Act, of 1887 (Nabokov, 1993). Similar to the allotment program for the nonimmigrating Choctaws of Mississippi in 1830, the concept was to remove land from the control of the tribes, and to grant each individual a small tract for personal support. The intent was to break the tribal structure, leaving only individuals to be absorbed into American society.

The Curtis Act of 1898, abolishing tribal governments, was the next logical step (Bode, 1957; Szasz and Ryan, 1988). It was followed and largely repeated by a 1901 amendment to the Dawes Act and the Five Tribes Act of 1906, in which the U.S. abolished tribal governments, principally by assuming control of tribal revenues (Prucha, 1984). No tribal treasurer could then receive or disburse money after this act. This loss of control of their funding eventually caused the closing of the tribal governments, including the schools (Bode, 1957; Debo, [1940] 1968; Szasz and Ryan, 1988).

However, the nations resisted such disbandment, and were resourceful enough to stall the inevitable closings for a considerable time (Prucha, 1984). By using donations, investments, saved money, and extending the lives of these existent funds through cautious management, combined with court fights and stubborn resistance, they effectively frustrated the federal plans. The Cherokee tribal government, including its schools, closed in 1913 (*Tulsa World*, 1914, June 30). The others held on even longer, with the last Creek school closing in 1928, Seminole in 1930, and Choctaw and Chickasaw in 1932 (Debo, [1940] 1968). For all practical purposes, they saw to it that they outlasted the allotment period and would survive beyond it.

Besides problems arising from the federal government, these school systems were never so well funded, outside of federal funds, that they could stand alone for any appreciable length of time. The Choctaw nation never provided a system of public taxation to support any of its governmental activities. Both tribes relied on funds from earlier land sales and compensations, supporting themselves entirely on the return from invested funds (Jackson and Galli, 1977; Layman, 1942). In this manner, between 1845 and 1855, the tribes were actually able to contribute more to the support of their schools than did the federal government (Jackson and Galli, 1977).

Both nations, the Choctaw in particular, were able to secure or provide funding to send their best graduates to colleges or academies in the east (Debo, [1940]1968; Debo, [1934]1961; Wright, 1991; Wright and Tierney, 1991). They drew on the civilization fund when available, although, being designated for Indians in general, it was spread quite thin (Jackson and Galli, 1977). During the early part of the century, the Scottish Fund, the legacy of Samson Occum, was still in existence. It was used to support a total of twelve Choctaw and Cherokee students at Dartmouth, beginning in 1838 (Wright, 1991; Wright and Tierney, 1991). In 1854, Joseph Folsom, a Choctaw, received his baccalaureate degree (Wright, 1991).

The Cherokee and Choctaw nations were very consistent about negotiating educational provisions in their treaties. The Doak's Stand Treaty of 1820 (Choctaw) contained a provision for funding schools and student support, as did the 1825 Treaty of New Echota (Cherokee) (Layman, 1942). The Treaty of New Echota contained, as part of the Cherokee's removal compensation, a provision of $6,000 annually for twenty years to support schools and "a literary institution of a higher order" (Layman, 1942; Thompson, 1978), indicative of the desires of the nation. It was never fully realized, although, in 1851, the Cherokee did establish two seminaries, male and female. They were very proud of these institutions and never allowed them under the supervision of the U. S. authorities. They were not even visited by the U. S. Department of Education until after June 30, 1898, the date of the Curtis Act. By 1906, the federal government had taken over the administration of the two of them. In 1909, they were made co-ed and combined, and purchased by the state of Oklahoma, to be made into the Northeastern State Normal School (Northeastern State University catalog, 1997).

Then, on March 10, 1910, a mysterious fire burned the Female Seminary building to the ground (Belgrade, 1992).

The biggest source of funds to support the Choctaw students of higher education came from the provisions of the Treaty of Dancing Rabbit Creek, 1830 (DeRosier, 1970; Wright, 1991; Wright and Tierney, 1991). This treaty was the last of seven forcing the westward removal of the Choctaws. The negotiations, conducted by Secretary of War John Eaton, lasted two days (White, 1990). The Choctaw were forced to sign away 10,423,130 acres to the United States, the last of their land east of the Mississippi (DeRosier, 1970; White, 1990). Disgusted with the proceedings, the majority of the Choctaw representatives left after the first day. Those remaining, the actual signers of the treaty, were primarily mixed bloods (White, 1990).

To sooth the injured feelings of those who refused, the U. S. agreed to grant individual allotments for those remaining in Mississippi. This effectively set up a division of the nation that endures to this day. Hundreds applied for these allotments. Several thousand others simply remained as illegal inhabitants, either unmindful of or uncomprehending of the government provision (White, 1990).

Only three hundred actually received the individual allotment. There very well may have been many more desiring to apply, but William Ward, the commissioner assigned to administer the allotment program, regularly ducked any contact with petitioners. Such was his animosity toward Native Americans, he was even reported to use the blank Choctaw application forms for toilet paper (White, 1990).

Article 20 of the Dancing Rabbit Creek Treaty addressed funding for Choctaw higher education. It provided funds to support forty students in Eastern colleges per year for twenty years. As each student completed his education, he was to be replaced by a new youth to maintain the number at forty (DeRosier, 1970). Provision was also made for $10,000 for the purpose of building a council house, several chiefs' houses, and three district schools/churches (DeRosier, 1970; Wright, 1991; Wright and Tierney, 1991). Finally, a total of $50,000, to be paid over twenty years, was apportioned for the support of the three schools (DeRosier, 1970).

The college fund provision was first used in 1841 for students at Ohio University, Jefferson College, and Indiana University (Wright, 1991; Wright and Tierney, 1991). The 1843 report from Commissioner of Indian Affairs Crawford mentioned twenty students being support by the fund, ten at Asbury University and ten at Lafayette College

(Wright, 1991; Wright and Tierney, 1991). It is not known how many completed their degree.

The fund was terminated, along with other federal funding, due to the Choctaw alliance with the Confederacy during the Civil War. In 1869, with tribal money raised to provide scholarships, the Choctaw resumed the practice of sending select students to Eastern academies and colleges. Twenty-two enrolled the first year (Debo, [1934] 1961).

The commitment of the Cherokee and Choctaw nations to education and higher education stands out in the history of Native American schooling. Their school systems, in terms of proportion of students, number of teachers, and quality of schools, have been described as superior to those in the adjoining states of Arkansas and Missouri (Szasz and Ryan, 1988). Such a description was justified by the fact that, as a result of their school and scholarship systems, the Cherokee and Choctaw nations at one time had both a higher level of literacy and a higher proportion of college graduates than their white neighbors in those states (Debo, [1934] 1961).

The Academies

With the cutoff of English funds resulting from the American Revolution, there was relatively little additional activity in Native American higher education during the early years of the United States. The notable exception was Dartmouth. By virtue of its Indian college reputation, and of being the de facto recipient of many of the federal funds either appropriated by Congress or included in treaty provisions, Dartmouth continued to welcome Indian students supported by such funds well into the nineteenth century. However, as indicated by the range of schools reporting Choctaw and Cherokee students, the tribes and the students had come to realize that the funds were attached to them, not the schools, and in the absence of any particular Native American special programs or curriculum, the choice of school was open.

The most noteworthy additions to higher education institutions serving Native Americans in the early nineteenth century were not colleges but certain academies. Although often closely identified with select tribes, they were not tribal institutions, but missionary or proprietary schools. While not chartered as colleges, the more significant ones did elect to offer a classical higher education curriculum and were responsible for educating many subsequently influential Native American leaders.

The Oneida Academy

When Samson Occum fell out with Eleazar Wheelock, feeling betrayed by Wheelock's failure to follow through on his professed focus on Indian higher education, he was not alone. In 1771, the Oneida tribe in general repudiated Wheelock's work (Smith, 1950). They elected to move to the west, locating in the area of what is now Oneida, New York. This was the move in which Occum arranged to legally register the tribal lands (Szasz, 1994).

The experience with Wheelock had not abated their interest in education. In 1794, the Oneida, along with the Tuscarora and Stockbridge, were signers of the first treaty with the United States to include educational provisions (Berry, 1969; DeJong, 1993; Layman, 1942). That same year saw the establishment of the Oneida Academy (Oppelt, 1990).

It was largely the effort of Samuel Kirkland, a long-time missionary among the Iroquois. He envisioned a major school to serve the six-nation Iroquois confederacy, with a system of feeder schools centered on it. The academy was chartered in 1793, although its building was not to be completed until 1799 (Layman, 1942). It actually opened in 1794, with an initial offering that began with elementary school.

Although ostensibly established to serve Indian interests, the white settlers in the area also supported and used the academy. They were more numerous and better able to support their students. As a result, the first class included only four Indian students (Layman, 1942; Oppelt, 1990).

Even with the whites, finances were insufficient, and the academy closed after only one year of operation. In 1799, with the completion of the building, it reopened. However, this time it had only one Indian student among the fifty in attendance (Layman, 1942; Oppelt, 1990). Kirkland reported several other Indians had applied, but they were not supported by funds (Layman, 1942).

In 1812, the academy offered its first college-level work and was granted a new charter as Hamilton College (Layman, 1942; Oppelt, 1990). It was then, as it is today, a predominately white, mainstream college, with minimal Indian involvement (Layman, 1942; *Lovejoy's College Guide*, 1995; Oppelt, 1990). The Hamilton experience was one of the earliest examples of what would become a frequent occurrence, that of an Indian school transforming into a predominately white college, due to the financial need to appeal to a broader base of potential students.

The Foreign Mission School

The Foreign Mission School, of Cornwall, Connecticut, was short lived and small. It opened in 1817 with twelve students, peaked in 1823 with only thirty-six students, and closed in 1827. It featured the usual mission school blend of Christian, agricultural-vocational, and academic training, although it did pursue much of the classical academic curriculum (Layman, 1942). It did prove influential beyond its short duration and small size. Many of its students became leaders of distinction, particularly in the Cherokee nation, for many years (Debo, [1940]1968; Layman, 1942).

The Choctaw Academy

The Choctaw Academy was the most influential of any Indian school of the treaty period. Although overseen by the Baptist Board of Foreign Missions, it cannot properly be called a mission school. It was proprietary, founded in 1825 by Colonel Richard M. Johnson, on his farm in Great Crossings (Georgetown), Kentucky (Berry, 1969).

Johnson had been a colonel in the War of 1812 and was reputed to have been the man who killed Tecumseh. He was a U. S. senator in 1819–1829, a U. S. representative in 1829–1836, and vice president under President Andrew Jackson in 1937–1841. His Indian school was a sideline of sorts, arising from his interest in Indian education (Layman, 1942).

Johnson's school began informally in 1816, with seven students. It was chartered by the Baptist Board of Foreign Missions in 1825. To his credit, Johnson's school focused on the standard academic subjects of reading, writing, and arithmetic, including "higher branches of literature" (Layman, 1942, p. 314). It added husbandry and domestic skills only to qualify for funds under the 1819 Civilization Act.

During its life, the Choctaw Academy was characterized by financial and political maneuvering, and by academic excellence. The financial/political issues centered on Johnson, his efforts to gain funding for the school, and the highs and lows of his political career.

In 1825, the Choctaw Council of Chiefs chose to apply the funds from the Doak's Stand Treaty (1820) and the New Echota Treaty (1825) to the education of their youth at some point "distant from the nation" (Layman, 1942, p. 318). This was in spite of treaty wording specifying use "within the nation" and several schools available closer to their lands (Layman, 1942, p. 318). Johnson later insisted he knew nothing of this plan and offered to educate any Choctaw boys sent to him.

Cyrus Kingsbury, missionary and superintendent of schools for the Choctaw nation, opposed the plan and contacted Secretary of War Barbour, requesting the establishment of a school in the nation for this purpose. Barbour approved this new plan, but the Choctaw chiefs did not. They went through with the plan to send eighteen to twenty boys to the "Choctaw Academy" and assigned the first annual treaty-provided grant of $6,000 to it. This commitment enabled Johnson to successfully persuade the Baptist Board to sanction his school, to be known as the Choctaw Academy (Debo, [1934]1961; Layman, 1942).

Besides Choctaw treaty funds, the academy later received funds for the education of students of the Pottawatomie, Prairie du Chien, Chickasaw, Seminole, Quapaw, Miami, Cherokee, Creek, and Chicago tribes. It also received some money from the civilization fund and was clearly the best funded of the Indian schools. It even sent representatives to treaty negotiations to press for educational provisions, to be channelled later to the academy (Layman, 1942).

On the surface, it would appear that Johnson was primarily interested in financial gain, since he was in debt at the time of the school's establishment. However, he did establish a very viable and successful school, one that stressed academics for Native Americans and was well received by the Indian community.

The academic strength of the school derived mostly from his superintendent of the academy, Thomas Henderson. Henderson was quite sincere and involved in the administration of the school (Layman, 1942). His original curriculum was impressive. It included mathematics, literature, English grammar, geography, astronomy, natural philosophy, history, moral philosophy, and music (Layman, 1942). He also looked to extracurricular activities, overseeing the establishment of the Lycurgus Court (self-government of the student body, including discipline) and the Napoleon Society (social skills, etiquette) (Layman, 1942).

In 1825, the academy had twenty-one students. This number grew to 101 by 1827. The highest enrollment was 174 students in 1835, a fairly large school for that time period (Layman, 1942). Of that class, seventy were Choctaw.

When the academy began experiencing difficulties, they came from several sources at once. Pressure from the government for more vocational and less classical education, relating to qualification for the civilization fund, led to mechanical and shop arts being added in 1832.

Then agriculture was added in 1837. Hezekiah Niles, publisher of the *Niles Register* and political opponent of Johnson's, questioned the advisability of educating Indian boys, in a clear but unacknowledged admission that assimilation into white society was not truly under consideration:

> Better it is that they should remain as they are than, by education, become unfit for savage life if such only we have resolved to allow them. (Layman, 1942, p. 336)

However, the changes in curriculum led to some negative response from parents, who supported the school intending a classical education for their sons (Layman, 1942). By 1838, the Choctaws began refusing to send their youth, followed by the Seminole, Cherokee, Quapaw, and Miami (Layman, 1942). This growing dissatisfaction with the curriculum was exacerbated by the increased distance to the school, a result of the removal to Indian Territory (Debo, [1934]1961; Layman, 1942).

About this same time, as Johnson's political career peaked, the publicity (and criticism) of the academy increased. When he lost the office of vice president in 1840, complaints about the school, its funding, and discipline problems increased further (Layman, 1942). In 1845, the academy was investigated by the U. S. House of Representatives on a complaint of mismanagement of Choctaw funds (Layman, 1942). The complaint was denied, but it was the deathblow to the school. The Choctaw voted to apply their funds in their own country, and the academy closed in 1846 (Berry, 1969; Layman, 1942).

The academy's history was one of much in the way of mercenary designs, political bickering, and dissatisfaction. From a historical perspective, Johnson's political positions may have created both much of the school's troubles and much of its strength. Certainly, Thomas Henderson's abilities and devotion as an educator stand out as having figured strongly in the school's contribution to the Indian community. Its difficulties notwithstanding, the Choctaw Academy did produce many important leaders among the Indian tribes for years to come.

The Federal Assimilation Policy

Virtually since the first contact between Europeans and Native Americans, the whites had debated over whether assimilation or removal would be the better way to deal with the Indian. With the exception of the token assimilationism of the educational policy, removal had almost always gained the upper hand as the whites pushed the Indians off the land, moving them ever farther to the west. Even so, removal was usually presented as some sort of compromise, a temporary step to allow time for assimilation to take place. Thus rationalized, this lightly named policy endured, resulting in frequent and repetitive uprooting of tribes and crowding them onto smaller tracts of land. In later eras, people in similar circumstances would be called refugees.

During the last years of the nineteenth century, assimilation at last began to supplant removal as the primary policy of the federal government. This occurred not so much because someone finally noticed the contradictory nature of removing the Indians from white society to assimilate them into it, but for the very simple reason that the nation was running out of places to remove them to. Due to a variety of factors, such as the California Gold Rush, population pressure in general, the Homestead Act, and the development of an extensive railroad system, the United States had at last become a transcontinental nation. As white immigrants continued to fill in the spaces across the country, the Indians found themselves forced onto smaller and less desirable parcels of land.

Both policies continued to attract supporters, and both continued to play a role. However, the rapidly diminishing available land and equally rapid expansion of the white society were making the so-called Indian problem much more intense, for both the whites and the Native Americans. Indicative of this intensity, the levels of both warfare and racism increased markedly.

During the Civil War, conflicts with the Indians, while not significantly different from previous conflicts all the way back to the attack on Columbus's garrison at La Navidad (Dickason, 1984), came to be seen as somehow conspiratorial. The government had long realized that conflicts and occasional violent uprising between Indians and settlers required a military presence all along the frontier. In spite of the pressures of the Civil War, this need continued. The desire to keep California securely in the Union resulted in such activities as the Pony Express, the transcontinental telegraph, the ongoing rush to construct a transcontinental railroad, and the general encouragement of westward immigration. All of these contributed to the tension between whites and Native Americans.

The fact that the United States had to fight any such Indian uprisings concurrent with the Civil War moved much public opinion away from the Indian cause. The 1862 Sioux uprising in Minnesota, in particular, led to a widespread fear of a conspiracy among the Indians to attack all along the frontier while the army was preoccupied with the Civil War.

However, except for the activity within Indian Territory, the concurrent wars with tribes on the frontier were largely unrelated to the Civil War (Prucha, 1984).

The alliances among the five civilized tribes with the Confederacy also fed this paranoia that the Native Americans would side with the Confederacy against the Union (Prucha, 1984). That the civilized tribes were feeling fairly vulnerable in dealing with a Confederate government that seemed to all but encircle them, or were hardly capable of mounting much of a threat to the Union army went unconsidered.

The traditional tendency of pro-Indian feelings being more prevalent on the east coast than on the frontier was heightened by such fears (Szasz, 1974). This white nervousness led to lost opportunities, misunderstandings, and occasional atrocities such as the killing of over 100 mostly women and children at the Sand Creek Massacre in Colorado (Nabokov, 1993, p. 330; Prucha, 1984). For twenty-plus years after the Civil War, warfare between Indians and whites in the southwest and on the high plains reinforced these anti-Indian feelings among the whites.

In the midst of this period of intensified conflict, the Indians found an unexpected supporter in President Ulysses S. Grant. His 1868 election was viewed with apprehension by many reformers and Indian leaders due to his militaristic image (Mardock, 1971). However, he was to prove far more favorably disposed toward Indians than earlier believed.

His true feelings should have been better understood by perceptive observers. In 1864, he had bluntly called the Sand Creek Massacre "a murder, not a battle" (Mardock, 1971). Once in office, he took the remarkable step of naming Ely Parker, a Seneca, to be the first Native American to serve as commissioner of Indian Affairs (Prucha, 1984).

Grant is well known for implementing the "Peace Policy" (Szasz and Ryan, 1988), having been influenced to do so by various Quaker groups. Even before becoming president, he established the Peace Commission to oversee a much more structured reservation system. The Commission was authorized to negotiate treaties in the southern and northern plains in an effort to bring about peace by locating the Indians on reservations (Prucha, 1984).

Grant advocated using army personnel to fill many Indian service positions, making the army a police force for the security of the Indians in an attempt to keep the two societies separated (Mardock, 1971). In 1871, Grant tried to strengthen his Peace Policy by naming a civilian Board of Indian Commissioners to oversee the U.S. Indian Bureau (Nabokov, 1993). Regarding Indian education, Grant still relied on

Christian organizations for schools and missions. However, more directly administered schools as a function of the federal government were just around the corner.

Grant's Peace Policy was an attempt at a major overhaul of the Indian policy. As much as he tried, Grant was unable to stem the warfare that characterized the plains and southwest areas during and after his administration. The Indians felt they were running out of options and had to resist in the face of relentless expansion of the whites into all available territories. The newspaper reports of battles and atrocities fueled public opinion against the Indians. The defeat of Custer, in particular, on the eve of the U. S. Centennial inflamed public opinion. It created much media and public sentiment against the Peace Policy in favor of what was now readily being called the War Policy (Mardock, 1971; Prucha, 1984).

The racism that tends to accompany such periods of animosity, the racism that reflected the negative public opinion that Grant tried to contend with, is readily evident in the public utterances and official statements of political and military leaders throughout the period. Easily the most famous is the inaccurate quote attributed to General Philip Sheridan that "the only good Indian is a dead Indian" (Nabokov, 1993).

In spite of Grant's peaceful approach and conservatism, Sheridan personified the war policy. When the Indians first saw Sheridan, with his short legs, thick neck, and long swinging arms, they thought he looked like a bad-tempered bear (Brown, 1970). At Fort Cobb, in December 1868, the first band of Comanches surrendered to U. S. forces, with Tosawi as their chief. When presented to Sheridan, desiring to make a good impression, he introduced himself as "Tosawi, good Indian" (Brown, 1970, p. 166).

Sheridan rather ungraciously replied, "The only good Indians I ever saw were dead." A Lieutenant Charles Nordstrom recalled the comment later and passed it on. In time, it became honed to the aphorism, "The only good Indian is a dead Indian," the effective motto of the entire war policy for the remainder of the century (Brown, 1970, p. 166).

But this remark was not a solitary sentiment. Secretary of State Henry Clay, arguing against extensive schooling or support for the Indians, stated they were "not an improvable breed." He saw them as destined to an extinction that "will be no great loss to the world" (Nabokov, 1993, p. 342). Theodore Roosevelt fully absorbed the frontier anti-Indian mentality, as evidenced by his remarks in an 1886 lecture:

> I don't go so far as to think that the only good Indians are the dead Indians, but I believe nine out of every ten are, and I shouldn't like to inquire too closely into the case of the tenth. The most vicious cowboy has more moral principle than the average Indian. (Dippie, 1982, p. 183)

Roosevelt did not subscribe to the exterminationist viewpoint and even accorded the Indians a rough measure of respect. But he was clear on one point; he considered the Indian a savage, one destined to vanish under the pressure of the superior civilization as the natural order of things (Dippie, 1982).

This propensity for public figures to make such blatantly racist remarks would continue for some time, and would be a part of the discussion of what kind of education should be provided for the Indians. Francis Leupp, commissioner of Indian Affairs under Theodore Roosevelt, would later describe the federal boarding school curriculum as appropriate for a "backward people" (Hoxie, 1992, p. 189). He argued that the colonial focus on offering higher education to Indians had been naive.

In 1909, Charles Dyle, an instructor at Hampton Institute, made a report to the National Education Association on the advisability of higher education for Indians. The Hampton Institute, later Hampton University, had opened in 1868 as a predominately black institution of higher education (*Lovejoy's College Guide*, 1995). It had been open to Indians since 1878 when Captain Richard Pratt had enrolled seventeen young Indian males (Trennert, 1988). Dyle's remarks as a member of the Hampton faculty are very telling:

> A knowledge of the race characteristics of one's students is fundamental. It is absurd to theorize about the propriety of a college education for the mass of Negroes, or Indians.... They lack the intellect to acquire it. (Hoxie, 1992, p. 199)

Such lamentable opinions were even supported by the social science of the time. Psychologist G. Stanley Hall provided a sense of scientific objectivity by postulating that the development of races was much like the development of individuals (Hoxie, 1992). Some races were simply less mature ("savage").

When writing his memoirs, Commissioner Leupp defended his view that it was advisable to set limits upon the education of Indians by the government. His position was that higher education is of no practical use to the Indians, and certainly not desirable in their case as in that of the whites. He contended that public debate and opinion in favor of it amounted to "[letting] theory usurp the place of practical acquaintance" (Leupp, 1910, p. 115). In doing so, he inadvertently provides a very rare admission that higher education for Indians was considered in some quarters, if effectively argued down.

Leupp defended his position, with no apparent intended irony, by pointing out that a lack of acceptance in white society invariably prevented an Indian trained in law, medicine, or theology from practicing his profession; and that similarly Indian society would prove no longer accepting of him as having gone over to the "white man's way" (Leupp, 1910, p. 116). He completely avoided the obvious example to the contrary, that his own predecessor under Grant, Ely Parker, had been just such an educated Indian functioning quite effectively in white society while simultaneously serving the Indians.

Having thus indicted, without comment, white society for not providing opportunities for such educated Indians, Leupp then devoted the next two chapters to a favorable assessment and critique of the government's system of reservation day schools, reservation boarding schools, and off-reservation boarding schools, and their industrial-agricultural-domestic arts curriculum (Leupp, 1910). He covered the advantages, current issues, and potential remedies or adjustments of the curriculum and system, insisting that it represented the most viable path for ultimate assimilation into the larger society.

This viewpoint held by Leupp represents the educational philosophy underlying the entire federal boarding school system, itself a reflection of the government's decision to hasten the assimilation of the Indians. Until 1870, efforts at dealing with the "Indian problem," whether by removal or assimilation, had been rather unfocused. Removals had occurred piecemeal and sometimes repeatedly, not by some overriding strategy, but due to the white needs of the moment and place. Education had likewise received no concerted attention, just sporadic funding and support. It was mostly left to interested religious organizations, institutions, and individuals.

In 1870, as part of Grant's attempt to overhaul Indian-white relations, the government seemed to decide to assert itself. That year, Congress appropriated $100,000 for the establishment of federal industrial schools for Indians (Wright and Tierney, 1991). For the first time, the government was to administer the Indian schools itself.

Behind this move was the federal decision on a policy of total assimilation of the Indians. However, such assimilation was still limited to very low-level vocational training, with no effort by the federal government to establish or encourage higher education for the Indians. That this was the case may quite reasonably be attributed to this largely unchallenged racism of the period. White society was feeling forced into assimilation by the shrinkage of available land, and was not in a particularly gracious mood because of it.

The avowed purpose of federal educational policy was to change the Indian system of values, to make them more like the white man (Szasz, 1974). This objective was never more succinctly put than by the Rainy Mountain School Superintendent Cora Dunn in an 1899 letter to Commissioner of Indian Affairs William Jones: "Our purpose is to change them forever" (Rainy Mountain School files, Indian Archives Division, Oklahoma Historical Society).

No doubt, Dunn meant this to sound like a lofty, high-minded goal. To the Native Americans, it must have sounded like cultural murder. While some Native Americans welcomed education, or simply faced reality and recognized its need, this was education under federal control, not local or community control as was the case for virtually the entire rest of the nation (Deyhle and Swisher, 1997). It was focused on government needs, not those of the Native Americans (Adams, 1988). Thus the government education-assimilation policy involved no change in curriculum and continued to consider only the lowest level of vocational training, certainly not higher education (Wright, 1991).

Much more attention dealt with the effort to destroy the Indian culture, the exact opposite of the more common educational objective of the transmission of culture from one generation to the next. This cultural denial was resented by the Native American community, creating a resistance to white education that was to be felt for generations. At the very beginning of this period of federally run education, Santana, a Kiowa chief, stated the case for his cultural identity at the 1867 Medicine Lodge Council:

> I love the land and the buffalo and will not part with it. I want you to understand well what I say. Write it on paper. I hear a great deal of good will from the gentlemen whom the Great Father sends us, but they never do what they say. I don't want any of the medicine lodges, schools, and churches out in the country. I want the children raised as I was. (Robbins, 1974, p. 88)

The government did nothing to take such a position into account. It attempted to assimilate not by direct contact in the community, or by a cooperative, participatory approach, but by a very paternalistic, compulsory one. The program was implemented by a series of agencies, with the Indians consigned to a passive role (Robbins, 1974).

This assimilation policy was two-pronged, land and education. The land element was not addressed until the Dawes Act (Allotment Act) of 1887. It was predicated on the belief that land ownership leads to good citizenship and responsibility (Szasz, 1974). More to the point, it was based on the assumption that putting land in the hands of individuals, instead of the tribe, would lead to self-sufficiency and a more easily broken control of the tribe. The belief was that not only were Indians both literally and culturally vanishing, but that the government could hasten this process by splitting up communal land holdings, and teaching the Indians how to farm. By creating individuals out of tribes, it was supposed that these individuals could be absorbed into the general population, the Bureau of Indian Affairs could be dismantled, and the Indian problem would be solved (Nabokov, 1993).

So confident was the government in this policy that along with individual land allotments, the newly individualized Indians were also able to apply for citizenship (Falmouth Institute, 1992). The period after the Allotment Act, in which the government passed several acts (1889, 1901, 1906) to take over the control of tribal funds and outlaw tribal governments, represents the attempt to follow through on this theory. The presumption was that without a land base, the tribal governments would lose their power (Falmouth Institute, 1992). In so doing, the federal government denied the sovereignty of the tribes that had existed and been recognized by all parties since well before the founding of the nation, not to mention by the U. S. Supreme Court. The fight to protect and reestablish that sovereignty would extend well into the twentieth century.

The second prong of this assimilation policy was education, in which the government was taking an active role for the first time. Previously, educational objectives had been set by the interested parties involved. The focus of colonial attempts had been to convert the Indians to Christianity. Through the early years of the nation, this was little changed. The religious and reform groups involved adhered to the hope that education and Christianization would civilize the Indian, broaden his ambition and views, stamp out pagan practices, and coincidentally destroy the tribal organization (Mardock, 1971; Wright and Tierney, 1991). The federal government in this period had largely ignored or neglected such educational efforts. Consequently, the educational focus seemed haphazard and unplanned (Szasz, 1974).

With the new focus on assimilation, the government was newly motivated to educate the Indian on its terms, in accordance with its needs (Adams, 1988). If the tribes were to be broken up into individuals, each with a plot of land to farm, they would need to be taught how to farm.

The first use of the federal funds to establish an off-reservation boarding school was to become the most famous, the Carlisle Indian Academy in Pennsylvania. It was founded by Captain Richard Pratt in 1879 (Stein, 1992; Szasz, 1974; Wright and Tierney, 1991). Pratt was in charge of a group of prisoners at Fort Marion, Florida. There they were basically marking time, due to the shaky issue of the army's right to prosecute Indian raiders in view of the government to government relations between tribes and the United States (Wescott, 1991).

In spite of his military position, Pratt was a champion of the Indian cause. In the limited fashion of the time, he was quite progressive, even liberal, in his view of the Indians. He understood the plight of the Indians, and his anecdotes show remarkable affection and empathy for them (Pratt, [1923] 1964). Yet he failed to appreciate their culture, and shared the nation's simplistic, shallow view of the ability to deny that culture (Wescott, 1991).

Pratt was an uncompromising zealot for assimilation and citizenship. He, Commissioner Morgan, and other reformers believed human beings were the products of their environment. They firmly adhered to the theory of the unity of humanity—that savagery, brutishness, and cultural differences were due to unfortunate circumstances, not any inherent defect of nature, a view that underlies much social philosophy to this day (Prucha, 1984). Pratt believed the Indian was very educable, a position shared by his superior, General S. C. Armstrong, as well as Commissioners Edward Smith, Morgan, and Price (Ellis, 1996; Szasz, 1974). Consequently, he believed the government should take a more active role in separating the Indians from their past and training them for a role in white society.

In 1878, Pratt oversaw the placement of seventeen young male prisoners at Hampton Institute, Virginia, as an experiment in just such a removalist approach to education for the Indians (Trennert, 1988). He was so pleased with their progress that the next year he obtained permission to use the Carlisle Barracks in Pennsylvania to set up an independent school, the first use of federal funds for an off-reservation boarding school (Prucha, 1984; Trennert, 1988; Wright and Tierney, 1991). The Carlisle Indian Industrial School was used as the model for virtually all subsequent off-reservation schools (Trennert, 1988).

The dominant approach focused on (1) removal from home and tribal influences; (2) strict military discipline, including short haircuts and uniforms; and (3) teaching of the Protestant work ethic (Adams, 1995; Wright and Tierney, 1991, p. 14). The curriculum emphasis was on manual arts, principally agriculture, mechanical, and domestic skills, not higher education (Wright and Tierney, 1991). The intent was to provide a very industrial, job-centered education with minimal academic training, usually limited to the sixth to eighth grade level (Trennert, 1988).

The outing system was used extensively, placing students with area farm families for educational purposes (Prucha, 1984), similar to the use of agricultural work for training purposes at Moor's Charity Indian School, and in a fundamental sense, to the work-study plan adopted at Antioch College fifty years later (Clark, [1970] 1992). The intended result was to produce Indians trained as domestics, laborers, unskilled workers, and self-sufficient farmers.

The success of Carlisle led to a Congressional appropriation in 1882 to expand the off-reservation industrial boarding school program (Szasz, 1974). Pratt promoted Carlisle and Indians in general constantly. In the 1890s, he was helped in this by the discovery that his students could play excellent football. Their schedule included Harvard, Cornell, Pennsylvania, and other well-known colleges. This led to an inaccurate public perception of the academic quality of the Carlisle program as being college level, rather than its true eighth grade/grammar/manual labor school character (Prucha, 1984).

Beyond Carlisle, the government developed an extensive system of such schools. As limited as their curriculum was, they were the top tier of schools under federal administration, the best funded, and, in a perverse sense, the most exclusive. In 1877, the federally administered school system consisted of 150 reservation day schools and reservation boarding schools (Jackson and Galli, 1977). In the 1900 annual report of the Commissioner of Indian Affairs, there were twenty-five off-reservation boarding schools with 7,430 students. The largest three were Carlisle with 1,000-plus, Haskell with 700, and Phoenix with 600. Next were eighty-one reservation boarding schools with an enrollment of 9,600, and 147 reservation day schools with 5,000 students. Outside of the government system were 250 students in twenty-two public schools, 2,800 in thirty-two contract schools, and 1,275 in twenty-two mission schools. The report made no mention of any college enrollment (Prucha, 1984).

With a total of only 26,355 school-age children recorded as enrolled in school, even in that year of a low of 237,000 Native American population, it is obvious that those in school probably represented only from one-third to one-half of the school-age children. Partly this apparent discrepancy may represent poor coverage relative to the need for schools. There was no provision for the education of younger students. The government was solely interested in teens and young adults capable of performing the industrial training (Trennert, 1988). As an example of the lack of coverage, in 1890, the Kiowa tribe was served by only three agency schools with a capacity of 190 students. These were responsible for a total of 1,045 school-age children on their reservation, 400 of whom were under active agency supervision (Ellis, 1996). The Kiowas pressed for more schools, but with little success.

The low attendance rates also clearly reflect an ongoing resistance to white education. There were instances of the hiding of children, runaways, and such (Ellis, 1996). At a minimum, parents were torn over whether to send their children to the schools. They tended to be unwilling to commit to the overall cultural change demanded by the government, but often were interested in gaining advantages for the young. Unlike the government, they distinguished between education and acculturation, seeing education not as a capitulation to a foreign culture, but as a pragmatic attempt to deal with change and disruption (Ellis, 1996).

Actually, it may be fair to say that the government distinguished between education and acculturation as well. The problem was the school system was being run to meet the needs of the government, not the students, and that need was acculturation, not education. That alone may explain the minimal level of academic content involved.

The level of cultural indoctrination, on the other hand, was substantial, beginning with the academic content itself. Besides being a meager curriculum in an academic sense, the subject matter definitely had a European slant. History began with the 1492 discovery by Columbus, then focused solely on the transplanted European culture and its spread across the continent. There was a full complement of Mother Goose and similar stories, but no mention of the great tradition of storytelling that was so much a part of Native American culture. Late in the boarding school period, native methods and subjects were broached in the areas of art only, a very slight crack in the facade of all-white culture (*Tentative Course of Study for U. S. Indian Schools*, 1915). Of course, the heritage of the tribes was not mentioned. Obviating any doubts that this was purposeful, Commissioner of Indian Affairs Morgan had stressed that teachers should "carefully avoid any unnecessary reference to the fact that they are Indian" (Prucha, 1973, p. 257; *Tribal Colleges*, Carnegie Foundation, 1989). He also admitted that American civilization "may not be the best possible, but [he believed] it was the best the Indians would get. They cannot escape it, and must either conform to it or be crushed by it" (Ellis, 1996, p. 11).

Language itself commanded special attention, so much so it has been labeled one of the primary objectives of the federal school system, along with manual labor training and Christian education (Prucha, 1984). The concern for language was equal parts the enforced use of English and the denial of native languages. So convinced were the federal administrators of the importance of language for cultural identity, an 1887 federal law even addressed the topic, forbidding Native American languages in the classroom (*Use of English in Indian Schools*, House Executive Document no. 1, 50th Congress, September 21, 1887).

The enforced use of English was considered of such importance that it drew comment from throughout the federal system. At various times, Secretaries of the Interior Teller and Schurz, Commissioners Hayt, Smith, and Atkins, and Superintendent of Education Benedict all expressed support for it (Prucha, 1984, p. 689). Benedict charged that tribal schools had been "guilty of conversing in native language" (Debo, [1940] 1968, p. 67). Schurz dismissed efforts to draw up Indian grammars and to instruct Indians in their native languages as "certainly very interesting and meritorious," but of little use to the Indians (Report of the Secretary of the Interior, 1877, pp. 10–11).

Commissioner of Indian Affairs J. D. C. Atkins was likely the most radical promoter of English usage, a matter of first principle to him. He saw the use of English, and the corresponding extinction of native languages, as a sort of cultural glue, a requirement of citizenship:

> Nothing so surely and perfectly stamps upon an individual a national characteristic as language. This language, which is good enough for a white man and a black man, ought to be good enough for the red man. (Prucha, 1984, p. 690)

Atkins helped push through the law on English usage and rejoiced that not one Indian student under the control of the U. S. government was permitted to study any language but English, "the language of the greatest, most powerful, and enterprising nationalities beneath the sun" (Prucha, 1984, p. 690).

The other principal tenet of the government approach to acculturation was the removal of students from the influence of home and tribe (O'Brien, 1989). The white view, in simplistic terms, was the fear that the children might be taught the curriculum of civilization by day, then instructed in "savagery" at night (Adams, 1988, p. 13). In typically racist tones, Commissioner Ezra Hayt (1877) expressed this perceived need to remove the children from

> the demoralization and degradation of an Indian home, which neutralizes the efforts of the school teacher, especially those efforts which are directed to advancement in morality and civilization. (Prucha, 1984, p. 689)

Because of this attitude, off-reservation boarding schools were considered superior to reservation day or boarding schools.

However, for all the ambitious effort at complete indoctrination, the assimilation policy was seriously flawed. For one thing, there was no rule compelling every Indian child to attend, creating the lack of coverage already mentioned (Ellis, 1996). Also, cultural identities were left intact to varying degrees on the reservations. Related to this was the complete lack of any sort of support or assimilation effort beyond the schooling itself.

By providing absolutely no avenue to open opportunities in white society for Indians to utilize their education, even at the manual labor levels, students in effect were left with only the choice of returning to their homes. "Going back to the blanket," as it was called (Adams, 1988, p. 13), was seen as a relapse of sorts and was a source of great disappointment for the federal school administrators. What seems remarkable is that they could not perceive that their policies insisted on it. With no entry available into white society, and no supporting economic development to implant a "white culture" on the reservation, there was no other choice (Trennert, 1988).

In a peripheral sense, this flaw, this lack of attention to socioeconomic opportunity or development may be seen as related to the lack of attention to higher education for Native Americans. Typically, it is higher education that trains the political, industrial, and social leaders, who then play significant roles in such social and economic development. By failing to provide schools for such leaders, the federal government ensured that the lower-level workers were being trained for an economy that did not and would not exist.

During this period, what little attention was paid to Native American higher education was done so by the tribes, religious groups, and at least one state, all with no assistance and not a little interference from the federal government. The federal government regarded higher education for the Native Americans in this period to be high school, possibly normal school for a few. A very few did attend such schools, although to do so meant resisting the restrictions on Indians going to public high schools. There were no such schools specifically for Indians, public or federal (Trennert, 1988).

The Allotment Act, with its avowed purpose of rendering the Native Americans self-sufficient, also seems flawed as an assimilation policy by this same line of reasoning. The Act is philosophically similar to the Homestead Act for whites. Yet the Homestead Act (1862) was passed in concert with the Morrill Act, which created land grant colleges. The intent of the Morrill Act was to generate colleges to provide the higher levels of training to create such leaders and professionals as would be needed to stimulate economic development into the future, creating a self-sustaining socioeconomic system (Key, 1996). In the case of Native Americans, both regarding the land and education elements of the assimilation policy, only the lowest levels were addressed. The program was flawed simply by being incomplete.

The off-reservation boarding school system, for all its limitations, proved remarkably durable. The government did not begin closing such schools until 1920, and then only slowly. Expectations to the contrary, only three evolved into Native American colleges. A few still survive today, functioning largely unchanged, providing a vocational education augmented by high school course work. Two of these are still in Oklahoma, the last to close having been Chilocco Academy in 1980. They serve mostly orphans, wards of the tribes or courts, and others with nowhere else to go (*Tulsa World*, 1997, June 15).

White Colleges Out of Indian Schools

The United States has over 2,500 institutions of higher education (*Lovejoy's College Guide*, 1995), a substantial number of which were founded in the late nineteenth century. A frequent pattern of development was not for colleges to be founded from scratch, but for them to develop out of lower level academies, seminaries, boarding schools, or proprietary schools, sometimes passing through a normal school phase (Rudolph, [1962] 1990). This pattern occurred with Indian schools as well as white, as in the case of the Oneida Academy becoming Hamilton College. However, again with Hamilton as an early example, when Indian schools were transformed into colleges, the results were rarely Indian colleges.

This movement away from a predominately Native American student body to a more mainstream position was usually based on financial considerations. A new college usually has a fairly straightforward need to appeal to as broad a population base as possible to ensure suffi-cient numbers of students. At times, this need to ensure the school's financial viability was no doubt encouraged by local population pres-sure as the white community responded to a perceived needed new col-lege in their midst.

As the following examples will illustrate, such a change in the mis-sion of the school may have occurred innocuously, even inadvertently. Or it may have been handled as something of a slap in the face of the Indian community, generating feelings of ill will within it.

Ottawa University

The experience of Ottawa University is one in which the move to a more mainstream position was not handled as well as might have been hoped. Today both the town of Ottawa, Kansas, and Ottawa Univer-sity are named in honor of the Ottawa tribe. However, the school of-fers no specific Native American programs, no specific Native Ameri-can mission, and has only about 2 percent Native Americans in its student body (*Lovejoy's College Guide*, 1995; *Ottawa University Cata-log*, 1995–1997).

The school was originally chartered in 1860 as Roger Williams Uni-versity, by the white community, but on Ottawa reservation land in Kansas (Oppelt, 1990; *Ottawa University Catalog*, 1995–1997). The Ottawa tribe had already been removed from the Great Lakes area to Kansas, and would later be required to move to Indian Territory be-tween 1867 and 1873 (Wright and Tierney, 1991).

As Roger Williams University, the school was not a financial suc-cess. The local white community was not capable of supporting a col-lege. But a group of three principal local promoters were not about to be so easily put off. They proposed the Ottawa Indian University in 1862 (Wright and Tierney, 1991), which itself was never actually real-ized. They then modified their plan, rechartering the existing school as Ottawa University (*Lovejoy's College Guide*, 1995; *Ottawa University Catalog*, 1995–1997; Wright and Tierney, 1991), affiliating it with the American Baptist Church.

The current Ottawa University catalog refers to the founders as "Bap-tist lay persons interested in education" (p. 2). Behind that innocuous statement are three rather unorthodox individuals. The first was John T. (Tauy) Jones, a mixed-blood Chippewa who was adopted by the Ot-tawa tribe (Oppelt, 1990). Tauy Jones has been described as having been involved in a series of minor indiscretions and questionable incidents in the East prior to coming to Kansas (Unrau and Miner, 1985).

Next was the Reverend Isaac C. Kalloch, a Boston Baptist minister, who moved west due to the scandal of a adultery charge (Oppelt, 1990). He would be named the first president of Ottawa University. The third was Clinton C. Hutchinson, an Indian agent who had been fired from the Sac and Fox agency due to an unaccounted-for $2,000 and frequent verbal abuse of his Native American charges. He had used his political contacts to gain a new appointment as the Ottawa tribe's agent (Oppelt, 1990; Unrau and Miner, 1985).

These three envisioned using the land currently controlled by the Ottawas to promote and expand the town of Ottawa, thereby strengthening the potential economic base of the college. The importance of Ottawa University in their plans is not known, whether their focus was the founding of the school, or if they saw it as an important asset for a growing community. Hutchinson and Kalloch formed a land corporation to handle legal and financial details, and to promote their land scheme for the development of the townsite to potential settlers and investors in the east (Unrau and Miner, 1985).

To get land to develop, they offered an affiliation between the tribe and the school in exchange for a grant of sixty-four acres on which to build the school itself and other lands for the support of the school. In exchange, any member of the tribe was to be able to attend tuition-free in perpetuity (Unrau and Miner, 1985). This provision was included in the treaty of 1867 which required the removal of the Ottawas to Indian Territory. This provision presumably would ensure that the removal would not deny the education of their children for which they had donated land (Unrau and Miner, 1985).

This treaty, like many others, provided for the forced sale of current tribal lands to raise funds for future tribal needs. However, the founders arranged, again due to their activities in the negotiations of that treaty, for 20,000 acres to be allotted for the support of the school (*Ottawa University Catalog*, 1995–1997; Unrau and Miner, 1985), and positioned themselves to be able to purchase other available land for one dollar an acre (Unrau and Miner, 1985). Hutchinson's father-in-law, J. W. Young, also managed to purchase 5,000 acres of the 20,000 acre grant for $1.25 an acre, the minimum price (Unrau and Miner, 1985).

Instead of developing or leasing the 20,000 acre grant, it was later sold to provide money for the college (Oppelt, 1990; *Ottawa University Catalog*, 1995–1997). Apparently all such revenue went into the general fund with none being set aside to fund the Ottawa tuition program. The lands purchased for one dollar an acre were also sold, for considerably more money, as part of the land development scheme (Oppelt, 1990).

Although named for the tribe and purporting to educate its children free of charge, the college was not otherwise related to the tribe. Consequently, the opening of the college and building of the campus proceeded unaffected by the removal of the tribe between 1867 and 1873. The first building, Tauy Jones Hall, was completed in 1869. To the Ottawas, it seemed much larger and more ornate than was necessary, even if they were not to leave Kansas. The Ottawas regarded it as evidence of how much they had been defrauded in the grant/sale and resale of lands (Oppelt, 1990).

To make matters worse, as the removal to Indian Territory neared completion, the university board of trustees began to refuse to provide free tuition to Ottawa children per the provision of the treaty. This, in turn, caused most Ottawas to refuse to send their children to the school. Before long, there was no evidence of Ottawa support of the school other than the involvement of Jones. In 1871, there was only one Indian student, Idelette Jones, Tauy's daughter (Oppelt, 1990). The college was effectively a white school from that point on. Jones himself was excluded from Ottawa tribal membership on April 24, 1869 (Unrau and Miner, 1985).

The Ottawas did more than simply refuse to support the school, and their complaints did have an effect, if an extremely belated one. Very early in the land scheme activities of the three founders, Secretary of the Interior John Usher inquired into some questionable aspects of the activities of Hutchinson as the Ottawa Indian agent. But he did not appear to perceive the complexity of the scheme unfolding in Kansas, and was likely busier with other concerns (the Civil War) at the time (Unrau and Miner, 1985).

The land scheme was later investigated twice by the Interior Department. The first investigation found nothing amiss. The second did, but nothing sufficiently important to require corrective action, other than the removal of Hutchinson as Indian agent in April 1867. Kalloch unabashedly applied for the vacant position but was rejected (Unrau and Miner, 1985). Several civil suits and government attempts tried to reclaim some of the land revenues, taking several years and with little results. Late in his life, Jones tried to distance himself from Kalloch and Hutchinson (Unrau and Miner, 1985). At his death, he left his $25,000 estate to the college (Unrau and Miner, 1985).

There the matter lay for several generations, until the 1946 establishment of the Federal Indian Claims Commission. This provided a means for the Ottawas to seek restitution. In 1951, a petition was filed, bringing twelve charges on the loss of lands and monies, three of which related to Ottawa University. These three charges were that the federal government (a) had permitted the organization of an illegal university board of trustees and sanctioned the operation of this board; (b) had failed to guarantee that Ottawa University would always be open to Ottawa children as provided by the treaty of 1867; and (c) had allowed a partial settlement of 1873, which had returned only a small fraction of the land or proceeds to the tribe (Oppelt, 1990).

The court case arising from this petition took until 1960 to be completed, with the plaintiff charges upheld. The case was complicated by the fact that the federal government had terminated its recognition of the tribe in 1956, due to its having no land base (Oppelt, 1990). Finally, on April 30, 1965, one hundred years after the founding of the college, the tribe received and disbursed to its 630 members the sum of $406,166.19, giving it legal, if not moral, restitution for the actions against it (Oppelt, 1990).

Sheldon Jackson College

The actions of Jones, Kalloch, and Hutchinson constitute something of an extreme case regarding insensitive treatment and failure to honor commitments to Native Americans in the course of establishing a college. Most Native American schools shifted to being predominately white schools far more inadvertently, even reluctantly. Such no doubt is the case of Sheldon Jackson College.

It was founded in Sitka, Alaska, the capital of Russian Alaska, in 1878 (*Lovejoy's College Guide*, 1995; Oppelt, 1990). At that time, it was an institute, not a college, associated with the Presbyterian Church, and served only Inuit or Eskimo-Aleut students (Oppelt, 1990). In 1944, it changed to a junior college, and found it necessary to admit white students as well. In 1981, it became a four-year college. The surrounding population is so sparse that the school has remained quite small, even as the Native American students slipped into a minority position. In 1990, Oppelt reported Sheldon Jackson's student body as 45 percent Native American. By 1995, Lovejoy's gives an 18 percent figure, with a total student body of only 200.

The University of Tulsa

The University of Tulsa may be one of the better examples of just how far from Native American roots a college can evolve. Today it is a small, urban private university, with ties to the Presbyterian Church, a reasonable degree of exclusivity, and a substantial endowment, thanks largely to close ties to the petroleum industry. It does offer a program within its law school specializing in Native American law (*University of Tulsa Graduate Bulletin*, 1994–1996). However, that program is more reflective of the specific interests of students and select faculty than of any strong sense of Native American roots, tribal ties, or mission.

Yet, in 1882, what would become the University of Tulsa was the Presbyterian School for Indian Girls, a boarding school in Muskogee, Indian Territory (Oppelt, 1990; *University of Tulsa Undergraduate Bulletin*, 1994–1996). In 1894, the school was rechartered as Henry Kendall College, a co-ed liberal arts school. It still had a substantial Indian student body and some support from the Creek nation, but was now open to whites. It was the second college in the relatively small town of Muskogee. The other was Bacone, which more purposefully served Native American students.

Kendall College struggled with financial problems for several years, including the loss of some support due to the federal termination of tribal governments. Meanwhile, a 1905 oil boom caused Tulsa, forty-five miles away, to grow substantially, eventually to become the largest city in the area. In 1907, the college administration voted to move from Muskogee to Tulsa (Oppelt, 1990).

While Tulsa, as was the case for all of Oklahoma, had a significant Native American population, it had been a small hamlet during most of the Indian Territory years. Tribal capitals had been located in Tahlequah, Muskogee, Okmulgee, and other towns that are now smaller than Tulsa. Consequently, the move to Tulsa had the effect of making Kendall College all the more likely to attract a predominately white student body.

Kendall next was faced with a familiar problem, a proposed second college, to be named McFarland after Robert McFarland, a local oil man. Representatives from both institutions agreed that even an enlarged Tulsa was unlikely to be able to effectively support two colleges. An agreement was reached to merge the two into the University of Tulsa in 1920 (Oppelt, 1990; *University of Tulsa Undergraduate Bulletin* 1994–1996). Today, its Native American population averages about 5 percent of its student body.

Northeastern State University

While the University of Tulsa is proud of its Native American roots, however small a role they may play in the university today, sixty miles east of Tulsa, in Tahlequah, is Northeastern State University. It has a similar history to the University of Tulsa, but has retained much more of the culture of and involvement with the Native American community. Northeastern State can trace its beginnings to the two Cherokee Seminaries established to fulfill the stipulation of the treaty of 1835 that an institution of higher learning be provided subsequent to their removal to Indian Territory.

In 1846, the Cherokee National Council voted to establish the National Male and National Female Seminaries (Fischer, 1974). They were operational by 1851. As discussed earlier, they were later taken over and combined by the federal government as part of the move to eliminate tribal governments.

Shortly after statehood, in 1909, Oklahoma purchased this institution from the government and chartered it as the Northeastern State Normal School, the first of many name changes to come (Oppelt, 1990). The school then offered four years of high school and two years of college. In 1919, it was renamed the Northeastern State Teachers College, and became a four-year institution.

The year 1939 saw the name changed again, to Northeastern State College. Master's degrees in various disciplines were added, beginning in the 1950s. In 1974, another name change resulted in Northeastern Oklahoma State University, and again in 1985 to the current Northeastern State University (*Northeastern State University Catalog*, 1996).

Although it is now a mainstream state institution with a white student body majority, having remained in Tahlequah its entire existence, Northeastern State retains close cultural and historical ties to the Cherokee nation. Native Americans remain a substantial presence at 16 percent of the student body (*Lovejoy's College Guide*, 1995), making Northeastern State one of only three universities in the United States with over 1,000 Native American students (Tierney, 1992; Wright, 1991).

Fort Lewis College

The history of Fort Lewis College of Durango, Colorado, contains elements of the histories of Northeastern State University and of Ottawa University. Fort Lewis started in 1878 as one of the federal government's off-reservation boarding schools. In 1911, it was taken over by the state of Colorado, and named the State School of Agriculture, Mechanical, and Household Arts (Oppelt, 1990). On the surface, this sounds like no change at all except for state instead of federal administration.

However, the state elected to open the school to whites as well as Indians. Possibly due to pressure from the Native American community or federal requirements attached to the state takeover of the school, in 1911, an executive order by Colorado Governor John Shaforth stated that "Indian pupils shall at all times be admitted to said school free of charge for tuition, and on terms of equity with white students" (Oppelt, 1990).

In 1933, the school was rechartered as Fort Lewis Junior College. It became a four-year school in 1962 (*Fort Lewis College Catalog*, 1995). True to form, the admission of white students quickly relegated the Native Americans to a minority position. By 1970, it had only 224 Indian students, 10.8 percent of the student body (Oppelt, 1990).

Having one in ten students not paying tuition created financial difficulties for the school. Consequently, in 1971, the Colorado legislature passed a bill to limit Native American tuition waivers to Colorado residents, not all Native Americans. The Bureau of Indian Affairs and other Indian organizations fought this development in court, eventually getting the bill rescinded (Oppelt, 1990).

Today Fort Lewis College maintains a substantial support and cultural program for its Native American students. Native Americans currently represent 12 percent or about 440 members of the Fort Lewis student body (*Lovejoy's College Guide*, 1995).

The Indian Colleges

In a nation with 2,500-plus higher education institutions, this pattern of Indian schools evolving into predominately white colleges has probably happened dozens of times. Although a few, like Northeastern State University or Fort Lewis College, have retained cultural ties or special programs for Native Americans, none evolved into exclusively Native American colleges. Only two such Native American colleges came out of the nineteenth century, both founded for just such a mission. They are Bacone College, of Muskogee, Oklahoma, and Pembroke State University, of Pembroke, North Carolina.

Bacone College

Founded in 1880, Bacone College is the oldest college in Oklahoma. Although it is traditionally and culturally Native American, and its mission is focused on Native Americans, it has never limited its enrollment to Native Americans. Over the years, the percentage of Native American students has varied considerably, even to being outnumbered by whites in 1895–1900 (Oppelt, 1990). Even so, it remains predominately Native American, now the oldest such college in the United States.

Bacone owes its existence to the efforts of Almon C. Bacone (1830–1896), a missionary-teacher-reformer, who was not merely interested in Native American higher education, but had a lasting impact on it (Bode, 1957). Many of Bacone's views and opinions were in conflict with those of his time, and generally considerably more progressive.

Bacone held a holistic view of education, a position generally more in keeping with Native American philosophy. Rather than favoring specialized learning or training in narrowly defined areas, he believed in broad applications of physical, intellectual, and moral education in unison (Williams and Meredith, 1980, p. 3). He also favored the integration of education with the student's home life, in opposition to the principle on which the federal boarding schools operated (Adams, 1995). He favored founding a college among the Indians, rather than requiring them to leave home to go east for higher education.

It is not too extreme to say the Indian cause was Bacone's passion. His personal motto was "Rescue the perishing," alluding to the troubling loss of Native American population at that time (Bode, 1957). Several statements by Bacone in the first catalog of the Indian University (Bacone College) pointedly took issue with the federal policies and programs common to that era. In the introduction to the new college and its mission, he stated "The extermination of a race is unworthy of a Christian people" (*First Annual Catalog, Indian University*, 1881, p. 6). In doing so, he called attention to this very troubling shrinkage of the Native American population, which would reach a national low of 237,000 in 1900 (U. S. Department of Commerce, June 1991). The federal policies of the time, if not necessarily genocidal, were equally unhelpful as the pressures of warfare, a lack of immunity to diseases associated with whites and removals to unfamiliar areas, and a generally impoverished lifestyle all contributed to the shrinkage of the Native American community. Bacone also stated that "a constant removal from the approach of civilization would never civilize" (Bode, 1957), a clear recognition of the contradictions of federal policy to prepare Indians for the white world, but to deny socioeconomic assimilation.

Bacone had immigrated from the East, and was serving as an instructor at the Cherokee National Male Seminary in Tahlequah when he first offered his idea for an Indian college. On October 10, 1879, he presented his concept to the Baptist Cherokee Association. It was so well received that later that same night a committee was formed to implement such a plan. Shortly afterward, a board of trustees was named for the proposed "Indian University" (Williams and Meredith, 1980).

The university opened in 1880, under the auspices of the American Baptist Home Mission Society through the Cherokee Baptist Mission (Bacone College Catalog, 1995; Debo, [1940]1968; Wright, 1991). It offered K-12 preparatory education and a four-year college curriculum. The college had three original students and was housed in the Home Mission Building of the Cherokee National Female Seminary (Williams and Meredith, 1980). Its mission was to serve the higher education needs of all Native Americans, and the founders envisioned the school as inclusive across the five civilized tribes plus the Delaware (Williams and Meredith, 1980).

The college very quickly outgrew its makeshift quarters. In October 1881, Bacone approached the governments of the Cherokee and Creek nations, seeking permission to move to Muskogee (Williams and Meredith, 1980). In 1866, the U. S. government had signed a treaty with the Creek nation to re-define their post-Civil War relations. Article 13 of that treaty had reserved 160 acres for the use of each religious society or denomination that would build and maintain an active mission within the lands of the Creek tribe (Bode, 1957). This provision was the basis of Bacone's appeal to the Creek Council for a land grant on which to build a new campus, since the university was a private Baptist institution, not of the tribal government itself.

His proposal was presented to the House of Kings and House of Warriors, the upper and lower houses of the Creek legislature. At the time, Creek feelings were still embittered about their earlier forced removal and the more recent post-Civil War treatment. This led to a heated debate on the acceptance of the proposal to build the university (Bode, 1957).

A young member rose with a bitter denunciation of the white man and his injustice to the Indian, stating, "We need nothing from the white man, either by way of education or religion, and we should give him nothing" (House of Warriors, Minutes #32616, October 29, 1881). The motion was subsequently tabled, but others were disappointed and pressed to reopen the issue. It was, and the supporters pointed out the potential future advantages of having such an institution in their own country. The proposal was opened to a vote and passed 39–35 (Bode, 1957).

Thereafter, the Creek council acted quickly to grant the college a new charter, as well as a land grant of 160 acres on which to locate the campus (Williams and Meredith, 1980; Wright, 1991). In effect, this made Indian University the first and only land grant college established by Native Americans themselves (Wright, 1991; Wright and Tierney, 1991). The Creek National Council specified that the school was to "be to the Indian Territory, as nearly as practicable, all that state universities are to the several states." It also was to be open to students of all Indian nations (Acts of the Creek Nation 1877–1882, #11, pp. 189–190; Bode, 1957, p. 23; Williams and Meredith, 1980).

The college flourished initially, granting its first baccalaureate degree in 1883. It had 109 students by the time of the move to Muskogee in 1885, and grew to 703 by 1895 (Williams and Meredith, 1980). In 1884, Bacone went east on a fund-raising tour. He had raised $3,000 before catching the attention of Mrs. J. D. Rockefeller. She prevailed on her husband to pledge $10,000, which paid for the construction of Rockefeller Hall, the original main building of the campus (*Bacone College Catalog*, 1995; Williams and Meredith, 1980). In 1887, the college began offering a master's degree, but no student ever earned one (Bode, 1957).

The college experienced a long, difficult period associated with the federal government's attempt to dissolve Native American tribal governments. On September 27, 1897, the U. S. government voided the original land grants of "Harrel Institute, Henry Kendall College, and Nazareth Institute in Muskogee, and Baptist University [*sic*] near Muskogee" (Bode, 1957, pp. 42–43; Williams and Meredith, 1980, p. 37), allowing each to retain ten acres only for school purposes. A second act (June 28, 1898) reduced this to five acres. On March 1, 1901, the government granted the schools the right to purchase forty additional acres.

Indian University filed suit against the federal government to protect its original grant and to evict the new landowner, one Quinton Garrett. The case took a long time and was contested to the fullest by both parties. The Oklahoma Supreme Court, then the U. S. Supreme Court, on May 27, 1914, upheld the university's claim, after seventeen years in dispute (Williams and Meredith, 1980).

During this period, enrollment dropped to 158 in 1905, of which only ten were college level. By 1909, enrollment was down to 110. The federal government had appointed a superintendent of the Indian national school system in 1903, and attempted to remove all Indian schools from local control, with closings starting in 1906. Part of the Indian University's court case was for recognition of its private, religious-affiliated status (Williams and Meredith, 1980), its principal avenue to protect itself from federal action.

In 1910, Indian University was renamed Bacone College in honor of the late founder (*Bacone College Catalog*, 1995). Enrollment continued to sag until 1916. By 1918, when B. D. Weeks was named president, Bacone was a college in name only. Weeks set about reestablishing the higher education program, offering sporadic college courses in the early 1920s. By 1927, he had restored the junior college department, having chosen to use the University of Chicago model of junior and senior college divisions. The senior division was attempted periodically, but was never successful, causing Bacone to evolve into a de facto two-year institution (Bode, 1957; Williams and Meredith, 1980).

In spite of the academic difficulties extending into the 1920s, that decade was quite profitable for the college regarding its endowment and physical plant. Thanks to the Oklahoma oil booms, many Native Americans in the general area found themselves extremely wealthy. A number of them made sizable gifts to Bacone College, raising its endowment to $900,000 by 1924 and providing a great deal of support for its building program (Bode, 1957; Oppelt, 1990). These gifts were often challenged by lawsuits from other interests, based on the view that Indians were not competent to thus dispose of their own wealth (Bode, 1957).

As recently as 1979, the prospects of reestablishing the four-year program at Bacone was discussed (Chavers, 1979), but it was not implemented. The high school program was discontinued in 1957. In the early 1960s, administrative control passed from the Baptist Church to the college itself. Today Bacone fluctuates around five to six hundred students. Enrollment is open to all, but Bacone retains a Native American student body tradition.

In some respects, Bacone maybe viewed as the prototype for the tribally controlled colleges of today. Its educational focus has long been in a strong liberal arts curriculum in the classical mode, but with a concurrent strong emphasis on their own Native American heritage (Williams and Meredith, 1980). This combination of objectives is notably similar to the mission and curriculum of our newer tribally controlled colleges. Also, this determined focus on Native American culture as part of the curriculum may be the reason Bacone successfully attracted Native American students and resisted the all-too-common tendency to evolve into a predominately white school.

For a small school with a history of limited enrollment, Bacone has graduated a remarkable number of influential alumni. Among its graduates are artists Acee Blue Eagle, Dick West, and Willard Stone. Political leaders from Bacone include Pleasant Porter (Creek leader) and Thomas Bartles, both of whom have Oklahoma towns named after them; as well as Arizona State Senator Lloyd House, Peter MacDonald, chairman of the Navajo Tribal Council, and Patrick Hurley, former secretary of war under President Hoover and ambassador to China (Oppelt, 1990; Williams and Meredith, 1980).

After its rather long, solitary existence as virtually the only one of its kind, Bacone continues to stand out among the newer generation of tribally controlled colleges. They both reflect, in their missions, and differ from, in being tribally controlled instead of private, Bacone College. Bacone's position in Native American higher education history is unique as the oldest, and for many years, the only traditionally Indian college in the United States.

Pembroke State University

To say the Bacone is the oldest and, for many years, the only Native American college is not to say it was the only one for the entire period from its 1880 founding to the advent of the new generation of Native American colleges in the United States. For many of those years, 1887 to 1954 to be exact, it shared the distinction of specifically serving Native American higher education needs with Pembroke State University of North Carolina (Beck, 1995). Pembroke is unique in being the first and still the only state college established specifically for Native Americans (Oppelt, 1990).

Pembroke was founded for the needs of a very specific tribe with a very unique history, the Lumbees of the Robeson County area of North Carolina. The Lumbees have only recently been recognized by the federal government, but have been by the state of North Carolina since 1885. Over the intervening years, thanks to resolutions of the state legislature, they have been known as the Croatans, the less imaginative Indians of Robeson County, the Robeson County Cherokees, the

Robeson County Tuscarora, the Robeson County Sioux, and, finally, the Lumbee, after a local river (*Dictionary of Indian Tribes*, 1980).

The origin of the tribe is lost in history and largely apocryphal. According to tribal tradition, they are the descendants of Sir Walter Raleigh's "lost colony" and a local band of coastal Native Americans (Dial and Eliades, 1971; *Dictionary of Indian Tribes*, 1980). In 1585, Croatan was an Algonquian or Hatteras village near Cape Hatteras, south of Roanoke Island, the site of Raleigh's colony (*Dictionary of Indian Tribes*, 1980, p. 423). The tribal tradition contends that the lost colony that disappeared between 1587 and 1591 disappeared from European view only (Gaillard, 1971). After an attack by hostile Indians, the remnants of the colony was accepted by the village, a possible explanation for the mysterious "Croatoan" carved on a tree as the only clue to their disappearance (*Dictionary of Indian Tribes of the Americas*, 1980). Together they eventually formed a new identity, the Croatans.

There is no physical, documentary, or other direct evidence in support of this legend. However, there is some reasonably compelling circumstantial evidence. The Croatan/Lumbee tribe racially is one of mixed blood, apparently Indian, white, and Negro, typical of many seaboard Indian groups (*Dictionary of Indian Tribes*, 1980). When they were discovered by Scottish settlers in the early 1700s, the Croatans were already speaking English, and many had brown hair and blue eyes. By 1708, Cape Hatteras Indian Town appears on maps in place of or very near the village of Croatan. The village itself appears on a 1585–1586 map (*Dictionary of Indian Tribes*, 1980).

Today, there are less than 100 surnames among the 40,000 Lumbees in North Carolina. Roughly one-half of these are surnames in common with those of the lost colonists (Gaillard, 1971). Besides sixteenth-century English names, the tribe retains many speech habits and customs that can be associated with England of that period (*Dictionary of Indian Tribes of the Americas*, 1980). Finally, Croatan was a real village and the tradition does offer the reasonable explanation of the mysterious "Croatoan" carving.

There is little official record of the Croatans until the 1835 North Carolina constitutional convention. It decreed that all peoples identified as Indians in North Carolina be classified as "free negroes," for lack of a better term, to recognize their free but non-white status (Stoutenburgh, 1960). Such nonwhites were to be denied many legal rights by the state. They could not vote, attend public school, attain more than a minimal education, own firearms, intermarry with whites, take part in court proceedings, or serve in the military. They could own land, but tended to fall prey to the fraudulent practices of whites who had a monopoly on legal rights (*Dictionary of Indian Tribes*, 1980).

They remained in such straits until 1868, when the post-Civil War amendments required the restitution of such suspended civil rights. Some time later, Hamilton MacMillan, the Robeson County State representative, investigated the origins of his Indian constituents, concluded the tradition of their origins was accurate, and came out as a champion of the tribe's rights (Dial and Eliades, 1971).

In 1885, MacMillan successfully enacted a bill to recognize the tribe, giving them the official name of Croatan (*Dictionary of Indian Tribes of the Americas*, 1980). He also included a provision to provide them with a state-supported school system. As a direct result, in 1887, the Croatan Normal School was founded and went into operation (Oppelt, 1990; Stein, 1992; *University of North Carolina at Pembroke Catalog*, 1997–1999).

Largely because of the trust responsibility assumed by the federal government regarding Native Americans, in 1890, North Carolina appealed to Commissioner of Indian Affairs T. J. Morgan for financial support of the school (Dial and Eliades, 1971). The request was denied. Lacking any historical claim of a land base, the tribe was not then and only very recently has been recognized by the federal government (U. S. Department of Commerce, June 1991).

In retrospect, the Croatan/Lumbees were fortunate to have had so little interaction with the federal government. They never fought a war, signed a treaty, or came under the jurisdiction of the Bureau of Indian Affairs. As a result, during a long period of federal control over most of the Native American community, the Croatan/Lumbees exercised a high degree of control over their own resources, including maintaining control of lands held, and input on their educational services and programs (Gaillard, 1971).

In spite of MacMillan's efforts, in its early years, Croatan Normal School was not well funded. It originally offered instruction at the elementary and secondary levels, granting its first diplomas in 1905. The two-year normal school program beyond high school actually was not added until 1926, with the first degrees granted in 1928 (Oppelt, 1990; *University of North Carolina at Pembroke Catalog*, 1997–1999). Prior to that time, normal school courses were offered only sporadically (Dial and Eliades, 1971). The 1926 establishment of the full normal school program resulted in accreditation by the state as a standard normal school, and the dropping of the K-12 program (Dial and Eliades, 1971).

Around 1911, Croatan became a label of derision (Dial and Eliades, 1971). As a result, the designated name of the tribe was changed to the rather generic Indians of Robeson County, with the school following suit as the Indian Normal School of Robeson County (Dial and Eliades, 1971; Oppelt, 1990). Two years later, a similar change in both yielded Cherokee Indians of Robeson County and Cherokee Indian Normal School of Robeson County (Dial and Eliades, 1971). The Tuscarora and Sioux appellations were used informally over time, as well. The Lumbee name would not be official until 1956 (*Dictionary of Indian Tribes of the Americas*, 1980).

General education college courses were added in 1931, with a full four-year program developing by 1939. The first baccalaureate degrees were granted in 1940; the first nonteaching degrees in 1942. The intervening year, 1941, saw a name change to Pembroke State College for Indians. "For Indians" was dropped in 1949 (Dial and Eliades, 1971; Oppelt, 1990; *University of North Carolina at Pembroke Catalog*, 1997–1999).

In 1945, the school made a major change in its mission, opening enrollment to all Native Americans instead of just the Lumbee tribe (Dial and Eliades, 1971; Oppelt, 1990; *University of North Carolina at Pembroke Catalog*, 1997–1999). This seemed the first of several such moves aimed at broadening the appeal of the school. In 1953, enrollment was opened to all races, with white enrollment limited to a maximum of 40 percent of the student body (Dial and Eliades, 1971; Oppelt, 1990; *University of North Carolina at Pembroke Catalog*, 1997–1999).

The very next year, the college administration moved quickly to comply with the 1954 Supreme Court *Brown versus Board of Education* ruling requiring the desegregation of public schools. Admission was opened to all, with Pembroke State quickly becoming mostly white (Dial and Eliades, 1971; Oppelt, 1990). The college experienced a 500 percent growth in the student body over the next eight years (*University of North Carolina at Pembroke Catalog*, 1997–1999).

Now Pembroke State University, the school as it exists today seems simply another, if belated, example of a Native American school evolving into a mainstream, predominately white school due to financial considerations. It has approximately 25 percent Native Americans among its 2,100 students (*Lovejoy's College Guide*, 1995). That actually represents something of a resurgence. The post-1954 growth was almost totally due to white enrollment. By 1971, Native Americans were only two to three hundred students out of a total enrollment of 3,000. At that time, the school had only three Native American faculty, and no special services, financial aid, scholarships, or Indian studies programs for Native Americans (Ackley, 1972). In fact, due to its emphasis on providing a typical college curriculum and training in the course of its existence, Indian culture has never played a primary role in the institution (Ackley, 1972; Dial and Eliades, 1971; Weinberg, 1977).

During the brief period from 1940 to 1954, Pembroke was the first and still the only state-supported four-year college for Indians in the nation (Dial and Eliades, 1971). The fact that only a single state college for Indians has ever existed emphasizes the perception that Indian higher education was seen as a federal responsibility, even though federal support has never been adequately forthcoming (Oppelt, 1990).

A strong sense exists in the Lumbee community that the push toward desegregation associated with the civil rights movement was detrimental to the Lumbee effort to maintain a separate school system, and through it, to enhance their cultural heritage (Gaillard, 1971). Our traditionally black colleges and universities have only recently begun to be pressured, by recent Supreme Court rulings, to open enrollment to whites (Wenglinsky, 1996). In the case of Pembroke, the state acted very precipitously, almost as soon as the 1954 desegregation was handed down. The state obviously used it as the opening to allow the enrollment of a wider population and ease the apparent financial burden imposed by the limited mission of the college.

Overview

The early decision to dwell on agricultural, mechanical, and domestic skills for the bulk of Indian education proved to be the most durable and descriptive aspect of the federal Indian education program. Why this proved to be the case is only minimally explained by the historical record. The reasoning that the colonial efforts at Native American higher education had limited results seems unduly simplistic. That, of nine colonial colleges, there were only three with Indian objectives, and a consistent lack of effective Native American recruitment, preparation, or properly supervised funding should not have been difficult to discern for anyone concerned with the direction of Native American education.

The early decisions to continue to recognize tribal sovereignty would seem to carry with it a recognizable need to provide for the preparation of the leaders required by such sovereign groups. Furthermore, the importance of colleges and universities as transmitters and repositories of culture should have struck a chord with those who believed Native Americans should be assimilated into the larger culture. As is the case in society as a whole, for Native Americans the colleges and universities would seem necessary to provide such leaders and to lead the way culturally, with the noncollege population benefitting from the trickle-down effects, from the teachers thus trained, and the leadership thus developed.

Why a government comprised of the mostly well-educated should have instead chosen a bottom-up, if not bottom-only, approach is effectively unexplained. The Native American was to be trained almost exclusively for a peasant lifestyle, one only minimally related to the American society. Even if one accepts such a choice as reasonable at the founding of the nation, that does not explain the continued adherence to that objective throughout the nineteenth and well into the twentieth centuries, as it became increasingly obvious that the United States was an industrial, market economy, and that the Indians must ultimately be included in the national society.

The most reasonable inference seems to be that the educational policy existed as a token to assimilationism during the early period otherwise guided by a removalist policy. And that a later realization that assimilation was becoming unavoidable was clouded by a rampant racism which interfered with any progressive change in established educational policy.

In choosing to administer the Native American schools from the national level, the fact that no one in government was prepared for such a task, or that a logical choice might be to model the federal system on the nation's localized educational system seems to have not been considered. The only concern seems to have been a remarkably simplistic means of gaining access to Native American lands, while providing a minimal form of retraining to enable the Indians to subsist on what land was to be given back to them. As we normally interpret education to mean the expansion of one's horizons and possibilities, such an educational program seems hardly deserving of the name.

Possibly the greatest fault with the federal program was not its chosen curriculum, but that it was a federal program. By not being under any sort of local control, as was the cases for virtually the entire rest of the United States educational systems, no input from the Native American community or locally responsive educators was forthcoming. Had local or self control been the case, arguments for a more elaborate introduction to the European culture, for concurrent attention to the Native American cultures, or for more effective leadership and professional training might have been forthcoming.

Several excellent beginnings in just such a direction existed within the tribal and missionary schools. However, the repeated disruption and necessity to begin anew associated with removals, the pressure to use the federally approved curriculum to qualify for funding, and the closing of schools as part of the abolishment of tribal governments all combined to negate any progress in the direction of local control.

Within the higher education scene itself, the pattern of select Indian schools evolving into colleges, only to leave their Indian roots behind, seems to stem mostly from simple financial need. With Native Americans representing such a small minority of the population, not to mention the lack of proper college preparation available to them, budding colleges had no choice but to broaden their appeal to the larger white community. Such a pattern of development could have been avoided only by a dedicated program of federal funding aimed at supporting the development of Native American colleges. Such an economically supportive approach was obviously a consideration in the development of the land grant college system (Key, 1996), and was instrumental in the development of traditionally black colleges (Wenglinsky, 1996). But regarding Native Americans, again one finds the unexplained absence of such insight, in favor of the continuing effort to transform the Indians into farmers.

The question of why Native Americans did not benefit from the widespread national urge to found colleges during the nineteenth century is a complicated one, likely best answered by a combination of three factors. Racism was certainly one. The United States, in this period, was considerably more racist, certainly more overtly and legally so, than since. The pronouncements of assimilation, given the subsequent experience of generations of Native Americans, now have a hollow ring to them. But such racism was not sufficient to deny the establishment of Native American colleges, as the concurrent founding of multiple excellent traditionally black colleges can attest.

Equally influential was the relatively small size (and wide dispersion) of the Native American population, well under a tenth of the black population now and even more so then. Colleges are not founded solely on good intentions. Financial concerns must be addressed if a school is to survive. Just as such issues fomented an apparent lack of commitment or consistency of professed Indian education objectives on the part of colonial colleges, so did it apparently lead quite a number of schools initially serving the Native American community to broaden the recruitment of their student body in the search for students.

Finally, the retaining of federal control and responsibility for Indian education at all levels added to the problem. The Native American community being served and the bulk of the nation's professional educators were thus excluded. The Army, secretary of war, and later secretary of the interior were addressing national security problems typical of their areas of expertise, not the problems of educational administration for which they had no particular skills or preparation.

At the turn of the twentieth century, only Bacone and Pembroke were specifically serving Native American higher education needs (Beck, 1995). Bacone was private, although with active tribal support, and fighting the federal government for its very survival. Pembroke was a state school for a nonfederally recognized tribe. It would later leap at the chance to broaden its base of potential students just as other schools had done. That there were only these two serves as a clear indicator of the completeness with which the federal government denied the need for higher education as part of its assumed responsibility for the education of Native Americans.

4

The Self-Determination Period

The twentieth century opened with the Native Americans in the worst position they had been in since the invasion of the Europeans. The years of warfare in the Plains and Southwest were finished, having accomplished little other than the loss of life and the turning of public opinion away from the Indian cause. Similarly, the Ghost Dance religious movements of the 1870s and 1890s had proven ineffective beyond voicing the desperation felt by Native Americans (Thornton, 1987).

The Native American population was at an all-time low of 237,000. The tribal governments had been outlawed, and the federal government had taken control of all aspects of Indian life, with the aim of eliminating their cultural identity once and for all. The Allotment Act had been in effect for thirteen years, ostensibly to split the tribes into individuals, but also enabling the whites to take over much of the remaining land (Espinosa, 1997, January 5), as in the cases of the Oklahoma land runs of the period. The federal Indian school system was geared to deny the Indian culture and accomplish little else, coincidentally rendering the Indians mostly little- or uneducated. This widespread lack of education, combined with the newly acquired individualized land holdings, made the Indians easy prey for land fraud and other schemes to deny them even these individual allotments (Ellinger, 1997, January 25).

Yet this century, which dawned with the Indians in such dire circumstances, was to see the most dramatic policy changes by the federal government regarding the Native Americans in the history of the nation, the shift to Native American self-determination (Wright, 1991). The change was slow in coming. The era of Native American self-determination is typically seen as having begun with the Indian Reorganization Act (Wheeler-Howard Bill) of 1934 (LaCounte, 1987; Szasz, 1974; Wright and Tierney, 1991), although it was only one of a series of reports and acts favorable to Native Americans (Deloria and Lytle, 1984).

The major impact of self-determination on Native American higher education was even slower in coming. Some changes were felt as early as 1921, when the Bureau of Indian Affairs (BIA) began to assume some responsibility for Native American higher education. Others occurred over a period of years. Increased higher education funding was part of the Indian Reorganization Act itself. Also, the number of Native Americans attending college increased substantially after World War II, as it did for the rest of the nation.

However, the real impact of self-determination on Native American higher education did not begin until the late 1960s, with the 1968 founding of the Navajo Community College, the Kennedy Report of 1969, and The Navajo Community College Act of 1971 (Prucha, 1984). That school's success as the prototype of the tribally controlled community college led to the 1972 Indian Education Act, the 1978 Tribally Controlled Community College Act, and others (Prucha, 1984), and the subsequent founding of thirty tribal colleges in the next twenty-five years.

The Stirrings of Reform

While these formal changes in the government's relations with Native Americans were still well in the future, the informal perceptions of Native Americans that would lead to such changes were beginning to appear at, and even before, the turn of the century. To their credit, a number of commissioners of Indian Affairs of that period expressed opinions in favor of expanding educational offerings to and safeguarding the culture of Native America.

At successive meetings of the Lake Mohonk Conference of the Friends of the Indians, Commissioner T. J. Morgan argued the case for improving Indian education. At the sixth annual conference, he offered the opinion that education was an indispensable instrument to "make the individual redman a member of the white man's civilization" (*Lake Mohonk Conference Proceedings*, 1888, p. 24). By itself, this statement could be seen as simply support for the boarding school program, but it was to signal a subtle beginning of a movement in favor of Native American higher education.

At the 1889 conference, Morgan presented a tentative ten-point plan, which he would refine over the next few years, for the revamping of the federal Indian school system (Ellis, 1996). His first point was a general call for the government to offer universal education to all Native Americans, to the fullest extent possible. To offer anything less, Morgan argued, would lead to social and economic degradation, of the type clearly evident in Indian life (Ellis, 1996). This constituted a remarkable admission that the impoverished lifestyles of most Native Americans could be traced directly to a lack of sufficient educational programs by the federal government.

Morgan's sixth point was much more specific. In so being, it went directly to the greatest weakness of the federal system.

> Sixth: The scheme should make ample provision for the higher education of the few who are endowed with special capacity and ambition and are inclined to leadership. There is an imperative necessity for this, if the Indians are to be assimilated into the national life. (*Lake Mohonk Conference Proceedings*, 1889, p. 16)

However, by the final form of the ten-point plan as presented in his 1891 annual report, this point had been limited to a general statement that the government could not shirk its responsibility to provide a full education program to the Native Americans (Ellis, 1996). Morgan did intend a four-tier educational system, as found in the white society, with higher education implicit in its structure. However, the inertia of the federal program led to little actual change in the agricultural-vocational focus of federal Indian education. Just prior to his death, Morgan strongly condemned the course of study and the persistent approach of only providing a rudimentary education for Indians: "Why should the national government offer to its wards so much less in the way of schooling than is offered by the states to the pupils of the public schools? The Indian child has a right to demand of the government, which has assumed the responsibility of his training, that he shall not be hopelessly handicapped by such an inferior training as for the competition for life's prizes." (Morgan, December 1902, p. 173)

In the early 1900s, successive commissioners W. A. Jones, Leupp, and Valentine began to resist the off-reservation boarding school program, arguing that the schools should not unduly push their acculturation agenda. They saw the offering of an educational experience more in keeping with what the Indian student's home life was like as being more reasonable, and more likely to be accepted in the Indian community (Ellis, 1996).

In 1904, Jones spoke of the fallacy of the theory that the Indian students' "reservation home is a hell on earth, when inevitably he must and does return to his home" (*Commissioner of Indian Affairs Annual Report*, October 17, 1904, p. 32). Jones pushed for an enlarged system of day schools to bring Indian education closer to the home setting— this just four months after having removed Pratt from his longtime position as head of the Carlisle school (and strong advocate of the off-reservation boarding school system) (Prucha, 1984).

Leupp, in spite of his frequent statements in favor of the federal system and the lower level vocational curriculum, expressed a view opposed to that of total assimilation in his first annual report as Teddy Roosevelt's Commissioner of Indian Affairs:

> I like the Indian for what is Indian in him. Let us not make the mistake, in the process of absorbing them, of washing out whatever is distinctly Indian. Our aboriginal brother brings, as his contribution to the common store of character, a great deal which is admirable, and which only needs to be developed along the right line. Our proper work is improvement, not transformation. (*Commissioner of Indian Affairs Annual Report*, 1905, p. 12; Hertzberg, 1971, pp. 17–18)

This statement hints of the coming of a changed view of the value of Native American culture and the need to preserve it. But, in spite of such sentiments, the longstanding programs of assimilation and vocational education continued. The eventual granting of something so seemingly obvious as citizenship to Native Americans was geared to encourage the government's assimilation process, but was inexplicably delayed in doing so. Native American citizenship was viewed as a welcoming of sorts into the white culture instead of as a birthright, and was frequently contingent on the simultaneous loss of tribal membership. In a 1901 amendment to the Dawes (Allotment) Act, the federal government conferred citizenship on all Indians in Indian Territory, coinciding with their individual allotments and the abolishment of tribal governments (Prucha, 1984). Prior to this, some Indians in other areas had accepted an offer of citizenship related to individual allotments, and later a few World War I Native American veterans had been given citizenship. Citizenship was not granted to all native-born Indians until the Indian Citizenship Act of 1924 (U. S. Commission on Civil Rights, 1973), by which time the move to abolish tribal governments was largely complete. This was a remarkably delayed action on the part of a government professing a desire to assimilate the Native Americans into the national society and culture.

Educationally, little change occurred in spite of the progressive rhetoric of past and present commissioners. The principal curriculum emphasis was still on agriculture and domestic skills, at a very low level. The policy manual called for intricate instruction on hammering, whittling, sweeping, even breathing, among many other similarly basic activities (*Course of Study for the Indian Schools of the United States*, 1901). Any curriculum change was incremental, limited to a slight move toward vocational training under Commissioner Sells, and some encouragement of native artistic work, indicating some budding sensitivity to native culture (*Tentative Course of Study for U. S. Indian Schools*, 1915).

Commissioner Leupp, in his effort to bring Indian education and home life closer together, argued in favor of putting more Indian youth into public schools. The closing of the boarding schools that began in 1919 and was very pronounced by 1920 had this as policy. Numerically, it had an effect. By 1928, there were 34,103 Native Americans in public schools compared to 25,274 in government schools and 7,621 in private or mission schools (Prucha, 1984).

However, the effectiveness of this push toward public schools was questionable for two reasons. First, there was no support system of counseling, remedial work, or tutoring such as would exist today for such an at-risk population. And the response in the Indian community was less than enthusiastic. The educational focus still seemed to lean toward assimilation, and to not to take into account the importance attached by the Indians to their own culture.

What was clearly needed was for the larger society, outside of the Native American community, to attach importance to the Native American culture. And that is just what happened. It would seem that the intellectual curiosity about the previously unknown histories, cultures, and societies opened by Columbus, itself long ignored in the rush to explore, conquer, and use the new continents, was finally to come into its own.

This began to occur about 1920, as a generation of intellectuals and reformers discovered the Pueblo Indian culture. They took up the Native American cause for cultural, not just humanitarian, reasons. Instead of adhering to the social Darwinist model of progressive stages of hunter-gatherer, herder, farmer, merchant, and so on, and the concurrent educational objective of training the Indians to start low and move up through the stages, they favored a multicultural approach of recognition and preservation of Native American culture (Deloria, 1993).

These reformers, including future Commissioner John Collier, proved very influential in legislative circles, leading to a number of acts supportive of Native Americans in the 1920s and thirties. They also appeared just in time to aid the Indian land claimants to fight the Bursum Bill.

In the midst of this growing interest in Native Americans, Bursum's Pueblo Lands Bill (1922) was to be the last major effort to push Native Americans off the land. Its objective was to remedy the problem of white squatters living on Pueblo land. Its solution was a proposed granting of the land to the whites who had settled there, forcing the Pueblos to prove their ownership through the Spanish, Mexican, and U. S. periods (O'Brien, 1989; Szasz, 1974). The successful resistance to the Bursum Bill assured the continued existence of what today is the largest remaining Indian reservation and marked the end of the uncontrolled government-sanctioned takeover of Indian land.

The New Deal Reforms

The Bursum Bill was unique in its era in being so anti-Indian. Several other contemporaneous measures contributed to a major overhaul of the government's relationship with Native Americans. The first was the Snyder Act of 1921. As a catalyst for change, the Snyder Act was actually fairly minimal. It authorized the centralization of educational programs and services through the BIA, serving as the primary legislative authority of the financing of the BIA school system (Thompson, 1978). Within these authorized services, were BIA grants to individual college students (LaCounte, 1987). The focus was similar to all that had gone before, support for students, rather than for institutions. However, it meant the BIA had at last begun to assume direct responsibility for the higher education of Native Americans. This centralization might seem a small point, but it was a necessary step on the road to broader support for Native American students and programs.

In 1924, the Indian Citizenship Act took the long overlooked step of granting citizenship to all Native Americans. Then, in February 1928, the Meriam Report was published. Officially titled "The Problem of Indian Administration," it was 900 pages of evidence and recommendations. It was very critical of the treatment, living conditions, and situation of the Indians at the hands of the government, including their education (Carnegie Foundation, 1989; Dippie, 1982; Falmouth Institute, 1992). With Collier as a principal contributor, it detailed the poverty and disasters which had beset Native Americans over the years, and blamed BIA mismanagement for the problems (*The Problem of Indian Administration Summary*, 1928).

Regarding education, the Meriam Report called for changes, but was relatively conservative. It advised dismantling the still-extant boarding school system in favor of the view that education should be more integrated into the natural setting of home and family life. Reservation day schools or, preferably, integration into public schools was promoted (*The Problem of Indian Administration Summary*, 1928).

Higher education was discussed, but less so. The report did state that higher education should be encouraged, not just allowed, by restructuring the federal schools to furnish adequate preparation, and by the provision of more financial aid and funding (DeJong, 1988; *The Problem of Indian Administration Summary*, 1928). It did not mention establishing specific institutions for Native Americans. Also, on the subject of higher education, the report addressed the problem of training Native Americans for posts in the BIA. Unfortunately, it led to a quick-fix approach, that of dropping the degree requirements rather than taking steps to increase the number of Native Americans obtaining degrees (Dippie, 1982).

The Meriam Report recognized the value of and strongly supported Native American culture and concepts. It observed that the Indians, both individually and tribally, had been dispossessed. Indian education likewise was labeled a failure, removal from the home environment being completely in conflict with modern educational theory on the importance of the natural setting of home and family life. The report was innovative in seeing assimilation and separation as valid options for Indians, a long overdue acknowledgement that the Indians, as both citizens and wards of the government, were entitled to a choice (Dippie, 1982). It signaled a change in federal philosophy and policy toward the Indian community (O'Brien, 1989; Thompson, 1978). The general movement toward ending federal paternalism in favor of self-determination drew heavily on the report. The Johnson-O'Malley Act, Collier Bill, and Indian Reorganization Act (Wheeler-Howard Act) all stemmed directly from the report (Deloria and Lytle, 1984; Dippie, 1982).

Some of the Meriam Report recommendations were translated directly into policy. High school education for Native Americans can be said to have begun in the 1920s. In 1924, there was only one federal Indian school with twelve grades, but high school was accepted as the norm by 1950 (Prucha, 1984). The issue of training for Native Americans to qualify for BIA posts was addressed in the Collier Bill (there were more Indians employed in the BIA in 1900 than in 1934). The Collier Bill also required Congress to promote and preserve Indian culture via grants and appropriations. This was the first direct federal move away from Native American cultural extinction (Deloria and Lytle, 1984).

Of all the bills of this period, the most significant was the Indian Reorganization Act of 1934. Its principal feature was a renewed recognition of tribal governments, and with it, tribal sovereignty, a sweeping reversal of past federal policy (Deloria, 1993; Wright and Tierney, 1991). Specifically, it ended the Dawes allotment policy, and allowed and encouraged the tribes to set up written constitutions. In rescuing the idea of tribal sovereignty and the status of "dependent domestic nations" from the past, the Act ruled these rights were inherent, having existed since before the existence of the United States. They were not granted by the United States as part of the guardian-ward relationship, but were retained by the tribes through past treaties that could not be extinguished (Deloria, 1993; Falmouth Institute, 1992; Prucha, 1984).

Eleven years later, New Dealer Felix Cohen reiterated this emphatic defense of Indian sovereignty in his *Handbook of Federal Indian Law*:

> Perhaps the most basic principle of all Indian law, supported by a host of decisions hereinafter analyzed, is the principle that *those powers which are lawfully vested in an Indian tribe are not, in general, delegated powers granted by express acts of Congress, but rather inherent powers of a limited sovereignty which has never been extinguished.* Each Indian tribe begins its relationship with the Federal Government as a sovereign power, recognized as such in treaty and legislation. The powers of sovereignty have been limited from time to time by specified treaties and laws designed to take from the Indian tribes control of matters which, in the judgment of Congress, these tribes could no longer be safely permitted to handle. The statutes of Congress, then, must be examined to determine the limitations of tribal sovereignty rather than to determine its sources or its positive content. What is not expressly limited remains within the domain of tribal sovereignty. (Cohen, 1945, p. 122, italics in original)

The Reorganization Act, along with the Johnson-O'Malley Act, also addressed higher education. It guaranteed federal provision of education and other services, to be administered by the BIA (*U. S. Congressional Hearings*, 1978, May 14, 28). The Reorganization Act's principal feature for higher education was the authorization of $250,000 for college loans (Szasz, 1974; Wright and Tierney, 1991). The Johnson-O'Malley Act similarly authorized $250,000 for vocational and trade school student loans, with a maximum of $50,000 of this to go to college students (Deloria and Lytle, 1984). This act also authorized contracts with the states for education and other services. This federal aid to the states was to ease the impact of state expenditures on tax-free Indian land (Thompson, 1978).

These acts, coming during Franklin Roosevelt's New Deal administration, were much more noticeably effective in enacting Indian self-determination regarding the reestablishment of the tribal governments than in education. The emphasis pertaining to education was more on voluntary, not forced, assimilation into the larger society, but it was still assimilation. The college curriculum was still not inclusive of Native American culture, as colleges were slow to alter or add programs or disciplines. In 1914, Senator Robert Owens of Oklahoma, the state with the largest Native American population, pushed for the establishment of an Indian studies program at the University of Oklahoma. Nothing came of it (Buffalohead, 1970). The effort was repeated in 1937, with a similar response by the university (Buffalohead, 1970; Weinberg, 1977). With little being done to make higher education more attractive or relevant as perceived by Native Americans, the federal support changes alone were not sufficient to cause a sudden surge in Native American college enrollment or federal participation in higher education (Belgrade, 1992, June). In that area, the effect was slow to start, accumulating over time.

In 1900, very few Native Americans had gone to college, in full awareness that success would mean an acceptance of American civilization and rejection of their own culture. In 1932, the BIA did a survey of Native American advanced education levels. They found, nationwide, only 385 Indians currently enrolled in college, fifty-two existing Native American college graduates, and five colleges offering Indian scholarships (Szasz, 1974; Wright and Tierney, 1991). By 1935, just one year after the Indian Reorganization Act, the BIA reported 515 active college students, still small, but a 34 percent increase over three years (Wright and Tierney, 1991).

In 1948, the BIA instituted a scholarship program. During that same period, some World War II Native American veterans entered college under the G. I. Bill. Also, some tribes began independently supporting higher education, usually with scholarship funds. By the late 1950s, there were twenty-four such tribal scholarship programs (Szasz, 1974). At that time, there were about 2,000 active Native American college students (Wright and Tierney, 1991). It is apparent that the pattern persisted of relatively few Native Americans attempting college, and those who did so being ill-prepared regarding preparatory education, cultural barriers, study habits, and supportive counseling. As late as 1961, there were only sixty-six Native Americans who graduated from college (Szasz, 1974).

This slow growth began to accelerate in the 1960s. Between 1961 and 1968, the number of Native Americans graduating tripled, and by 1965, there were some 7,000 active Native American college students (Szasz, 1974; Wright and Tierney, 1991).

The slow pace of the growth of Native American higher education after the very supportive start of the New Deal measures seems to have been affected by several factors. Unavoidable delays, inertia on the part of the BIA , and a lack of subsequent federal support and funding all seem relevant. Of an unavoidable nature, the period between the New Deal shifts in policy, and the growth of Native Americans in college in the 1960s and the subsequent founding of the tribally controlled colleges included the protracted effects of the Depression and World War II. The attention of the nation, for much of the time, was simply elsewhere.

Regarding the inertia, resistance, and longevity for which federal bureaucracies are often maligned, justly or unjustly, the BIA educational programs after World War II offer a striking example. Having finally moved away from the objective of making self-sufficient farmers out of individual Indians, the BIA educational system used the decision to try to relocate them into urban areas as another avenue to justify a vocational orientation.

W. W. Beatty, the director of Indian Education beginning in World War II, stressed in 1944 that the primary job of Indian education was to prepare them to earn a living by means of their own resources and skills. In 1951, this same director spoke of the concern of the school system for the "mastery of the material culture of the dominant race" (Prucha, 1984, pp. 1060–1061).

During the 1950s, the BIA educational focus was primarily on adult vocational education. In 1955, a program was initiated on five reservations (Papago, Fort Hall, Turtle Mountain, Seminole, Rosebud Sioux) consisting of strictly vocational training and English language instruction. By 1958, this program had expanded to seventy-nine Native American communities (Prucha, 1984). Besides the job training and English mastery goals, the program's objectives included orienting Indians and their children to a "time-conscious, acquisitive, and competitive world" (Prucha, 1984, p. 1067). Not only do such positions and programs discount over a half century of policy pronouncements and changes, and the movement toward higher education in the general society at that time, they harken back to a Eurocentric view of Native American culture dating from the onset of the colonial era.

Not that such concerns slowed this vocational training thrust of the BIA school system. Beginning in 1956, BIA Department of Education Director Hildegard Thompson pushed the vocational focus into the high school and post-high school institutions, effectively trying to transform the Department of Education into an adult job training agency (Szasz, 1974). By 1963, there were 2,911 such adult vocational students, growing to 8,000 by 1968 (Jackson and Galli, 1977).

The BIA resistance to becoming involved in higher education was evident right up until the dawn of the modern era of unprecedented growth in Native American colleges. In 1962, on the eve of this next major reform period in Native American self-determination, the BIA operated 263 schools. Most were elementary schools. Within the system were only twenty-seven high schools, three technical institutions, and no colleges (Jackson and Galli, 1977).

Regarding support, the Native American programs fared best under Roosevelt, and later under Kennedy and Johnson. Funding was noticeably curtailed during the Eisenhower years and during the administrations of Reagan and Bush. Beginning in 1954, at the request of the administration, Congress authorized a program of accelerated termination of federal trust responsibility for Native Americans, seeking to reduce federal expenditures that were already minimal and poorly executed (Deloria, Jr., 1991; Prucha, 1984; *U. S. Congressional Hearings*, 1978, May 14, 28). This termination policy was an attempt to rid the federal budget of the BIA expense and let the Indians manage their own affairs, notwithstanding the long-term lack of a higher education system to enable them to develop the leaders necessary for such a move (Jackson and Galli, 1977). The result was the termination of federal recognition (funding) of over 100 tribes, and a concurrent push to relocate them in urban areas (Falmouth Institute, 1992).

In 1957, Congress appropriated $70,000 for tuition grants to Native American students, less than a third of the 1934 figure. Tribal funds plus some private or institutional funding no doubt equaled or exceeded this federal figure (Prucha, 1984). Later, the Reagan-Bush era interpreted self-determination to mean that Native Americans could administer their own programs (Deloria, Jr., 1991). Consequently, appropriations were cut back, following the precedent set in the 1950s. Conversely, the New Frontier and Great Society programs stressed Native American economic development, with education seen in a supporting role (Deloria, Jr., 1991).

The Tribally Controlled Colleges

During the 1960s, for the first time in the nation's history, Native Americans began enrolling in colleges on a large scale (Havighurst, 1981). But that increased Native American interest in higher education is only one contributing factor to the changes that have occurred since then. In many ways, the Native American reform movement that began in the New Deal days seemed to experience a rebirth in the late 1960s and 1970s.

In 1966, Robert Bennett, a member of the Oneida tribe, was named BIA Commissioner, the first Indian to head the Bureau since Ely Parker nearly a century earlier. His tenure signalled a major shift in direction for the nation's Indian affairs, labelled the "new trail" (Prucha, 1984). The emphasis was to be on the application of Indian self-determination, the actual taking of control of aspects of Indian life previously in the hands of the federal government.

This renewed drive to implement Indian self-determination was very pronounced in education. For the first time, education was prominent among the issues to be dealt with, instead of something to be included almost as an afterthought. Quite a number of the Congressional acts that would follow dealt directly with Native American educational support.

During the 1960s, the development of Indian Community Action Programs within the Office of Economic Opportunity allowed the tribes increased latitude to administer their own programs and initiate their own reforms (U. S. Congressional Hearings, 1978, May 14, 28). This opened the way for tribes to be able to successfully control their own affairs, without the interference of the paternalistic/assimilationist policies of the past (Wright and Tierney, 1991).

Early in this period, some tribes began providing space for local community colleges to deliver Indian-centered education. However, this program failed to achieve the expected results. The educational focus still was not sufficiently inclusive of Native American culture (Raymond, 1986).

In 1966, the Rough Rock Demonstration School was founded on the Navajo Reservation. It was funded by the federal government and run on a contract basis by the tribe (Prucha, 1984). This was viewed as an experiment in Indian control of education, and led directly to the founding of the Navajo Community College in 1968, the first college controlled and directed by Indians.

From 1968 to 1971, the Navajo Community College was housed in the Many Farms High School. It clearly served as a prototype and a successful argument for an expanded program of Indian community colleges. In 1971, Congress passed the Navajo Community College Act, appropriating $5.5 million to construct its campus (Prucha, 1984). Although the curriculum was roughly one-third academic and two-thirds vocational, this college is seen as the true beginning of Native American self-determination in higher education, albeit with necessary federal funding (Jojola and Agoyo, 1992; U. S. Congressional Hearings, 1978, May 14, 28). It served as the model for all subsequent tribally controlled community colleges, and led directly to the passage of the Tribally Controlled Community College Act of 1978 (Prucha, 1984).

During the same time frame, on November 3, 1969, the report of the Senate Special Subcommittee on Indian Education was issued. Commonly known as the Kennedy Report, the committee having been chaired by Robert, then Edward Kennedy, this report in many ways was reminiscent of the Meriam report. In general, it called attention to the poverty, lack of economic development, and overall lack of progress within the Indian community (DeJong, 1993).

However, very pertinent to the budding example of the Navajo Community College, the Kennedy Report dwelled on education itself. It cited a high school dropout rate among Native Americans of 49 percent, with only 28 percent of the remainder attempting college (Fries, 1987). The BIA was actively providing financial assistance to college students, but in the year of the report, only 3,500 took advantage of the assistance.

Although at the time the BIA had chartered the Institute of American Indian Arts in Santa Fe as a junior college, the first of the federal schools to evolve into a college with two more to follow shortly, the report touched on the lack of operation or support of specific institutions by the Bureau (Jackson and Galli, 1977). For the most part, however, the report's focus was still on the individual student, citing inadequate academic preparation, remedial needs, lack of sufficient funding and aid, and the high dropout rate, not on the availability of Indian colleges (Prucha, 1984).

Even so, coming as the report did during the first years of the Navajo Community College, the interest in Indian education was heightened by both developments (Horse, 1982). This led to a number of federal task force and General Accounting Office studies and reports on the specific problems of Indian students, covering such issues as academic preparation, cultural barriers, socialization, and finances. The 1970s also saw the passage of several bills in support of Indian education. They included the Indian Education Act of 1972, the Indian Self-Determination and Educational Assistance Act of 1975, the Education Amendments Act of 1978, the Tribally Controlled Community College Act of 1978, and the Higher Education Act of 1978 (Wright and Tierney, 1991).

There was a concurrent increase within the Native American community of higher education activity. From the 1969 level of 3,500 students, by 1973 the BIA was providing aid to 13,500 (Jackson and Galli, 1977), a fourfold increase in four years. This increased interest leveled off but still grew, reaching 14,600 undergraduate and 700 graduate students by 1979. Of these, 1,639 undergraduate and 434 graduate students received their degrees that year (Wright and Tierney, 1991). Also during the 1970s, the proportion of all Native American adults with high school diplomas increased from 20 percent to 33 percent (Jackson and Galli, 1977). But these heartening increases in Native American educational activity and attainment were not, in and of themselves, the most significant development in Native American education.

Without a doubt, the most striking development to come out of this self-determination policy was the appearance of the tribally controlled community colleges. Stemming from the reception and success of the Navajo Community College, over the following twenty-five years, thirty tribally controlled colleges were founded. Clearly the Native American community harbored an unrealized desire for higher education that did not deny Native American culture. Armed with the host of federal acts of the 1970s in support of Indian education and the freedom to implement their own programs, several tribes acted to establish their own colleges.

In 1972, the Indian Education Act provided for changes in federal funding and school administration, mostly at the K-12 level, addressing the dropout and academic preparation problems (Prucha, 1984). The Indian Self-Determination and Educational Assistance Act of 1975 brought K-12 Indian education under more localized control by strengthening the parents' input on school matters and academic content. The Education Amendments Act of 1978 served to correct some deficiencies of the 1975 Act, with the focus still at the K-12 level (Prucha, 1984).

At the higher education level, the Higher Education Act of 1978 provided for increased financial aid for Native American college students, as well as grants for Native American programs and studies. The most significant of the federal acts, however, the cornerstone of the tribally controlled college phenomenon, was the Tribally Controlled Community College Act of 1978.

Drawn directly from the success and federal support of the Navajo Community College, the Tribally Controlled Community College Act established direct federal support to higher education institutions for Native Americans (Pease-Windy Boy, 1994; Prucha, 1984). The act provided for "the operation and improvement of tribally controlled community colleges to insure continued and expanded educational opportunities for Indian students" (Prucha, 1984, p. 1147). It provides direct support to the tribal colleges in the form of per-student operational funds. Eligibility is determined based on a charter granted to the college by a recognized tribe, an Indian majority governing board, and an Indian majority student body (Pease-Windy Boy, 1994). Details of these eligibility requirements included an operating philosophy and plan of operation designed to meet the needs of Indian students (Prucha, 1984). The financial support was originally in the form of a $4,000 grant to the school per year per full-time student (Prucha, 1984). Congress later increased this authorized support to up to $6,000 per student (Wright and Tierney, 1991).

The founding of other tribally controlled colleges began even before the passage of the Tribally Controlled Community College Act, reflecting the interest generated by the Navajo Community College as an example of educational self-determination. The second tribally controlled college, Sinte Gleska University, in South Dakota, was founded in 1970. It was followed in 1971 by D-Q University and Oglala Lakota College. This was the beginning of a surge of college openings that saw one to four schools established each year except two of the period from 1970 to 1988. Three more were established in 1992 and 1993.

Besides the colleges themselves, an administrative infrastructure has developed around them. In 1973, the American Indian Higher Education Consortium (AIHEC) was founded. Its original purposes were to provide assistance to the tribal colleges, serve as the lobbyist organization for the colleges, and serve as a possible precursor to a tribal accrediting agency, in support of the cultural and native languages curriculum (Stein, 1990). In the mid-1990s, this accreditation function was set up as a separate agency, as a means of dealing with the special needs (cultural, tribal relations, student support) of the tribal colleges (Crazy-Bull, 1994). In 1989, the American Indian College Fund was established, again within the AIHEC. It has grown to a $3 million annual budget of funds in support of the tribal colleges and their students (Nicklin, 1995, September 8).

A recent addition to the authorized federal funding was the 1994 extension of the Morrill Act, granting land grant status to the tribal colleges, seen as justified by the analogies between the mission of the tribal colleges and that of the land grant institutions. In light of the long history of white takeover of Indian land, it was more than a little ironic that this land grant support came in the form of endowments instead of land, due to a lack of federal land available to be granted (*U. S. Congressional Hearings*, 1993, November 18).

Although the tribal colleges are as diverse as the tribes themselves, the colleges do share common goals and exhibit remarkable unity of purpose (Pease-Windy Boy, 1994). Chief among these are to safeguard and promote the tribal cultures, histories, and language development (Belgrade, 1992, June; Raymond, 1986). The preservation of Native American languages, in particular, has been recognized as of prime importance in the promotion, maintenance, and preservation of native cultures (Arizona State Department of Education, 1983). To a large extent, the past federal attempts to suppress native languages in favor of English might well have succeeded in extinguishing Native American cultures had a follow-through program been in place to prevent students from returning to their reservation homes. Now, native languages occupy a central position in tribal and cultural studies. At the Little Big Horn College, in Crow Agency, Montana, 75 percent of the students have Crow language as their first language. Consequently, all business office and student service functions are conducted in the Crow language (*Little Big Horn College Catalog*, 1997–1999).

Cultural preservation is only one of several concurrent purposes served by the tribal colleges. They are colleges, and as such, are concerned with providing a suitable education to enable their students to go out into the larger society and compete for jobs and positions on an equal footing. This creates an inherent difficulty in their missions. They must contend with two knowledge bases, that of western civilization and that indigenous to Native American cultures (Horse, 1982). Considering the small size, and limited faculty and resources of the tribal colleges, to devote a major effort to promoting native cultural ideals, yet to strive to function as part of and provide a knowledge of mainstream America is a formidable undertaking.

The cultural curriculum is often the most problematic. Issues of accreditation, funding, needs, and a residual lack of Indian scholars persistently impact and constrain tribal college efforts in the cultural areas. This makes curriculum development more complex than the norm. Most opt for a sort of dual curriculum, including the use of many comparative courses (Badwound, 1990; Ramirez-Shkwegnaabi, 1987; Rosh, 1986). Critical thinking, synthesis, analysis, and other classical higher education processes are addressed, but not always with classical subject matter. In support of such an approach, many higher education writers now acknowledge that there is no universally satisfactory definition of the curriculum:

> An elementary caution on the way to understanding the curriculum may be to assume…that maybe there is no such thing as *the* curriculum. (Rudolph, 1977, p. 2).

Beyond these two major objectives, tribal colleges strive to serve the same sorts of needs within their communities as do mainstream colleges. The training of future tribal leaders, the strengthening of the economies of Indian communities, the support and defense of tribal sovereignty, and the strengthening of the tribal social fabric, as well as relations with the larger society all play important roles in the operations and future plans of tribal colleges (Belgrade, 1992, June; Humphrey, 1997, April 7).

Tribal colleges are also concerned with special needs pertaining to their student bodies. Stemming from the long history of poor educational service provided to Native Americans, tribal college students are usually the first generation in their family to go to college, and are often in need of particular attention to cultural and personal support systems, financial aid, study assistance, remedial education, and vocational training. Also, since a majority of tribal colleges are two-year institutions, a great deal of attention to and support of transfer programs is present (Raymond, 1986).

As rapidly as the number of tribal colleges grew, their story is not one of unqualified acceptance and uninterrupted success. Four of them have failed to survive: the Lummi School of Aquaculture, Lummi, Washington; the Inuipiat University of the Arctic, Barrow, Alaska; the College of Ganado, Ganado, Arizona; and the Keeweenaw Bay Ojibway Community College, Baraga, Michigan (Belgrade, 1992, June).

A lack of funding is still a major concern for the tribal colleges. Given their student bases and local environments, it is a fact of life for the tribal colleges that their tuition and local support tend to be low. Consequently, federal funding is of primary importance to them. During the Reagan era, although Congress had authorized $6,000 per student per year in support, the amount actually released slipped to $1,900 (Wright and Tierney, 1991), providing minimal support for this most at-risk student population. In 1988, a survey of 110 administrators in Native American higher education found lack of funding to be their number one problem (Tippeconnic, 1988).

In the 1990s, some calls for improvement have been heard. The White House Conference on Indian Education (1992, January 24) issued multiple resolutions calling for increased federal funds in support of the tribal colleges, Native American students, graduate studies, matching of state funds, and research into tribal cultures and histories. Within these resolutions was a bare call for full funding as authorized in the Tribally Controlled Community College Act. Coming at the beginning of the last year of the Bush administration, there was little response to these resolutions.

By 1997, the total federal Indian education program budget was $1.6 billion. Of this, only about $20 million goes to the tribal colleges. However, in an era concerned with balancing the federal budget, this figure was still being curtailed. This was justified as reflecting the move to greater self-sufficiency, citing 1996 profits from Indian bingo and casino operations of $3.5 billion (Fink, 1997, June 29).

In the face of such pressure, calls for greater support persist. The Carnegie Foundation for the Advancement of Teaching recommends the increase of federal money to the tribal colleges to $40 million, double the current figure. Such a move would actually represent only the release of the amount authorized by the 1986 extension of the Tribally Controlled Community College Act (*Chronicle of Higher Education*, 1997, May 30). The Foundation also encouraged the states to provide funds as authorized by the 1994 expansion of the Morrill Act, and called for increased private support. Related to such an appeal, the W. K. Kellogg Foundation in 1997 announced grants of $22.2 million over the next five years (*Native American Colleges*, 1997).

There is a possibility that some of the lower than authorized release of federal funds relates to political misperceptions and turf battles arising from the growth of the tribal colleges. The development of the tribal colleges represented a major movement of Native American education away from BIA control at about the same time that the BIA finally established some colleges of its own. Today there are three such BIA-chartered colleges, all developed from past BIA schools. They are the Institute of American Indian Art, Santa Fe, chartered in 1962; the Haskell Indian Nations University, Lawrence, Kansas, chartered in 1970; and the Southwest Indian Polytechnic Institute, Albuquerque, 1971 (Belgrade, 1992; Oppelt, 1990). Just as Carlisle was the most famous Indian school of the nineteenth century, Haskell is the best known of the contemporary schools. Originally a boarding school established in 1884, it became a high school in 1921, then a vocational-industrial school before becoming a junior college in 1970 (Oppelt, 1990).

Until the establishment of these three schools as junior colleges, the federal government provided no degree granting institutions for Indians. Judging from the burst of interest in the tribal colleges, the three BIA colleges and the past BIA financial assistance to individual students represented too little too late to satisfy the nascent Native American interest in higher education. The BIA found it had lost ground quickly. With the growth of the tribal colleges, local control of Native American higher education, even considering the rapid growth of Native Americans in mainstream higher education, is now a reality. There are more tribal schools than BIA schools, effectively comprising the first true higher education system for Native Americans (Deyhle and Swisher, 1997).

The tribal colleges enroll approximately 25,000 students (*Chronicle of Higher Education*, 1997, May 30; Humphrey, 1997, April 7), or about a fifth of the 127,372 Native Americans attending colleges and universities (*Chronicle of Higher Education*, 1996, September 2). Compared to the numbers in tribal colleges and in mainstream schools, the BIA is responsible for only a small portion of Native American higher education.

While the growth of the tribal colleges represented a loss of BIA control of Native American higher education, the 1979 establishment of the Department of Education at the cabinet level effectively did the same for K-12 education. The Indian educational program was transferred from the BIA over protests from it and from the Indian community. As dissatisfied as Native Americans tended to be with the BIA, some did feel that it best understood their needs and offered a viable route to self-determination if it retained responsibility for their education system (Prucha, 1984).

Not only was there initial resistance to the tribal college movement from the BIA, there were some misperceptions within the government that the movement was associated with the very assertive American Indian Movement (AIM). AIM did include education within its many pronouncements and demands. In 1969, a group called "Indians of All Tribes" seized Alcatraz Island in a very visible protest movement. It called for the island to be used for an Indian university (Moguin, 1973). Later, during the 1972 takeover of the BIA headquarters and confrontation with the government in Washington known as the "trail of broken treaties," AIM issued a document called *The Twenty Points*. Point 20 asked for more funding and better management of a variety of programs, including education (Deloria, 1993). During the formative years of the tribal college movement and the founding of the AIHEC, the government challenged both as being associated with AIM, backed up by the BIA testifying that higher education services were already being provided (Roach, 1997, April 7).

Such an interpretation of the coinciding of the tribal college movement with the rise of AIM and any statements by it on education is overly simplistic. Besides the fact that the confrontational nature of AIM was not in keeping with the more typical Indian characteristic of reticence, it would assume a monolithic Indian movement not in keeping with the nature of Native Americans. With less than one percent of the nation's population spread over approximately 600 tribes, and a history and cultural background that encourages leadership by persuasion and allows dissension and splinter group separation, it seems unlikely that such an extremist group as AIM would or could presume to speak for all Native Americans. Such diversity and individualism within the Native American community is more likely to result in a wealth of viewpoints and difficulty in arriving at a consensus.

An indication of this disparity of viewpoints reflects the tribal college problem of striving to cover both Western knowledge and native culture in the curriculum. Dissension exists in the Native American community over whether the best education is one that focuses on their own culture and traditions, or one that contributes to economic marketability and advancement within the larger society (Hirschkind, 1983). As a result, there are Native Americans who advocate higher education as offered by the tribal colleges and those who firmly believe a mainstream education is the better choice. This is a conflict as old as white-Indian relations. It was the basic problem wrestled with by Samson Occum in his attempt to blend the two worlds, by Eliot's towns of praying Indians removed from both their own and the white people, by such "best of both worlds" advocates as Crow Chief Plenty Coups (c. 1848–1932), and by the tribal colleges in attempting to blend both into their curriculum.

The Tribal Colleges within the Push toward Diversity

The appearance and growth of today's tribally controlled colleges corresponds roughly with the timing of the civil rights movement. Among many other societal objectives during the 1960s and 1970s, a combination of legislative, executive, and judicial influences brought pressure to bear on colleges and universities to increase the participation rates of select under-represented minority groups (Richardson and Skinner, 1991, p. 3). The broad focus was on ending discrimination, principally by increasing access. Indeed, the emphasis on access that characterizes today's higher education system in the United States may be said to have begun in the 1960s (Richardson and Skinner, 1991, p. 8).

At first glance, the appearance of the tribally controlled colleges seems at odds with the civil rights movement. It was an unusual time to be founding specialty colleges, a time when, since 1954, movement away from the "separate but equal" doctrine was paramount in education. Other specialty colleges, principally black and women's colleges, began to experience pressure to expand their constituencies. But a little analysis may relieve the sense that the rise of Native American colleges was an anomaly, placing it more in agreement with the civil rights issues of the day than it seems on the surface.

First, a simple consideration of the civil rights and affirmative action requirements reveals them to be far less sweeping, particularly in colleges, than is commonly supposed. Discounting public perceptions, there are real differences among equal opportunity or nondiscrimination as required by law, affirmative action, and so-called "reverse discrimination" (Carnegie Council, 1975, p. 103).

Reverse discrimination is a frequent misnomer for affirmative action, an erroneous belief that the federal government requires that an employer or institution must favor the targeted minority group, even to the point of recruiting and selecting less qualified job or student applicants (Leap and Crino, 1993, p. 78). Quotas are a frequent part of such a belief, arising from incomplete or mistaken information. No federal requirement exists for quotas. The closest thing to one is the so-called 80 percent rule used by the Equal Employment Opportunity Commission (EEOC) to determine the presence of discrimination.

Briefly, the EEOC, in response to a charge of discriminatory practices, may look at the rate of hire for minority applicants relative to that of the majority (Leap and Crino, 1993, p. 97). If the minority rate is 80 percent or more of that of the majority, it is seen as one indicator that discrimination is not present. All it represents is one after-the-fact piece of evidence for or against discrimination. Although firms and institutions may elect to monitor and adjust their own such ratio of selection rates, and this technique may be reapplied to indicate whether any court-ordered change in policy has been implemented, active use of the 80 percent rule does not appear as any federal requirement. It is a guideline only (Leap and Crino, 1993, p. 97; Carnegie Council, 1975, p. 127).

Ignoring for the moment the post-Civil War amendments and acts, the bulk of federal nondiscrimination requirements is in the form of the various EEO acts. They include the Equal Pay Act of 1963, the Civil Rights Act of 1964, its Educational Amendments of 1972, the Rehabilitation Act of 1973, the Vietnam Era Veterans Readjustment Act of 1974, and the Americans with Disabilities Act of 1974 (Leap and Crino, 1993, pp. 92–94; VanderWaerdt, 1982, p. 77). These are largely enforced by the EEOC and apply mostly to employment.

Higher education is specifically addressed by Title VI of the Civil Rights Act of 1964, and by Title IX of the 1972 Educational Amendments, which are enforced by the Office of Civil Rights (OCR) within the Department of Education (VanderWaerdt, 1982, p. 77). Both deal with student programs and have primarily been enforced regarding admission levels and athletic programs for women.

Affirmative action programs are generally more limited than perceived publicly. Affirmative action is defined as "the obligation for organizations with government contracts to make a special effort to recruit, hire, and promote job-qualified members of a targeted minority group (Leap and Crino, 1993, p 77). All generalized federal affirmative action requirements deal with employment.

Only two pieces of legislation require affirmative action and they apply to the handicapped and to Vietnam-era veterans. All other general federal affirmative action requirements stem from executive orders. Executive order no. 11246 (September 24, 1965), amended by no. 11377 (October 13, 1967) and no. 12086 (October 8, 1978), covers race, sex, religion, color, and national origin. No. 11141 (February 12, 1964) covers age. No. 11478 (August 8, 1969) addresses direct federal employment. No. 11701 (January 24, 1973) addresses veterans, no. 11935 (September 2, 1976) deals with citizenship, and no. 12125 (March 20, 1979) deals with direct federal employment of the handicapped (Leap and Crino, 1993, pp. 88–89).

Although it may occasionally appear as a specific requirement in response to a court finding of discrimination in a particular case, there are no other broad federal affirmative action requirements. Some state and higher education institutions have implemented their own modified affirmative action programs, most visibly the recently rescinded program in California public colleges. In such cases, the selective use of lowered admission standards to manipulate levels of admission by group has contributed to the public perceptions of reverse discrimination, and to the pressure to rescind such programs.

Such moves go against the federal affirmative action practice of requiring special effort to include the targeted group, but not of relaxing qualifications. Such manipulation of academic requirements has also fueled the controversy surrounding the use of affirmative action in colleges. An ongoing debate in higher education circles has centered on the perception of quality (defined as meeting traditional standards) and diversity (increasing minority participation) as conflicting goals in the view of many in the field (Richardson and Skinner, 1991, p. 3).

Although it has been less publicly noticed than the Title IX enforcement of gender equality on athletic programs, there has been some federal affirmative action focus on higher education. However, in keeping with the above comments on federal affirmative action, it has dealt chiefly with employment of faculty and staff on the nation's campuses. This was in response to the not-too-distant (late 1960s and before) practice of mentoring of and networking by white males as prime avenues to fill such positions. The academic grapevine once frequently precluded the need to advertise to recruit new faculty (VanderWaerdt, 1982, p. 1). As a result, in the mid-1970s, the Office of Civil Rights became involved in enforcing non-discriminatory hiring practices, principally on issues of gender, and requiring affirmative action to do so (Carnegie Council, 1975, pp. 125–127).

Within this less-than-clear-cut history of affirmative action being applied to higher education, some factors and characteristics of the Native American population has served to limit any pressure on higher education to be more proactive in recruiting Native American students. First, higher education can legitimately claim to have included and sought out Native American students since colonial times. The educational efforts on behalf of Native Americans by the original colonial colleges were real, if less than ideal in hindsight. Second, the Native American resistance to white education, now so ingrained by generations of reinforcement as to be nearly a part of their modern culture, no doubt served to limit any pressure being applied by the Native American community to increase access to that education.

Third, since Native Americans represent less than one percent of the general population, their numbers in college populations were unlikely to generate as much concern or effort for increasing their representation. African Americans historically represented 11 to 13 percent of the nation, and were so clearly excluded from mainstream higher education institutions (and so vocal about seeking social redress) that just as clearly something needed to be done.

Native Americans, on the other hand, were and are such a smaller minority that all too often, particularly at smaller schools, a virtual handful of students could give the impression of near-parity of representation. A bare consideration of their presence, of course, does not address such issues as their lack of support at several levels, of preparation, completion rates, or greater numbers in two-year programs.

Finally, the uniqueness of the Native American position in American society may not only have made them less interested in support from mainstream higher education and more so in founding their own colleges to safeguard and promote their own cultures. It may have made an equally unique contribution to the diversity sought by the higher education system and society at large.

Birnbaum (1983) takes the position that diversity itself has more than one definition and can operate at several levels within higher education. He argues that educational diversity should exist not just in terms of the student body, but of institutional variation. Specific forms could extend to faculty, types of institutions, programs, student services, disciplines, and areas of concentration.

Birnbaum sees value in such institutional diversity at three levels. At the institutional level, issues of curriculum development and the meeting of student needs would more readily be served. At the societal level (the focus of the civil rights movement itself), such diversity could fulfill political, social, and economic objectives, and permit mass and elitist education simultaneously, encouraging social mobility. And at a systemic level, such institutional diversity could enable higher education to remain stable, yet evolve in response to environmental or social changes (Birnbaum, 1983, pp. 2–17).

In support of such a position, Birnbaum makes the point that traditionally New Jersey exported more students than any other state, the majority of which left to seek institutions with specific characteristics not found in the New Jersey selection (1983, pp. 4–5). To Birnbaum, this is indicative of the need for a diverse system to serve both student needs and the public interest.

The appearance of the Native American colleges serves to both expand Native American access to higher education, yet to function as cultural repositories and centers for academic inquiry. Clearly they fall under this heading of increased institutional diversity as promoted by Birnbaum, and just as clearly have contributed to the growth of diversity within higher education.

Overview

Certainly the most important factor influencing the growth of the tribally controlled colleges and other events of the self-determination period is the one from which the name is drawn, the self-control by Native Americans of their educational system. This self-determination, in turn, can be inferred to have developed due to several contributing factors.

In the early twentieth century, Manifest Destiny was a fact. The United States had expanded to fill in all the real estate blanks from coast to coast. No longer were there available vast tracts of land to which to remove the Indians. With removal no longer feasible, the long-avoided need to assimilate took on new meaning.

Also, with U.S. growth into new lands complete, the Indians no longer represented an impediment to that growth, a "problem." Now, they could be assimilated based on treatment as people, as citizens. And being treated as citizens meant having a say in matters, however grudgingly conferred, just like other citizens.

At about this same time, the reformers and intellectuals of the 1920s and 1930s awakened the nation to the merits of a multicultural approach to dealing with and accepting such a diverse group within the citizenry. This represented a first distinction between legal, social treatment, where uniform and equal treatment is desired and necessary, and cultural recognition, where diverse approaches can and should be welcomed. Such a view of the contribution and desirability of cultural diversity is now the professed norm in our society.

This, too, strengthened the move to self-determination. In recognizing and seeking to conserve the cultures of Native America, a natural opening strategy is to seek out input from Native Americans as obvious experts in their own culture. From this cultural recognition, it is a simple step to granting and encouraging self-control of their educational system and objectives to Native Americans due to the role of an educational system as a repository and transmitter of that culture. After centuries of being treated as a problem or worse by the white society, this recognition of the importance of Native American culture and of the input pertaining to it by Native Americans carried with it a sort of blanket recognition of the ability and need for Native Americans to control their own destiny. The net effect was the recognition of Native Americans as culturally diverse but intellectual equals within the society as a whole.

5

Black Higher Education: A Brief Comparison

In tracing the development of the tribally controlled colleges, there is a tendency to compare them to other specialty colleges, particularly those that have traditionally or historically served the African American student population. Similarities and differences abound, beginning with the barest description of the two populations. Both are clear minorities in American society, historically oppressed and denied access to mainstream American life on the grounds of race. Yet the Native Americans held something, the land, desired by the white society, and were in a position, however poorly served, circumvented, or abused, of being legally entitled to it. Even the most unreconstructed Eurocentric land grabber would grudgingly admit that they were here first, even if that was to be subsequently ignored.

Conversely, the blacks were brought here by the whites. All they had that the whites wanted was their labor, to be gained with as little expenditure as possible, social or economic. American black education, including higher education, may be considered to have passed through four distinct stages in terms of public policy (Myers, 1989). These stages are prohibition (prior to the Civil War), development (roughly the remainder of the nineteenth century), segregation (legally defined as from *Plessy versus Ferguson*, 1896, to *Brown versus Board of Education*, 1954), and desegregation or integration (beginning with the civil rights movement of the 1950s and 1960s).

Prohibition

The prohibition period covers the entire period of slavery in the United States. There were strict laws in the South prohibiting the teaching of blacks, laws that were only occasionally broken when a favored house or personal slave might be given some rudimentary home schooling, usually in reading and writing. Sometimes the slaves tried to pick it up on their own and to teach others. In either case, such schooling was always done surreptitiously.

The basis for such laws was the clear need to stifle any desire for freedom, to keep the slave population totally subjugated. A chronic fear of a slave uprising was a given in the old South, and an educated slave represented a potential leader or instigator of such an occurrence (Myers, 1989). No amount of increased value stemming from a slave having an education could counter such a perceived threat.

Northern colleges felt within their rights in admitting blacks, but slave ownership had to be recognized, however grudgingly, as a legal property right within the nation. Basically, Northern colleges only dealt with a very limited population of free or freed blacks, and they were few and far between. The first black college graduate in the United States was John Russwurm, from Bowdoin College, Maine, in 1826. He later founded and published *Freedom's Journal* (Johnson, 1938).

Black college graduates totalled only seven more in the next twenty years and twenty-eight overall by 1860 (Johnson, 1938), roughly the same number enrolled in colleges from the Choctaw nation at any given time during that period. This is a particularly minuscule representation when one takes into account that the total American black population was several times that of the Native American.

Development

To say that blacks in higher education only became more than sporadic social and educational outliers after the Civil War is a major understatement. The Civil War proved to create as sudden and total a change in black education as it did in their legal standing. What was previously prohibited was now not only free to development, but vigorously encouraged and supported in certain quarters.

Religious activist groups and philanthropists began pressuring to create institutions to educate blacks in the period just prior to the Civil War. The first black college, Lincoln University in Pennsylvania, was founded in 1854. By 1865, many religious organizations, as well as philanthropists, the Freedman's Bureau, the reconstructionist state governments, and even some newly freed slaves were busily establishing schools and promoting education for blacks. A significant number of traditionally black colleges were established during the subsequent reconstruction period (Myers, 1989).

Since the overwhelming majority of blacks lived in the South, most black colleges were in or quite near the old South, with Lincoln University in Pennsylvania as the farthest north and Langston University in Oklahoma Territory the farthest west (Hill, 1985). A typical pattern would be to establish a college with its own captive elementary and secondary feeder schools or divisions. Of necessity, most early black colleges were of such an elementary nature that the designation of "college" was more a gesture of hope than an indication of advanced education (Johnson, 1938, p. 7).

The motivation for these religious and missionary efforts was the desire to implement some measure of religious and social leadership for the recently emancipated slaves. The Northerners sought to provide higher education to educate those blacks who would then teach others (Wolters, 1975, p. 3), much like the colonial college Native American programs attempted to provide Native American teachers for their own communities. Such a top-down strategy for the cultural development of the target population, while typical of educational policy in general, is diametrically opposed to the federal system of providing rudimentary vocational training to the Native Americans as a means to promote their assimilation into mainstream society.

The numbers of black college students increased steadily each year. By 1900, blacks had been awarded a total of 5,358 degrees, including 2,541 bachelors, 2,731 professional degrees, 77 masters, and 7 Ph. D. degrees (Johnson, 1938, p. 8). Clearly, the growth of higher education for and among blacks had quickly taken hold and outstripped that concerning Native Americans.

Even allowing for a black population then some fifteen times that of Native Americans, the figures from the early 1930s reveal how remarkably quickly black higher education grew compared to Native American higher education. Recalling the 1932 BIA survey identifying 385 active Native American college students and only fifty-two existing college graduates (Szasz, 1974; Wright and Tierney, 1991), during the period 1931–1935, blacks received 9,960 bachelors, 862 professional, 154 masters, and 20 doctorate degrees for a total of 11,663 graduates (Johnson, 1938, p. 8).

Not unexpectedly, the majority of early black college graduates were first-generation college students. This was also true of Native American graduates, and for largely the same reason since the parents of both had enjoyed little opportunity to go to college. Yet, the urge to partake in American society and the view that education was the avenue to do so was far stronger among the black community. As a result, black college students were far more likely to be supported in their educational aspirations that their Native American counterparts. By the 1930s, while only 0.4 percent of the black population were college graduates, they were in turn producing about 25 percent of the then current black college students. In the words of Dr. Charles Johnson of the University of North Carolina, Chapel Hill (1938), "college graduates are, on the whole, not the product of one but of two or more generations of education" (pp. 74–75).

Segregation

This rapid growth in black colleges undoubtedly fed the fear in the white South that blacks would someday demand equal social treatment and economic opportunity. Following the withdrawal of federal troops from the South at the end of the Reconstruction period, the white Southern society countered with the doctrine of segregation. Ongoing resistance to black participation in white society resulted in the development of the "separate but equal" concept. This policy of segregation, solidly established in law and custom, even found support in Supreme Court constitutional interpretation with *Plessy versus Ferguson* in 1896 (Myers, 1989). For more than the first half of the twentieth century, "separate" was usually rigidly enforced, while "equal" treatment was just as obviously violated.

Even so, this "separate but equal" doctrine had the perverse effect of strengthening the numbers and development of the black colleges. The pressure within the black community for higher education was certainly there, and denied access to white colleges, it just as certainly contributed to the growth of the black colleges. The first federal report on black higher education, in 1915, described three "college-grade" institutions—Howard University, Meharry Medical College, and Fisk University (Hill, 1985, p. xii). Thirty other institutions offered college-level work but were considered to be primarily secondary schools.

Following this 1915 survey, the increasing demand in the black community for higher education, coupled with the opportunity to found black land grant colleges under the 1890 Morrill Act and the continuing social policy of requiring separate black schools, created a new wave of founding black colleges. By 1927, the 1915 total of thirty-three such colleges had increased to seventy-seven (Hill, 1985, p. xiii; Wolters, 1975, p. vii).

Although most black colleges emphasized much needed teacher education, this time frame saw the development of a curriculum distinction between private and public black colleges that led to a period of campus unrest and upheaval among them during the 1920s. Broadly speaking, the private colleges emphasized a traditional academic curriculum, while the public institutions offered more vocational training.

This pattern reflected the major source of support for the two types. The private schools continued to benefit from and reflect the objectives of the Northern philanthropists and religious activists, who sought to provide academic, cultural, and social elevation for the black community. The public colleges, mindful of their dependence on the larger white society in which they functioned, were in the position of having to acquiesce to the white Southern view of blacks as inferior, not by the effects of slavery and oppression, but by nature. The Southern view sought to restrict black education to a vocational level, in clear recognition of the menial roles accorded them in society (Wolters, 1975, p. 4).

This prevailing postreconstructionist view that if blacks were not innately inferior, at a minimum they were in a primitive state of cultural evolution drew heavily on the doctrine of Social Darwinism then in vogue (Wolters, 1975, p. 5). It formed the basis for the belief that a traditional higher education curriculum ignored the limited aptitudes and capacities of blacks. Rather than stressing a curriculum designed for people in the highest degree of civilization, the reasoning went, it was believed that the curriculum should be adjusted accordingly, a remarkably similar argument to that earlier used in favor of vocational education for Native Americans.

The black public colleges (and the Northern philanthropic foundations aiding them) found themselves in a delicate position during the early years of the twentieth century. Not that they agreed with such reasoning, they often still felt it necessary to shift to an agricultural/vocational training emphasis to prevent the loss of public support and the onset of possible restrictions (Wolters, 1975, p. 8). As a matter of survival, it was believed necessary to work within the traditions and framework of the white society, seeking to accomplish what could be done without alienating the white South rather than following the earlier Yankee missionary goal of what should be done.

Within the black community, while there were those who agreed that economic necessity made such vocational training a valid objective, many began to see their supporters as well as detractors as trying to limit black education to keep blacks in their place. The more outspoken black leaders argued that the prevailing segregation meant black schools must provide the future leaders for the black community, proving the need for advanced education. By the 1920s, there was increasing pressure to strengthen such a focus on higher education, not on vocational training.

The two sides of this conflict were effectively embodied by major figures in the development of black education. W. E. B. DuBois, then with Atlanta University, represented the black intellectual. He led the debate in favor of classical higher education, arguing that black colleges should become centers of social and historical research in the black experience (Wolters, 1975, pp. 18–28). He believed that races as well as individuals contributed to culture.

DuBois's equally renowned counterpart was Booker T. Washington, president of Tuskegee Institute until his death in 1915. Washington held a strongly pragmatist and materialist view, and his stature was such that his influence continued well past his death. He believed that black economic progress was the key to social progress (Thornbrough, 1969, pp. 10–12). Consequently, he came out in favor of vocational or "manual" training, arguing that establishing an economic base was of more immediate concern.

Washington's was clearly an appeasement approach, seeking to gain and solidify what gains could be made. Washington even went so far as to state in his autobiography that the Ku Klux Klan was a phenomenon of the reconstruction period and had ceased to exist in the South past that time (Washington, 1937, p. 79). Much of the debate and animosity between these two views centered around the fact that Tuskegee enjoyed comparative lavish financial support from the government and private money, while Atlanta University was chronically financially strapped (Wolters, 1975, p. 25).

This debate created several riots and incidents on black campuses throughout the decade of the 1920s as black students and faculty members pushed to realize a true higher education system for themselves. This response was undoubtedly heightened, particularly where students were concerned, by a tendency of the black colleges to impose a very strict lifestyle on their student bodies.

Again very much echoing the experience of the Native American community, the majority white teachers and administrators in the black colleges believed learning was hampered by the continued influence of black culture and home life. In pushing their students to break away from such influences and to assimilate the values of the white culture, schools frequently required campus residence and implemented a very regimented lifestyle. The students' dress, hours, meals, social life, activities, and behavior were very strictly controlled, supervised, and regulated (Butler, 1977, pp. 22, 58; Wolters, 1975, p. 12). While the students grew restive under such conditions, the black educators likewise resisted the pattern of white teachers, and even more clearly, white administrators being the norm. This wealth of conflicting issues and positions led to a number of remarkable confrontations.

At Fisk University in Nashville, president Lafayette McKensie (a white) pushed to build a financial base to make Fisk a true university, raising a million dollars in endowment. Yet, he did so with a draconian student lifestyle, one that even forbade student organizations. There were no clubs, no fraternities, no sororities, no NAACP chapter; not even a student paper was allowed (Wolters, 1975, p. 29). DuBois, invited to speak at the 1924 commencement, startled McKensie and the rest of the administration by openly and emphatically confronting them as denying black freedom to assemble, enjoy a public forum, or to speak and think for themselves.

This issue festered through a semester before resulting in a riot, February 4, 1925, of just over 100 students. Faced with what seems a relatively small disturbance, and in an era of lynchings and other violence in black-white relations, McKensie made the career-ending mistake of calling out the white Nashville police. Such a potentially bloody blunder led to pressure that would not subside and he resigned (Wolters, 1975, pp. 63–69). His successor, Thomas Jones (also white), was nevertheless able to enjoy a twenty-one-year tenure as president, largely as a result of establishing policies at the onset directly counter to those of McKensie.

Howard University, Washington DC, has long been and was then the preeminent black university, devoted to a traditional, classical education. However, it too experienced difficulties directly attributable to black acceptance of a white administration. Howard held many black educators, but was governed by a white president and trustees.

Many of Howard's professors pushed for the acceptance of black studies as a discipline. They urged the development of academic treatment of and research into black culture and history with such efforts as the founding of the Association for the Study of Negro Life and History by Carter Woodson in 1915 (Wolters, 1975, p. 84).

However, president James Durkee and his trustees resisted, both in policy and funding, at times bordering on having a condescending attitude. Durkee most clearly seemed to not have the best interests of the black community at heart when he accepted a simultaneous position as head of the Curry School of Expression in Boston. Curry was well known for explicitly banning black students and Durkee did nothing to change, contest, or even express an opinion on this policy (Wolters, 1975, pp. 110–111).

Influenced and likely encouraged by the professors, Howard students became caught up in the fight for the study of black life, culture, and history. They went on strike from the school in May, 1925; a strike which threatened to effect the congressional appropriations for the school (Wolters, 1975, p. 113). The alumni association so feared such a consequence of the ongoing conflict that they called for Durkee's resignation. He resisted, eventually enduring a hearing on eight charges of harmful action to the university. This hearing saw some unusually direct denunciation, in a public forum, of the president by several professors.

Durkee ultimately resigned, in March 1926, amid demands that the next president be black. He was—Mordecai Johnson was a pastor with degrees from Morehouse, Chicago, and Harvard. The selection was delayed due to a perceived need to avoid any internal candidate as being too likely to be involved in the factionalism of the Durkee years (Wolters, 1975, pp. 133–134).

Even Tuskegee, in its earnestness to appease the white South, did not escape an incident of conflict with white control. In fact, it experienced what may have been the most dramatic such incident of the period.

Following the death of Booker T. Washington in 1915, president Robert Moton continued the appeasement policies to ensure a similar (and elevated) continuance of financial and political support (Butler, 1977, pp. 56 ff, 81–82). Not unexpectedly, this resulted in increased criticism for going along with the Southern white policy of only providing minimal training for blacks to fill lower socioeconomic positions.

To be fair, in retrospect, such a path, at least by some black schools, may have enabled black education to survive a very tense period. To confront and conflict directly with Southern white attitudes of the day would have probably invited inestimable social and political strife and violence. Even today, many programs for postsecondary education of at-risk populations take this same position of placing extreme importance on enabling the targeted population to economically strengthen themselves by training to get and hold a job.

Moton did make some quiet headway, establishing a separate college curriculum during the 1920s (Butler, 1977, p. 93; Wolters, 1975, p. 141). However, his moment in the glare of publicity arising from black resistance to white dominance came in relation to a new federal hospital built in connection with Tuskegee (Wolters, 1975, pp. 151 ff).

The hospital was to serve black veterans of the Great War (World War I), but Southern white political pressure was felt on two points. The first was simple economic gain—it was argued that the civil service jobs represented by the hospital should go to whites. The second was the fear that somehow such a cluster of disabled black veterans (trained fighting men!) combined with a black administration and staff would constitute a possible physical threat to the Southern white suprematist way of life.

That both positions constituted logical absurdities seems to have drawn little comment. First, Southern custom prohibited white nurses and doctors from handling black patients, so short of no care at all, black staffing seems a foregone conclusion. Second, how a group of disabled men in need of hospitalization who were restricted to low-level service jobs while in the military were expected to combine with doctors and nurses to somehow create a fighting force capable of an uprising against the greater numbers of Southern whites (or why) invites neither comment nor rebuttal. It invites (or should have) derision.

In any case, Moton countermanded his usual conciliatory style and insisted on a black or integrated staff and administration. This eventually led to a direct confrontation with the Ku Klux Klan who threatened to destroy the school. The Klan held a major demonstration on July 3, 1923, marching two miles through the streets of Tuskegee. They burned a cross, then continued marching on through the Institute to the new hospital (Wolters, 1975, pp. 173–175). Militant area blacks took up positions along the route, professing an intent to protect the school. However tense the atmosphere, cool heads prevailed and no conflicts or outbreaks occurred. The Klan eventually just went home.

These were the major disturbances in black higher education in the 1920s, but by no means the only ones. Nathan Young (a white) served as president at both Florida A and M College and Lincoln University in Missouri during the decade. He led a protracted struggle to establish a classical curriculum in place of vocational training at both, and was forced to step down from both schools. Both schools experienced student rebellions as a result of this struggle, including the destruction or damage of six buildings by fire at Florida in the Fall semester of 1923 in response to Young being fired (Wolters, 1975, p. 200).

Hampton Institute had a long, proud history of educational service, including the original group of Native American students that eventually were prominent in the founding of Carlisle Academy. Hampton was very similar to Tuskegee in being financially well endowed, in being focused on vocational education, and in being soundly criticized by W. E. B. DuBois.

Entering this conflictual period, in 1918, James Edgar Gregg, a white minister educated at Harvard and Yale, was picked to head the Institute. Like Jones at Fisk, Gregg seemed an unlikely choice to placate black critics. Yet he was very active in giving blacks a larger role, and in raising the numbers of blacks in teaching appointments, including the chairs of various departments. He established programs in black and African studies, black culture and history, launched the West African Student Union, and established the *Southern Workman* with the publication of over sixty articles on Africa (Wolters, 1975, pp. 232–233).

Gregg steered a very progressive course for Hampton, with his college division experiencing strong growth. This raised comments along the usual white alarmist position that education might excite racial pride and present a threat to the established Southern order of race relations. Gregg probably could not have agreed more.

Besides educational reforms, Gregg instituted remarkably progressive social relations at the school. Faculty, staff, and administration, black and white alike, ate in common dining halls, mingled at social events, and were seated together at school functions and gatherings, an unheard-of thing in the white South. This led to predictable outrage and pressure to adhere to the traditional Southern segregation. There was even a state law (the Massenberg Law in 1926) requiring it (Wolters, 1975, p. 244).

The Institute tried to counter this reaction (and the law) by placing such racial intermingling behind closed doors. It also tried to placate fears by tightening an already structured, regimented student lifestyle. Although this was a very common method of allaying white fears in the 1920s, the students felt the faculty and administration were weakening in their resolve. As a result, even such a progressive administration endured a student rebellion and strike, October 11-18, 1927, during this tumultuous period (Wolters, 1975, p. 247).

There were a number of other such student strikes, rebellions, and incidents on black campuses; Talladega College, Alabama, 1914; Morehouse College, Atlanta, 1917; Shaw University, North Carolina, 1919; Storer College, West Virginia, 1922; Livingstone College, North Carolina, 1923; Bowie College, Maryland, 1923 (faculty); Lincoln Institute, Kentucky, 1925; Johnson Smith University, North Carolina,

1926; St. Augustine Junior College, North Carolina, 1927; and Alcorn A and M College, Mississippi, 1929 (Wolters, 1975, pp. 276–277). Obviously, black higher education experienced a system-wide revolt during the 1920s against both the paternalistic policies and industrial emphasis imposed by white society.

In pushing for black representation in faculty and administration, in pushing for true higher education for the black community, and in the nascent move to establish black studies, this period may be considered to have begun the move to integrated higher education that would feature so prominently in the civil rights movement of the 1950s and 1960s. Several lawsuits beginning in 1935 challenged the "separate but equal" principle in higher education, as evidenced by the lack of public graduate and professional schools for blacks in states with dual educational systems (Hill, 1985, p. xiii). That it took until *Brown versus Board of Education* (1954) for the Supreme Court to declare that "separate educational facilities are inherently unequal" probably says more about the readiness of the court and white America to recognize the obvious than about the desire and effort of the black community to establish and support education for itself at the highest level.

Integration

As clearly as *Plessy versus Ferguson* defined the legal recognition of the segregation stage of black education, so did *Brown versus Board of Education* mark the onset of the desegregation or integration phase. The highlights of the civil rights movement of the 1950s and 1960s— *Brown versus Board of Education*, the Little Rock high school confrontation, the marches and barricades of the 1960s—are well known scenes, etched in the collective consciousness of the nation. Although resistance was to last legally well into the 1960s, and socially beyond that, the clear direction of black education and higher education in this period has been away from specialty institutions and toward enrollment in mainstream schools and colleges.

By the 1970s, the focus was shifting to solidifying the gains made, on filling in the blanks as it were. In 1970, the NAACP filed a class action lawsuit (*Adams*) that resulted in the traditionally black colleges being enhanced, and requiring affirmative action to increase the number of black students and faculty on the campuses of traditionally white colleges. Interestingly, such ongoing pressure to open mainstream higher education to blacks has led to pressure on the traditionally black colleges.

Today there are 105 such traditionally black institutions, forty-three of which are public. Stemming from a 1992 Supreme Court case requiring the state of Mississippi to "educationally justify or eliminate" all vestiges of segregation (Wenglinsky, 1996, p. 91), the traditionally black colleges find themselves likewise being forced to broaden or justify the racial make-up of their student bodies.

Within educational circles and within the black community, black colleges have their defenders and detractors. Detractors insist they are echoes of the segregated era and should now integrate, merge, or close rather than continue to exist as an outdated artifact of a darker time. This argument is based on the "common school" model of education, drawn from the assumption that mixed student types will benefit educationally.

Defenders of the black colleges see their continued existence as a viable and desired option, insisting that students learn best when they are with like-minded peers, reducing conflict stemming from differing origins and being more consistent regarding values and culture. This position sees black colleges as valuable in serving as repositories of black culture, pride, and identity within the larger society (Wenglinsky, 1996, p. 91–92).

Such a position, of course, featured prominently in the development of the tribally controlled colleges. However, the momentum of the move to desegregate black higher education has resulted in pressure away from separate black schools during the same period that separate Native American colleges have enjoyed expanded social support and federal assistance.

Overview

The development of black higher education within the United States has been markedly different from that of Native Americans. Not surprisingly, differences between the two communities' experiences far outweigh the similarities. As given by the government survey of black higher education in 1915, the period roughly of the late nineteenth century saw the establishment of thirty-three black colleges. Today, within approximately the same time frame, the late twentieth century has seen the development of thirty-two traditionally Native American colleges.

The development of the tribally controlled colleges drew heavily on a developing interest in Native American cultures, and still is fueled largely by an urge in the Native American community and the larger society to preserve and study Native American history, culture, and lifestyles. Early black higher education was chiefly focused on education as a tool for economic gain and social progress. It was only with the pressure of the 1920s in favor of black studies, reiterated by the recent threat to the continued existence of the black colleges posed by federal integration requirements, that black colleges have been recognized in some quarters as potential safe havens for black cultural study and preservation (Wenglinsky, 1996).

There are at least five very striking differences of experience between black and Native American higher education, any one of which could have created profoundly different outcomes. Taken together, it is remarkable that any similarities, even superficial ones, exist between the two today.

One, of course, is the simple matter of who was administering the education of the two groups. During the federal period, the government oversaw Native American education, regardless of the fact that such was not the case in other segments of society, and that the federal government did not have sufficient experience in education, higher or otherwise. True to form, the government program was rather one-dimensional, a monolithic "solution" to a problem, rather than a varied set of provisions for the educational needs of Native Americans. Conversely, the development of black education and higher education (as well as that of Native Americans during the colonial and the self-determination periods) followed the normal pattern of various interested private groups and the pertinent state and local governments working to establish the range and variety of institutions that seemed called for to satisfy the needs of the community.

Next, there is the matter of financial support, public and private. Compared to the Native American experience all the way back to the Boyle fund, black colleges as a group have been consistently and relatively well funded since the Civil War. This, no doubt, will come as a shock to past and present administrators of black colleges. But it is only necessary to glance at the figures to reveal the difference in favor of the black schools. Of today's 105 traditionally black colleges, forty-three are state schools. No such Native American school exists and only one has done so in the history of the nation.

Certainly the Southern states provided considerably less for their black schools than for their white, and certainly they pressured for vocational education rather than a classical curriculum. But provide they did, as did private sources, which is more than can be claimed regarding the Native American students. Only when the federal government began to provide funds did the burst of tribally controlled college foundings occur, much like the post-Civil War philanthropic and religious support fueled the then new growth of black colleges.

Third, the development of black higher education occurred in a much more concise manner. A larger and far more cohesive target population, a more clearly defined geographic area (the old South), and a more simplified time frame—the freeing of the slaves—seemed to have brought both the need and the desire to provide for black higher education into sharper focus. Overnight a large population was to be somehow assimilated into the national life. Their educational needs stood out clearly, sufficiently so as to motivate those in some quarters to strive to provide for such needs.

Comparatively, the need to assimilate the Native Americans into white society was a drawn-out, piecemeal affair, lending itself well to a national procrastination. It was not thought remarkable that removal seemed a truly viable option. There always seemed to be enough land on which to push them back. Not only were there less Native Americans, but they were widely dispersed and could be dealt with in much smaller tribal groups, not as a whole. Unknown to those who coined the term, the "Indian problem" of the nineteenth century quite possibly owed a great deal to this drawn-out chronic nature of the nation's relations with the Indians.

The fourth difference was reflected in the disruptions on black college campuses of the 1920s. One of the issues creating conflict within black colleges during that period was the debate over whether black higher education should be focused on providing a classical education or on vocational training. Superficially, this looks like a clear similarity, recalling the policy of vocational education to the exclusion of nearly all else being provided Native American students during the entirety of the federal period. The professed objective or justification in both instances was the providing of job training as a matter of economic necessity to aid in their assimilation into mainstream society. Other apparent similarities relate to this objective. The respective requirements to live on campus rather than in black homes or on reservations, and the use of rigidly restricted student lifestyles which were expected to aid in the assimilation of white culture and values fit this description.

It may also be argued that, in both cases, one may find a more basic commonality in that the professed goal of assimilation for either group was a sham. The lack of economic opportunity available within mainstream society for Native Americans, and the experiences of and justifiable belief within the black community that vocational education was intended to "keep blacks in their place" support this view. In both cases, the real objective seemed to be to deny access to all but the most menial positions in society.

However, there is a large difference underlying this collection of apparent similarities. In the case of the Native Americans, the vocational training efforts were supported principally by those considered to be their supporters. The nineteenth-century debate over removal or assimilation tended to cast detractors of Native Americans into the camp of those wanting to push them off the land and out of the way. Native American supporters clung to the belief that vocational training would lead to the ability to make a living within the white society, which would lead to the desired assimilation. That no such economic opportunity was afforded, or that a top-down educational approach would have proved more effective, even with the example of the historical efforts of the colonial colleges, never drew much comment or support.

Conversely, during the period of and leading to the debate in black higher education over vocational training versus a traditional curriculum, the vocational education side was that of their detractors. Having fought a bitter civil war involving the issue of freedom for blacks, their detractors apparently realized that no training at all was simply not a feasible option. Interestingly, removal of a sort did see some debate, as post-Civil War plans to transport the blacks back to Africa were discussed in some quarters. However, the sheer numbers involved, the desires of the newly freed blacks, the mood of the nation, and the fact that many if not most were several generations removed from their African roots made it a simplistic and untenable idea.

As a result, most detractors of blacks in the white community supported the low-level vocational training, not without cause seen by the black community as designed to keep them in a relatively subjugated position. Just as obviously, black supporters of vocational training, however strongly they felt the importance of economic progress, tended to be viewed as engaged in the appeasement of whites.

The last difference between the black experience and the Native American experience regarding higher education may be the most influential. It is certainly the most durable. It is the level of attraction or resistance to education found within the target community. Blacks as a community found themselves newly freed from, yet still economically and socially burdened with a severe level of subjugation. They perceived education as the means with which to deal with their collective situation. Consequently, they embraced education at all levels with remarkable quickness, even the vocational training offered by apparent detractors. This created a swelling of community support for education that contributed significantly to the rapid development and expansion of black higher education.

On the other hand, the Native Americans emphatically resisted white education from the start. Neither option, removal or assimilation, appealed to them. The policies of the federal government reflected the needs of the government, not the needs of the Native Americans. Consequently, the Native Americans correctly saw such education as focused on denying and eliminating their culture while converting their children to the views and values of the white society. Education was opportunity to the blacks; to the Native Americans it was cultural genocide. This led to a pattern of resistance to white education that persists to this day, and was no doubt instrumental in minimizing support within the Native American community for education of any sort. Only with the coming of Native American self-determination on educational matters can this resistance be said to have abated.

6

Compendium

In considering the history of Native American higher education, one is struck by a sense of what might have been. The conquistadors made an extremely promising beginning 460 years ago. The Jamestown colonists professed a desire to build not just our first college, but our first Indian college, 380 years ago. Yet, not until twenty to thirty years ago did an effective system of Native American higher education begin to develop. The cost of such a delay is incalculable. With a truly effective educational structure contributing to a maximum exchange of knowledge and awareness between the two cultures, what changes might have been realized. The endlessly repetitive removals, land thefts, and warfare, the progress of white-Indian relations, the position and status of Native Americans in today's society might all have been unrecognizably different.

There is a temptation to give the colonists credit for addressing Native American higher education, but they did so only in a limited sense. The apparent colonial interest in Native American higher education was an artificial one on the part of both the interested English public and the educational administrators themselves. The typical educational objectives underlying such interest were not paramount.

The contributing public's real interest was in converting the natives to Christianity in a purely proselytizing sense. Education was seen as a necessary element subservient to that end, not an end in itself. This religious interest generated donations, leading to an awakening of interest by the colonial educators in Native American higher education as a means of gaining access to these funds. Neither group could be said to have been primarily concerned with the intellectual advancement of the Indian community, certainly not with including that community in the setting of its own educational objectives. "Spreading the faith" and "civilizing the savages" are not typically synonymous with classical educational objectives, and one clearly does not ask the savages for their input.

These colonial educators were not fraudulent. They had valid educational objectives and attendant financial needs. The problem was that Native American higher education figured far more prominently in their financial activities than in their educational objectives. A scholarly interest in Native American cultures, the application of European educational models within Indian life, or simply that the inhabitants of this world might profit from and simply be interested in learning of the history, culture, and extent of the European world for its own sake appears to never have crossed anyone's mind.

The primary characteristic influencing Native American higher education in the colonial period was one that would set a precedent that would be a long time in overcoming, the lack of local or self-control. The colonists devoted a great deal of effort to Indian education, but did so without consulting the Indians. Consequently, the Indian community had no input or influence on curriculum or objectives. The education offered was designed to serve the needs and objectives of the educators, whether religious proselytizing or financial gain, not the needs of the educated. That colonial Indian education had limited results should have been no surprise to anyone aware of the lack of supervision over funds raised, or the response of Native Americans to education so lacking in attention to their needs and desires.

Factors such as the urge to convert the natives to Christianity, or the financial motivations underlying virtually all the colonial college Indian objectives can be subsumed under this broader factor of educational offerings determined by white control without any input or cooperative involvement from the Indian community. The only other influential factor is the simple focus of that era on the exploration and exploitation of this new world.

So strong was the urge to explore, claim, and profit from the newly discovered countries, it is remarkable that education for the natives even came up for discussion. That much is owed to the religious motives of the era. The haste to occupy and profit from the new world represents a possible cause for the minimal attention paid to informing the natives of a complex world foreign to them, and to the reverse, the study and learning of the native societies unknown to the Europeans.

During the federal period, the federal takeover of Indian education represented a more direct way of achieving their ends. The question of why the loss of the colonial interest in Native American higher education goes to the point about colonial efforts having proselytizing and civilizing purposes instead of more classical educational objectives.

The interest in dealing with what would later be termed the "Indian problem" remained. What changed was not so much a loss of interest in higher education, but a change of the method for dealing with the "problem."

The concern by Jefferson, Washington, and others for the lack of results in the colonial period indicates a desire to try a different solution. Had the first solution (higher education) been effective, it would have been retained. Or, had higher education been the direct objective instead of the means to the government's ends, it would have been retained and even strengthened.

During the federal period, the Indians were still being taught according to the dictates of the whites, just with different objectives. The single minded federal concern for using education for assimilation seems to have obscured any awareness of other, more typical objectives. Education for Indians was still not designed to broaden their awareness of the world or to develop Indian leaders.

Considering the degree to which the federal government was devoted to assimilating the Indian, it is also remarkable how short-sighted and one-dimensional the program was. Indian education was preparation for only the lowest levels of society, not a comprehensive, top-to-bottom approach at educating Indians in the white manner. There was a complete lack of socioeconomic opportunity within the white society, even after such a minimal preparation for entering it.

The attempt to assimilate the Native Americans, yet keep them at a social distance may be interpreted as not dissimilar to the removal policies. Both seem to reflect a desire to reestablish a distance between white and native cultures that was lost with the establishment of the U.S. national government. These elements should have made the eventual failure of the program evident to even casual observers.

The federal period may be accurately characterized as one of multiple unacknowledged contradictions. Contradictions that apparently went unrecognized then now seem to leap off the page. Thomas Jefferson, instrumental in the founding of the University of Virginia and an early advocate of using college trained administrators in government, had no apparent difficulties with calling for Indian education to be vocational. He was an early supporter of what would become the land grant college phenomenon, seeing higher education as a necessary catalyst for economic development (Key, 1996), yet he failed to apply that reasoning to the recognized problem of a lack of economic development among the Indians.

The nation's educational system, widespread and locally controlled, certainly was effective in preparing its own citizens for membership in and service to society. Counting on that system, or using it as a model for an Indian educational system would seem to have been a natural choice. Instead, the government, untrained and inexperienced in education, elected to run Indian education itself. Indian education was often overseen by the Army, unsure of whether it was dealing with combatants, prisoners, or students. The Indians were not a responsibility or a duty, certainly not an opportunity. They were a "problem."

The assimilationist objective itself was so poorly conceived and implemented as to guarantee its failure. Indians were encouraged to become acquisitive and economically competitive. Yet their education was designed to consign them to a peasant or laborer lifestyle at the very bottom of the social ladder, not at all a full participation in the expansive, capitalist society with which they were supposed to join. In case any should doubt the emptiness of the assimilation being offered, the Indians were then denied the opportunity to function in white society even at these minimal levels, finding themselves ostracized or isolated on reservations instead.

At the broadest level of analysis, the principal factor influencing and limiting the direction of Indian education in the federal period was still the fact that it was outside of local or self-control by the Indians. Instead of religious or financial motives, the federal objectives were to move the Indians off the land and out of the way of the expanding nation. The curriculum selected was one designed to enable the Indians to subsist on the lands left to them, or to take lower-level jobs to support themselves. Had the Indians administered their own education, such low-level vocational and agricultural training would surely have had a place in their system. However, judging from the Choctaw and Cherokee school systems of the nineteenth century and the tribal college movement of today, such training would not have defined their educational objectives and program. These federal objectives determined the type of education provided to the Indians and were very limited. But, in the broadest sense, the problem was that the objectives were determined by the government, to serve its needs, with little input from or concern for the desires and goals of the Indians.

The concurrent growth of the nation's colleges and universities was not enough to draw attention to the need for such institutions for Indians. The federal government's concern with its own objectives of removal and access to land, the contributing effects of racism, and the widely dispersed and quite small, in absolute numbers, nature of the Native American population all served to isolate the Indian community from participating in and benefitting from the nineteenth-century growth in higher education.

So concerned was the government with its myopic view of assimilation, it completely missed and actually curtailed the most effective moves toward Indian assimilation of the period. The nineteenth-century efforts of various tribes to develop and maintain their own school systems in the face of continuous disruptions, closings, and removals merit special recognition. Similarly, the efforts to open and operate colleges for Indians were nothing short of heroic. Their limited impact on Native American economic progress and cultural recognition reflects only their rarity, not the level of their effort or accomplishments. Possibly no greater indication of a willingness to assimilate could exist than the patterning of Indian governments and schools on that of the white society. Imitation is the sincerest form of flattery, yet no one noticed. Instead of encouraging and supporting such efforts, white policies caused the Indians to build from scratch over and over again. That the twentieth century dawned with tribal schools in disarray and closing, and with only two extant Indian colleges struggling for survival, reflects not an Indian resistance to assimilation, but a lack of white recognition of the assimilation taking place.

Just as the overriding factor affecting the course of Native American higher education in the colonial and federal periods was the lack of local or self-control over their own educational objectives and system, the most influential factor of the self-determination period is the Indian control of their own education that gives the era its name. The history of Native American higher education is a monument, not only to exploitation, but to bureaucracy. Nearly 200 years of control at the federal level had not only failed to address classical educational objectives, it had failed to achieve, and at times even stifled, the federal objectives.

This new-found ability on the part of Native Americans to control their own educational destiny stems from several supporting factors. The United States in the twentieth century no longer had vast areas available to which to remove the Indians, and was finally feeling the pressure to truly assimilate them into the general society. Prompted by the intellectual awakening to the value of Native American cultures by the reformers of the 1920s and 1930s, the nation was also shifting to an acceptance of a multicultural approach, leading to an assimilation policy based on the treatment of Native Americans as citizens, not a "problem." A natural outgrowth of such a multicultural position is the input from Native Americans themselves as obvious experts on the elements of their own cultures. In turn, this just as logically leads to self-control on the part of Native Americans regarding educational objectives and administration due to the role of any educational system as a cultural repository and transmitter.

One possible overlooked contribution to the weak academic heritage behind today's Native American college students is the long-term past equating of education with assimilation (Warner and Hastings, 1991). Presenting education as an either-or proposition, either give up your culture and adapt, or lose the opportunity to share in society's wealth, doubtless did little to endear education to generations of Indians (Horse, 1982). By providing an education that sought not to instruct but to assimilate, seeking no input from the Indian community nor from the academic world, the federal government committed, in the words of David DeJong (1993), "educational malpractice."

The recent development of tribal colleges represents the first true regard within United States Indian education for Indian values, perspectives, and culture (Horse, 1982). This not only reflects Indian control, but the cessation of one-way-only education for Indians. Historically, Indian education has been "built on the premise that the Indian has a great deal to learn from the whites" (Deloria, Jr., quoted in Thompson, 1978, p. 10). White religion, economics, justice, history, and culture were all presented as superior, representing the highest achievement in social evolution. Even more than the lack of willingness to truly provide a full range of education to Native Americans, this realization that whites had much to learn from and about the Indians was very late in arriving. To quote Lubomir Bic, director of the American Indian Summer Institute in Computer Science, "More academic progress has been made since the advent of the reservation-based college than in the preceding four centuries" (Gustafson and Knowlton, 1993).

Given the positive strides made during this self-determination period, there remains a sense that the federal government still does not fully comprehend the nature of Indian education or the government's role within it. Much has been made of the argument that self-determination represents the means by which the Indians will assume control of their own destiny and the federal government will no longer need to intervene. Attempts to accelerate this process led to the curtailment of funding during the Eisenhower and Reagan-Bush administrations. The conclusion can be drawn from this that the federal government has not, now or in the past, accurately recognized the nature of its self-avowed trust responsibility for Native Americans.

The federal support of the tribal colleges represents an expansion of the federal-Indian trust relationship, not a prelude to its disappearance (Pease-Windy Boy, 1994). In the past, by serving its own needs in seeking to deal with Indians as simply impediments to national expansion, the government unwittingly ignored this trust responsibility. The first rule of a trust relationship is that the administrator of a trust serves the needs of the trustee, not of the administrator.

In the modern era, self-determination means the Indian community is now empowered to determine its own educational objectives and direction. It does not excuse the federal government from all involvement. Just as the government has a trust relationship with all its citizens, so it does with its Indian citizens. Federal support of mainstream schools, in terms of research grants, contracts, and student financial aid, is a given in our society (Kerr, 1963; 1995). To grant Native Americans the same rights to set their own educational course should not be an excuse to deny the responsibility to support the needs of these citizens.

7

The Current Status of Native American
Higher Education

As a result of the reforms and efforts of the last thirty-five years, today Native American higher education is directly served by a wealth of institutions, both tribal colleges and mainstream schools. There are thirty-two colleges that traditionally or purposefully serve Native Americans. They include the twenty-six tribally controlled colleges and the three federally chartered schools, as well as three private schools (Bacone, Nazarene Indian Bible College, and the American Indian College).

Most of these are two-year institutions. According to their catalogs, six offer bachelor's degrees. They are Sinte Gleska University, Oglala Lakota College, Salish Kootenai College (all tribal), Haskell Indian Nations University (federal), Nazarene Indian Bible College, and American Indian College (both private). Two of these offer master's degrees as well, Sinte Gleska and Oglala Lakota.

There are twenty-five mainstream colleges and universities offering a wide variety of specific programs or disciplines for Native Americans. Among these are Harvard and Dartmouth, still holding true to their early Indian missions, the lackluster colonial performance notwithstanding. They also include the Native American law specialty program at the University of Tulsa Law School (*University of Tulsa Graduate/Law School Bulletin*, 1994), the American Indian Scientific and Engineering Society founded by Clarkson University of New York (Wright, 1991), and the newly established Ph. D. program in American Indian Studies at the University of Arizona (*Chronicle of Higher Education*, 1996, December 20). Due to the prevalence of two-year programs at the tribal colleges, several mainstream schools work closely with them in support of transfer programs. Montana State University probably maintains the most comprehensive support system for Native

145

American students. It houses a center for Native American study, coordinates with the tribes and the seven tribal colleges in Montana on transfer issues, and provides financial aid and personal support for its Native American students (Wright, 1991). Northern Arizona University is another school that coordinates its program with area Indian colleges and is very supportive of its Native American students.

• There are eighty-five mainstream schools with over 5 percent Native Americans within their student bodies (*Chronicle of Higher Education*, 1996, September 2). They are mostly medium to small schools; only seven enroll more than 500 Native American students. Even including the tribal colleges, all small as well, there are only three colleges that enroll more than 1,000 Native American students. They are Navajo Community College (80 percent Native American), Northeastern State University of Oklahoma (16 percent), and Northland Pioneer College of Arizona (22 percent) (Fries, 1987; Wright, 1991).

Virtually all of the Native American colleges and three-fourths of the mainstream colleges with Native American programs are in the western half of the United States. Of the tribal colleges, two-thirds of them are in the northern plains states, mostly in Montana, North Dakota, and South Dakota.

With the advent of such a wealth of institutions serving Native American higher education, much of the current focus has shifted back toward the individual students. It is worth recalling that until the mid-twentieth century, federal officials believed that vocational education was sufficient for even the most intellectually able Indian youth, as evidenced by the chartering of the three BIA junior colleges at the very end of the federal control period, approximately 100 years after the founding of Howard University and other colleges for freed Blacks. The overt prejudice against Indians in higher education was generally not as strong as against blacks, but the lack of response on the part of federal officials and the conditions of reservation life combined to make generations of Native Americans the most underrepresented minority in United States higher education (Astin, 1982; Oppelt, 1990).

Such a long-standing deficiency of educational services has caused some consistent and difficult problems within the Native American college student population. Even though Native American educators report their main problems are funding and the inability to expand programs and services that stems from a lack of funding (Tippeconnic, 1988), various reports and studies have identified Indian student needs and reasons for a lack of college success as mostly individually centered problems (Guyette and Heth, 1983: Kirkness and Barnhardt, 1991, May; McIntosh, 1987). Typical issues identified include a persistently high dropout rate during or before high school (Tierney, 1992); a low proportion of high school graduates entering college (Belgrade, 1992); a strong sense of isolation and of insurmountable cultural barriers (Richardson and Skinner, 1991); a general lack of academic preparation and skills, a lack of role models, financial problems, negative cultural pressure (Guyette and Heth, 1983); culture shock, lack of motivation, English deficiency, unrealistic career goals, distrust of the institution, and a general lack of support, socialization, and counseling (LaCounte, 1987; McIntosh, 1987; Wright, 1991).

Specific solutions have been offered as numerous as the problems. They include a much expanded recruitment program extending to the family as well as the student, and to those out of high school for a few years; a much more elaborate socialization and orientation program; attention to monitoring of progress and ongoing support; the development of Native American faculty; and job experience by the students (LaCounte, 1987; McIntosh, 1987). Obviously, a number of directly applicable remedies could be developed. However, in virtually every case, more funds and resources would need to be committed. Reflecting this, frequently the oft-repeated call for increased funding is made, if combined with specified applications (Houser, 1991; Wright, 1991).

Much of the difficulty experienced by Native American college students seems to be traceable to cultural causes of two types. The first is the generally unsupportive situation in which such students find themselves. They tend to come from high schools that themselves are poorly funded, lacking special programs and support services. Once at college, almost all Native American students tend to feel isolated, usually trying to go home each weekend. Leaving home for these students is traumatic due to their expanded family and community involvement.

Furthermore, this expanded sense of membership in family and community tends to carry with it little in the way of encouragement to go to college. The low level of higher education experience in past generations has resulted in a significantly high incidence of first-generation college students among Native Americans. They suffer from a distinct lack of role models and traditional family support, encouragement, and understanding of the college experience (Thompson, 1990; Tierney, 1992). All too often, going to college is treated as leaving behind one's background and upbringing.

The second cultural basis for Native American college difficulties is much more deeply ingrained. It stems not from the lack of collegiate experience in the Native American community, but from the Native American cultural heritage itself. It goes directly to differences between the white and native cultures. Native American students tend to have a more holistic frame of reference concerning themselves and the world. The fragmentation of knowledge that characterizes the academic pattern of separate and distinct disciplines conflicts with their tendency to see knowledge as an interrelated whole. When forced to function in this compartmentalized academic style, they react with a sense of incompleteness and inadequacy to such an apparently reductionist approach (Deloria, Jr., 1991; Kirkness and Barnhardt, 1991).

Native American students also tend to be less comfortable within the requisite formal educational organization structures that emphasize individual status and competitiveness over consensual decision making and group identity (Badwound, 1990; Ramirez-Shkwegnaabi, 1987; Rosh, 1987). They respond to the typical classroom situation differently. In such group situations, they tend to be reticent and noncompetitive, shrinking from calling attention to themselves in ways that affect their success (Deloria Jr., 1991; Kirkness and Barnhardt, 1991). Even nonreservation students, those schooled in mainstream public schools, still have less academic success than the norm in college. Such a pattern may reflect their resistance to the Eurocentric view of history that still predominates, or to a differing cultural view of time, affecting such issues as commitment, study habits, course load, and attendance (Thompson, 1990).

The mainstream colleges themselves are seen as tending to perpetuate policies and practices that have been shown to be nonproductive for Native American students. They tend to be institution-centered, taking a coming-to rather than going-to view of the college experience. Such a traditional viewpoint contributes to the tendency to identify problems in terms of the individual, such as low achievement, high attrition, poor retention, weak performance, or poor study habits (Kirkness and Barnhardt, 1991).

Dealing with the problems that arise from this cultural clash between Native American students and higher education institutions is exacerbated by unreliable statistics concerning Native Americans in higher education. As the smallest U. S. ethnic minority at less than 1 percent, Native American samples are usually so small as to create validity and reliability problems, or are grouped into "other" (Tierney, 1992; Wright, 1991). Important information on Native Americans in higher education suffers accordingly. How many go on to college, how many go several years after high school, how many take longer than four years or return after dropping out, and particularly how many who enter college actually eventually graduate are all important questions about which less than ideal information is available.

One piece of data about Native Americans in higher education that is clear is that most of them are in two-year schools. The *Chronicle of Higher Education* reports (1996, September 2) that, nationwide, two-year enrollments account for about 39 percent of the total enrollment figure. For Native Americans, about 55 percent are in two-year programs (Astin, 1982; Olivas, 1979). This high incidence of Native Americans in two-year schools is reflected in the degrees awarded. Of Native American graduates in 1989 and 1990, 40 percent received associate's degrees, compared to 30 percent for Blacks and Hispanics, and 20 percent for whites and Asians (Pavel and Colby, September 1992). Overall, while representing .8 percent of the population, Native Americans are granted .9 percent of the associate's degrees, but only .5 percent of the bachelor's and .4 percent of the graduate degrees (*Chronicle of Higher Education*, 1996, September 2).

This preponderance of Native Americans in junior and community colleges may reflect a tendency toward self-selection on the part of an at-risk population. Native American students may choose two-year schools as a means of dealing with perceptions of poor preparation, or fears of larger, more distant schools. Also, to some extent, it reflects the fact that most of the tribal colleges are two-year schools, since they account for about 20 percent of Native American college students.

The large proportion of Native Americans in two-year schools may also reflect pressures related to the less than fully supportive environment preceding their college careers. Studies have shown that Native American high schools tend to promote community colleges for much the same reasons that the students may self-select. Community colleges are presented to the students as a means to lessen the confusion and tendency to be overwhelmed in the transition to college. Such arguments are often presented instead of unqualified information, assistance, and contacts for the full range of college choices (Tierney, 1992).

In some respects, Native American students may be better served in two-year schools. Wright (1989) reports an extensive survey of students in tribal colleges. He found the colleges were perceived as doing a superior job of meeting student needs relating to financial support, counseling, orientation/socialization, academic support, and cultural support. McIntosh (1987) similarly cited findings of community colleges to be more community oriented; to be socially, culturally, and economically more inclusive; to be cheaper; and to provide more counseling.

Others cite characteristics of community college Indian students that may reflect the more supportive and accessible nature of the community college. Thompson (1990) notes that among community college Indian students, both full-time and part-time students carry heavier class-hour loads and seem more committed. Houser (1991) describes the typical tribal college student as nontraditional (usually older or a returning student), more likely to be female, lower income, having children, and having a GED, rather than a high school diploma.

Such indications of a more student-friendly approach by community colleges and a positive response by clearly more at-risk students would seem to bode well for the use of junior and community colleges to serve first-generation Native American college students. Chavers (1979) notes that the tribes and the BIA tend to promote going to local community colleges as a means of stretching funds and lessening the breaking of one's bonds at home and in the community. However, there are others who tend to see junior and community colleges in a far less positive light.

The original concept of a junior college was as an associated feeder school to a larger university, not a free-standing, degree-granting institution. William Harper, at the 1892 founding of the University of Chicago, presented a new model of the university. The junior college division, the first two years, was to be more collegiate and preparatory; the senior division more advanced and scholarly (Rudolph, 1962; 1990). Harper expected three-fourths of existing colleges to become junior colleges as a response to the expanding appeal of education, yet offering a way to address the perceived lack of serious scholastic interest on a large part of the population (Rudolph, 1962; 1990).

By 1930, the junior college was well on the way to being recognized, not as the first two years of a typical baccalaureate career, but as serving the needs of "the non-academically minded high school graduate" (Snyder, 1930). By their recent appearance, as well as by the non-academic background underlying most Native American students, Stein (1992) places the tribally controlled community colleges solidly within this general junior/community college movement.

Today, junior and community colleges are seen as serving two prime functions. For those desiring to transfer after two years to a four-year college or university to complete their baccalaureate, they offer a cheaper, local, less overwhelming means of completing the first two years. For those not desiring a four-year degree, but wanting more advanced training or education for a career, they offer certificate and associate degree programs. However, many argue the transfer function is no longer very credible. They see a major de facto function of community colleges to be that of "cooling out" the students, of deflating perceived unrealistic academic or career goals and steering the students into settling for something more easily within reach (Clark, 1960; Dougherty, 1987; Zwerling, 1976).

True or not, attendance at a two-year institution has been shown to have a negative impact on the likelihood of eventually attaining a baccalaureate degree. Pascarella and Terenzini cite consistent research findings that students entering a four-year institution are substantially more likely than those at a two-year institution to persist in their education, obtain their baccalaureate, and/or to attend graduate school (Pascarella and Terenzini, 1991). They argue that the need to repeat the process of entering a new institution, requiring another socialization and orientation period; the availability of an "out," of stopping at the associate level; and the missing out on the residential part of the collegiate experience by living at home and going to the local community college may all contribute to a decreased probability of attaining the degree.

If one accepts this negative view of two-year colleges, the fact that most of the tribal colleges are such schools could lead to the conclusion that they are somehow developmentally stunted, following the long-held pattern in Native American education of vocational training over academics, and are something of a disservice to Native Americans. However, it is arguably more reasonable to take a balanced view of two-year and, within them, tribal colleges. They are not necessarily an unqualified answer to students in need of support in making the adjustment to higher education. Nor are they necessarily some sort of Marxist plot (Zwerling, 1976), designed to promise, yet deny, socioeconomic mobility to the masses.

More than anything else, the preponderance of two-year schools among the tribal colleges may reflect their newness. In the past, a common developmental pattern among colleges was for a school to be a normal school first, later to attain full college status. Today that same pattern exists with some schools starting as junior colleges before expanding to four-year, then graduate programs. Within the tribal colleges, the three that offer bachelor's degrees are among the oldest schools, particularly the two that offer master's degrees as well. It seems reasonable to expect this pattern to continue. As the tribal colleges progress through the coming years, one would expect more and more to expand to four-year, then graduate programs. At the present time, the characteristics of two-year schools that tend to benefit first generation students from less than ideally supportive circumstances should serve to make the tribal colleges all the more responsive to the needs of their growing student constituencies.

Future Implications

In light of the gains of recent years, a natural question arises at this point of what of the future of Native American higher education? Where does it go from here?

A recurrent proposal since the 1822 report of Jedidiah Morse (Unrau and Miner, 1985) is that of the establishment of a national Indian university, a large central school with four-year and probably graduate and/or professional programs. Some hints of such a concept exists in the earliest views of Bacone (Indian University) as a school for all the civilized tribes, and in the brief period of open enrollment for all Indians at Pembroke. Some consideration has been given in the recent past to developing Haskell or Bacone into such a centralized institution (Chavers, 1979). It was also the basic proposal offered by the "Indians of All Tribes" at the Alcatraz takeover to use the island for such a central Indian university (Moguin, 1973).

In 1982, a number of tribal college administrators indicated they were generally favorable to such a concept, but many believed it should be a senior level school (Oppelt, 1990). As such, it would not offer the first two years, but would take students from the tribal colleges on a feeder basis, similar to Harper's original concept at the University of Chicago (Rudolph, 1962; 1990).

Realistically, such a concept is probably too simplistic in failing to take the nature of the Native American community into account. With under one percent of the nation's population scattered over six hundred tribes, it is probably unrealistic to expect a single institution to be able to effectively serve such a diverse constituency.

Two likely problems seem evident. First, the Native American population is approximately two million strong. Nowhere else in our nation does the situation exist of one school, even a large central school at the top of a feeder system, serving such a large population base. By way of comparison, Oklahoma, with a population of approximately three million, has forty-four higher education institutions, twenty-seven of which are four-year schools (*Tulsa World*, 1996, November 11).

Second, in attempting to function as a cultural repository for the community it serves, such a central Indian university would be overwhelmed. The range and diversity of the cultures within Native America would preclude adequate representation of all but a few at such an institution. The current twenty-six tribal colleges, even allowing for some multitribe associations, represent well under a tenth of the existing tribes.

This does not mean we are going to end up with six hundred tribal colleges. Smaller tribes, their cultures and languages will continue to be absorbed, disappear, or at the least, be minimally maintained and represented. The cost of the white rush to take over the continent continues. The tribal colleges that do exist constitute a reasonable representation of Native American cultures and certainly are a welcome reversal of the long-standing attempt to eradicate the Native American contribution to the human experience. They no doubt will grow and strive to preserve Native American culture as they do so. But much has been lost and probably cannot be regained.

Vine Deloria, Jr., a noted Indian scholar, predicts (1991) that the tribal colleges will begin to attract the non-Indian. As a discipline, the study of Native American culture, including the opportunity to study with tribal elders and scholars, will grow to the point of attracting the interest of scholars without regard to their own ethnicity.

Deloria further sees the number of four-year and graduate colleges within the tribal colleges increasing, as the tribal colleges advance to become greater sources of scholarly output and publishing. Simultaneously, they are expected to assume more prominent roles in tribal economics and political activities. At that point in the development of Native American higher education, self-determination will become ubiquitous, taken for granted. Native American higher education will have assumed the natural role of education in Indian affairs.

Appendix A

Chronology of Important Events in the History of Native American Higher Education in the United States

1492	Discovery of New World by Columbus.
1495–1520	Debate in Europe on the nature of American Indians; hostile savage versus noble savage.
1536	Spanish colonists open Tlaltelolco, the most successful of several academies, in Santa Cruz (Mexico City) as a college for the Indians with 60 students.
1548	Tlaltelolco turned over to Indian alumni to administer (lasted until c. 1568).
1550–1551	Bartolome de Las Casas, Dominican friar, argues against the application of Aristotle's doctrine of natural slavery to Indians; argues in favor of the use of religion and education as the means to civilize them.
1568	The Jesuits establish a school in Havana for Florida Indians.
1616	Pocahontas party travels to England to raise funds for Indian education.
1617	King James I instructs the church to raise funds for the proposed Henrico College for Indians in Virginia.
1617–1622	Funds for Henrico College continue to come in, funds are consistently 'invested' in the Virginia Company.
1622	Indian uprising kills 347 colonists, Henrico College subsequently forgotten.
1636	Founding of Harvard.
1643	Harvard tract issued calling for funds for Indian education to be sent directly to President Dunster.
1645	John Eliot (founder of a system of towns of "praying Indians") sends two young Indian students to Harvard to be prepared for college.

1649   Founding in England of the President and Society for the Propagation of the Gospel Among the Indians in New England and Parts Adjacent; it would support missionary work.

1650   Harvard charter changed to include education of Indian youth as part of its purpose.

1653   First Harvard Indian college student, John Sarsamon (killed by own people, thought to be a spy against the upcoming King Phillip's War).

1656   Harvard builds Indian College building.

1665   Caleb Cheeshateaumuck (Cheeschaumuk?), first Indian to get degree from Harvard (died shortly thereafter).

1693   Founding of William and Mary College, charter gives purpose as for Indian education.

            Harvard Indian College building razed, had only four students with one graduate during its 37-year existence.

1700   Founding of the Society in Scotland for Propagation of Christian Knowledge (to support missionary work).

1701   Founding in England of the Society for Propagating the Gospel in Foreign Parts (to support missionary work).

1705–1721   Only years with evidence of Indian enrollment at William and Mary.

1714   Benjamin Larned, last colonial-era Indian student, at Harvard.

1723   Brafferton Building (to house Indian students) built at William and Mary.

1733   Start of the "Great Awakening," largest religious revival of the colonial period. Prompts many, including Eleazar Wheelock, to become interested in teaching and conversion of the Indians.

1743   First Indian student at William and Mary after the building of Brafferton (20 years later).

1744   Iroquois chiefs turn down offer during treaty negotiations to send their sons to William and Mary college.

1751   First Indian student at College of New Jersey (Princeton), died while in school.

1754   Wheelock founds Moor's Charity School for Indians (preparatory).

1756   Founding of Dartmouth, stated purpose for Indian education.

1759   Second Indian student at Princeton, expelled.

1765–67   Wheelock sends Rev. Whitaker and Samson Occum to England to raise funds—very successfully, raised over 12,000 pounds, most to date for Indian education.

1769   Founding of Dartmouth, charter stated for the education of "Indian youth, and also of English youth".

1769–1893   Dartmouth has total of 58 Indian students, 11 graduates.

1773   Third and last Indian student of the colonial period at Princeton, forced out by loss of support due to American Revolution.

1774   Scottish fund raised by Samson Occom is exhausted.

1775   Continental Congress appropriates $500 for support of Indians at Dartmouth.

1776   William and Mary Indian school closed, had total of 16 students.

c. 1776   Access to Boyle fund and any other English support for Native American higher education cut off by American Revolution.

1777   Daniel Simmons, first Indian graduate from Dartmouth.

1778   Reorganization of William and Mary by Thomas Jefferson; lists Brafferton but no mention of Indians.

Treaty with the Delaware, first of the treaty period.

1779   Continental Congress appropriates an additional $925 for support of Indians at Dartmouth.

1780   Peter Pohquonnoppect, second Indian graduate from Dartmouth in colonial and early U.S. period.

c. 1780   Washington and Jefferson come out in favor of vocational education instead of higher education as valuable for Indians.

1781   Lewis Vincent, third and last Indian graduate from Dartmouth in colonial and early U. S. Period.

1791   U. S. Government makes promise to Senecas for two government-supplied teachers of husbandry and agriculture.

1793   Oneida Academy chartered.

1794   Oneida Academy closes, lack of funds.

First treaty, with Oneida, Tuscarora, and Stockbridge Indians, with educational provision—for a grist mill and sawmill, and training in both.

1799   Oneida Academy reopens as Hamilton-Oneida Academy; 50 students, only one Indian.

1812   Hamilton-Oneida Academy chartered as Hamilton College, minimal Indian involvement.

1817   Foreign Mission School, Cornwall, Conn., opens; closes by 1827, peak of 36 students in 1823, yet students were leaders of distinction, particularly among the Cherokees, for many years.

1819   Indian Civilization Act; most important piece of legislation in the treaty period; provides $10,000 annually to support teaching of agriculture to Indians (the "civilization fund").

1820–1890   U.S. Indian policy split between gradualists and removalists (later roughly equivalent to the Peace versus War policies).

1825   Choctaw Academy in Tennessee established; has a very classical curriculum.

1830   Indian Removal Act.

Treaty of Dancing Rabbit Creek, authorizes $10,000 annually to support Choctaw students at Eastern colleges.

1831   *Cherokee Nation versus Georgia*; establishes tribes as sovereign but "dependent" nations.

1841   First use of funds provided by the Treaty of Dancing Rabbit Creek for education of Choctaw youth at eastern colleges.

1846   Choctaw Academy closes.

1851   Cherokees establish their male and female seminaries to provide basic and higher education.

1860   Roger Williams University is chartered (Ottawa, Kansas).

1862   Ottawa University (Kansas) is proposed.

1865   Roger Williams University rechartered as Ottawa University.

1867   Ottawa University opens, funded by the sale of lands granted to the school by the Ottawas, and land bought from them at one dollar an acre but sold for much more.

1867–1873   Ottawas removed to Indian Territory (Oklahoma).

1868   On meeting Tosawi, Comanche chief, General Phillip Sheridan remarks, "The only good Indians I ever saw were dead."

1869   President Grant names Ely Parker (Seneca) to be Commissioner of Indian Affairs (first Indian in the position).

1870   First Ghost Dance movement, from a vision by Wodziwob, mostly in California, Nevada, and Utah.

U. S. Authorizes $100,000 for industrial boarding schools.

1871   Close of treaty period; over 400 total, including 97 with educational provisions.

1878   Richard Pratt takes 17 Fort Marion Indian prisoners to Hampton Institute, Virginia for school.

Sheldon Jackson Institute, Sitka, Alaska; opens, all-Indian student body.

Fort Lewis boarding school, Durango, Colorado, opens.

1879   Pratt moves his industrial boarding school for Indians to Carlisle Barracks, Penn. (first free-standing off-reservation boarding school).

1880   Indian University (Bacone), Muskogee, Indian Territory, founded by Southern Baptist Association.

1882   Presbyterian School for Indian Girls established at Muskogee.

1884   Founding of Haskell Institute.

Founding of Croatan Normal School (North Carolina; exclusively for Croatan-Lumbee Indians)—first and only state-supported higher education institution for Indians.

1885   160-acre land grant to Indian University (Bacone) made by Creek Nation.

1887   Allotment Act.

Federal law forbids use of Indian languages in schools; only English allowed.

1890   Second, larger Ghost Dance movement, from a vision by Wovoka, covers most of western U. S.

1894   Presbyterian School for Indian Girls chartered as Henry Kendall College, enrollment open to all, not just Indians.

1900   Commissioner of Indian Affairs report; contrasting general versus higher education, lists 25 industrial boarding schools (7,430 students), 81 reservation day schools (9,600), 147 day schools (5,000), 22 public schools (500), 32 contract schools (2,800), and 22 missionary schools (1,275); no mention of Indians in college, or of colleges serving Indians.

Indian population at 237,000; all-time lowest.

Only Indian University (Bacone) and Croatan (Pembroke) serving Indians exclusively.

1906   Five Tribes Act; U. S. Government takes control of funds and governance of the five civilized tribes, causing closing of tribal schools as funds and/or gifts run out.

U. S. Government takes over Cherokee seminaries.

1907   Henry Kendall College moves to Tulsa.

1909   State of Oklahoma takes over Cherokee Seminaries, combines and changes them to Northeastern State Normal School (enrollment open to all).

1910	Indian University at Muskogee renamed Bacone College.
	Former Cherokee Female Seminary burns.
1911	Croatan Normal School changes to Indian Normal School of Robeson County.
	Fort Lewis boarding school changes to Fort Lewis State School of Agriculture; still offers typical curriculum of agricultural, mechanical, and household arts; Indian students tuition-free.
1913	Last Cherokee school closes.
1919	Northeastern State Normal School changes name to Northeastern State Teacher's College.
1920	Henry Kendall College merges with the proposed Robert McFarlin College to form the University of Tulsa.
1923	Snyder Act.
1924	Indian Citizenship Act.
1925	Meriam Report.
1928	Last Creek school closes.
1930	Last Seminole school closes.
1932	Last Choctaw and Chickasaw schools close.
1933	Fort Lewis school changes to Fort Lewis Junior College.
1934	Indian Reorganization Act (Wheeler-Howard Act); re-establishes tribal governments; establishes fund for student loans; BIA begins support of Indian education.
1939	Oklahoma's Northeastern State Teacher's College changes to Northeastern State College (to Northeastern Oklahoma State University in 1974, and to Northeastern State University in 1985).
1940	Indian Normal School of Robeson County changes to Pembroke State College for Indians.
1944	Sheldon Jackson Institute changes to Sheldon Jackson Junior College; enrollment open to all.
1945	Pembroke State College for Indians opens enrollment to all Indians (previously for Robeson County or Lumbee Indians only).
1949	Pembroke State College for Indians changes name to just Pembroke State College.
1953	Pembroke opens enrollment to all, white enrollment allowed to maximum of 40 percent.
1954	Pembroke drops restriction of white enrollment in voluntary response to desegregation ruling from *Brown versus. Board of Education*, Indian students quickly drop to a very small minority.

1960	Ottawas win $400,000+ for land fraud associated with the founding of Ottawa University.
1960s	Native Americans begin enrolling in college on a large scale for first time.
1962	Fort Lewis Junior College becomes Fort Lewis College; now about 12 percent Indian.
	Founding of Institute of American Indian Arts, New Mexico (federally controlled).
1968	Founding of Navajo Community College, Arizona; first tribally controlled college (TCC).
1969	During AIM occupation of Alcatraz Island, they call for it to be used for an Indian University.
1970	Founding of Sinte Gleska University, South Dakota (TCC).
	Haskell Indian Nations University, Kansas chartered from the U.S. Indian Industrial Training School; in operation since 1884 (federally controlled).
1971	Navajo Community College Act.
	Southwestern Indian Polytechnic Institute, Albuquerque, chartered as Community College (controlled by the BIA).
	Founding of D-Q University, Davis, California (TCC).
	Founding of Oglala Lakota College, South Dakota (TCC).
1972	AIM Movement confrontation with government at Wounded Knee, lists twenty points of demands, 20th is increased funding of variety of programs, including education.
	Indian Education Act.
	Founding of American Indian College, Phoenix (private).
	Founding of Turtle Mountain Community College, North Dakota (TCC).
1973	Founding of American Indian Higher Education Consortium.
	Lummi School of Aquaculture, Washington, opens; now closed.
1974	Founding of Cankleska Cikana Community College, North Dakota (TCC).
1975	Indian Self-Determination Act.
	Inupiat University of the Arctic, Barrow, Alaska, opens; now closed.
	Founding of Nazarene Indian Bible College, Albuquerque (private).
	Founding of Dull Knife Memorial College, Montana (TCC).
1977	College of Ganado, Arizona, opens; now closed.

Founding of Salish Kootenai College, Montana (TCC).

1978   Tribally Controlled Community College Act.

Higher Education Act.

Keeweenaw Bay Ojibway Community College, Michigan, opens; now closed.

Founding of Cheyenne River Community College, South Dakota (TCC).

Founding of Fort Peck Community College, Montana (TCC).

Founding of Nebraska Indian Community College (TCC).

1979   Founding of Blackfeet Community College, Montana (TCC).

1980   Founding of Little Big Horn College, Montana (TCC).

1981   Sheldon Jackson Junior College becomes Sheldon Jackson College; now only 18 percent Native American.

1982   Founding of Lac Courte Oreilles Ojibwa Community College, Wisconsin (TCC).

1983   Founding of Northwest Indian College, Washington (TCC).

1984   Founding of Stone Child Community College, Montana (TCC).

Founding of Bay Mills Community College, Michigan (TCC).

Founding of Fort Belknap College, Montana (TCC).

Founding of Sisseton Wahpeton Community College, South Dakota (TCC).

1986   Founding of Sitting Bull College, North Dakota (TCC).

1987   Founding of United Tribes Technical College, North Dakota (TCC).

Founding of Fond de Lac Tribal and Community College, Minnesota (TCC).

1988   Founding of Fort Berthold Community College, North Dakota (TCC).

1989   American Indian College Fund established; $3 million annual budget.

1990   Indian population at 1,959,000; roughly 0.8 percent of U.S.

1992   Founding of Leech Lake Tribal College, Minnesota (TCC).

1993   Founding of Crownpoint Institute of Technology, New Mexico (TCC).

Founding of the College of the Menominee Nation, Wisconsin (TCC).

1997   University of Arizona establishes first Ph. D. program in American Indian Studies.

Appendix B

Presidents, Secretaries of War/Interior, and Comissioners of Indian Affairs to 1980

President	Secretary of War	Commissioner
George Washington April 30, 1789	Henry Knox September 12, 1789	
	Timothy Pickering January 2, 1795	
	James McHenry February 6, 1796	
John Adams March 4, 1797	James McHenry (con't.)	
	Samuel Dexter June 12, 1800	
Thomas Jefferson March 4, 1801	Henry Dearborn March 5, 1801	
James Madison March 4, 1809	William Eustis April 8, 1809	
	John Armstrong February 5, 1813	
	James Monroe October 1, 1814	
	William Crawford August 8, 1815	
James Monroe March 4, 1817	John C. Calhoun December 10, 1817	Thomas L. McKenney[1] March 11, 1824
John Quincy Adams March 4, 1825	James Barbour March 7, 1825	Thomas L. McKenney (con't.)
	Peter Porter June 21, 1828	

Andrew Jackson March 4, 1829	John Eaton March 9, 1829	Thomas L. McKenney (con't.)
	Lewis Cass August 8, 1931	Samuel Hamilton[1] September 30, 1830
		Elbert Herring[1] August, 1831 July 10, 1832[2]
		Carey Harris July 4, 1836
Martin Van Buren March 4, 1837	Joel Poinsett March 14, 1837	Carey Harris (con't.)
		T. Harley Crawford October 22, 1838
William H. Harrison March 4, 1841	John Bell March 5, 1841	T. Harley Crawford (con't.)
John Tyler April 6, 1841	John Bell (con't.)	T. Harley Crawford (con't.)
	John Spencer October 12, 1841	
	James Porter March 8, 1843	
	William Wilkins February 20, 1844	
James K. Polk March 4, 1845	William Marcy March 8, 1845	T. Harley Crawford (con't.)
		William Medill October 28, 1845

Secretary of the Interior

Zachary Taylor March 4, 1849	Thomas Ewing March 8, 1849	William Medill (con't.)
		Orlando Brown June 30, 1849
		Luke Lea July 1, 1850
Millard Fillmore July 10, 1850	Thomas Ewing (con't.)	Luke Lea (con't.)
	Alexander H. H. Stuart September 16, 1850	

Franklin Pierce March 4, 1853	Robert McClelland March 7, 1853	George Manypenny March 24, 1853
James Buchanan March 4, 1857	Jacob Thompson March 10, 1857	George Manypenny (con't.) James Denver April 17, 1857 Charles Mix June 14, 1858 James Denver November 8, 1858 Alfred Greenwood May 4, 1859
Abraham Lincoln March 4, 1861	Caleb Smith March 5, 1861 John Usher January 1, 1863	William Dole March 13, 1861
Andrew Johnson April 15, 1865	John Usher (con't.) James Harlan May 15, 1865 Orville Browning September 1, 1866	William Dole (con't.) Dennis Cooley July 10, 1865 Lewis Bogy[3] November 1, 1866 Nathaniel Taylor March 29, 1867
Ulysses S. Grant March 4, 1869	Jacob Cox March 9, 1869 Columbus Delano November 1, 1870 Zachariah Chandler October 19, 1875	Nathaniel Taylor (con't.) Ely Parker April 21, 1869 Francis Walker November 21, 1871 Edward P. Smith March 20, 1873 John Q. Smith December 11, 1875
Rutherford B. Hayes March 4, 1877	Carl Schurz March 12, 1877	John Q. Smith (con't.) Ezra Hayt September 20, 1877 Roland Trowbridge March 15, 1880

James A. Garfield March 4, 1881	Samuel Kirkwood March 8, 1881	Hiram Price May 6, 1881
Chester A. Arthur September 20, 1881	Samuel Kirkwood (con't.) Henry Teller April 17, 1882	Hiram Price (con't.)
Grover Cleveland March 4, 1885	Lucius Lamar March 6, 1885 William Vilas January 16, 1888	Hiram Price (con't.) John Atkins March 21, 1885 John Oberly October 10, 1888
Benjamin Harrison March 4, 1889	John Noble March 7, 1889	John Oberly (con't.) Thomas Morgan June 30, 1889
Grover Cleveland March 4, 1893	Hoke Smith March 6, 1893 David Francis September 4, 1896	Daniel Browning April 18, 1893
William McKinley March 4, 1897	Cornelius Bliss March 5, 1897 Ethan Hitchcock February 20, 1899	Daniel Browning (con't.) William A. Jones May 3, 1897
Theodore Roosevelt September 4, 1901	Ethan Hitchcock (con't.) James R. Garfield March 4, 1907	William A. Jones (con't.) Francis E. Leupp January 1, 1905
William H. Taft March 4, 1909	Richard Ballinger March 5, 1909 Walter Lowrie Fisher March 7, 1911	Francis E. Leupp (con't.) Robert G. Valentine June 19, 1909
Woodrow Wilson March 4, 1913	Franklin Knight Lane March 5, 1913 John Barton Payne March 13, 1920	Cato Sells June 2, 1913

Warren G. Harding March 4, 1921	Albert B. Fall March 5, 1921 Hubert Work March 5, 1923	Cato Sells (con't.) Charles Burke May 7, 1921
Calvin Coolidge August 3, 1923	Hubert Work (con't.) Roy O. West January 21, 1929	Charles Burke (con't.)
Herbert Hoover March 4, 1929	Ray L. Wilbur March 5, 1929	Charles Rhoads April 18, 1929
Franklin D. Roosevelt March 4, 1933	Harold Ickes March 5, 1933	Charles Rhoads (con't.) John Collier April 21, 1933 William Brophy March 6, 1945
Harry S. Truman April 12, 1945	Harold Ickes (con't.) Julius A. Krug March 18, 1946 Oscar Chapman January 19, 1950	William Brophy (con't.) John R. Nichols April 13, 1949 Dillon Myer May 5, 1950
Dwight D. Eisenhower January 20, 1953	Douglas McKay January 21, 1953 Frederick Seaton June 8, 1956	Glenn Emmons August 10, 1953
John F. Kennedy January 20, 1961	Stewart Udall January 20, 1961	Philleo Nash September 26, 1961
Lyndon Johnson November 22, 1963	Stewart Udall (con't.)	Philleo Nash (con't.) Robert Bennett April 27, 1966
Richard Nixon January 20, 1969	Walter Hickel January 24, 1969 Rogers Morton January 29, 1971	Robert Bennett (con't.) Louis Bruce August 8, 1969 Morris Thompson December 3, 1973

Gerald Ford August 9, 1974	Rogers Morton (con't.)	Morris Thompson (con't.)
	Stanley Hathaway June 11, 1975	Benjamin Reifel December 7, 1976
	Thomas Kleppe October 9, 1975	
Jimmy Carter January 20, 1977	Cecil Andrus January 23, 1977	William Hallett December 14, 1979
	Forrest Gerard[4] October 13, 1977	

1. Head of Bureau of Indian Affairs
2. Appointed Commissioner of Indian Affairs
3. Not confirmed by the Senate
4. Assistant Secretary of the Interior for Indian Affairs
Source: Prucha, F. P. (1984). *The Great Father*, vol. 2, pp. 1211–1216. (Lincoln: University of Nebraska Press).

Appendix C

Current United States Tribal and Traditionally Native American College

Name, location, year founded or chartered	Degrees offered
Tribally Controlled Colleges	
Bay Mills Community College Brimley, Michigan 1984	Associate's
Blackfeet Community College Browning, Montana 1979	Associate's
Cankdeska Cikana (Little Hoop) Community College Fort Totten, North Dakota 1974	Associate's
Cheyenne River Community College Eagle Butte, South Dakota 1978	Associate's
College of the Menominee Nation Keshena, Wisconsin 1993	Associate's
Crownpoint Institute of Technology Crownpoint, New Mexico 1993	Associate's
D-Q University Davis, California 1971	Associate's
Dull Knife Memorial College Lame Deer, Montana 1975	Associate's

Fond du Lac Community College
Cloquet, Minnesota
1987   Associate's

Fort Belknap College
Harlem, Montana
1984   Associate's

Fort Berthold Community College
New Town, North Dakota
1988   Associate's

Fort Peck Community College
Poplar, Montana
1978   Associate's

Lac Courte Oreilles Ojibwa Community College
Hayward, Wisconsin
1982   Associate's

Leech Lake Tribal College
Cass Lake, Minnesota
1992   Associate's

Little Big Horn College
Crow Agency, Montana
1980   Associate's

Navajo Community College
Tsaile, Arizona
1968   Associate's

Nebraska Indian Community College
Winnebago, Nebraska
1978   Associate's

Northwest Indian College
Bellingham, Washington
1983   Associate's

Oglala Lakota College
Kyle, South Dakota   Associate's, Bachelor's,
1971   Master's

Salish Kootenai College
Pablo, Montana
1977   Associate's, Bachelor's

Sinte Gleska University
Rosebud, South Dakota   Associate's, Bachelor's,
1970   Master's

Sisseton Wahpeton Community College
Sisseton, South Dakota
1984   Associate's

Sitting Bull College
Fort Yates, North Dakota
1986   Associate's

Stone Child Community College
Box Elder, Montana
1984   Associate's

Turtle Mountain Community College
Belcourt, North Dakota
1972   Associate's

United Tribes Technical College
Bismarck, North Dakota
1987   Associate's

Federally Chartered Colleges

Haskell Indian Nations University
Lawrence, Kansas
1970   Associate's, Bachelor's

Institute of American Indian Arts
Santa Fe, New Mexico
1962   Associate's

Southwest Indian Polytechnic Institute
Albuquerque, New Mexico
1971   Associate's

Private Colleges

American Indian College
Phoenix, Arizona
1972   Associate's, Bachelor's

Bacone College
Muskogee, Oklahoma
1880   Associate's

Nazarene Indian Bible College
Albuquerque, New Mexico
1975   Associate's, Bachelor's

References

Acts and Resolutions of Creek National Council 1877–1882. Acts of the Creek Nation, no. 11, 189–190. Indian Archives Division, Oklahoma Historical Society, Oklahoma City.
Annual Report of the Commissioner of Indian Affairs. (1887). U. S. Department of the Interior.
Arizona State Department of Education. (1983). *American Indian Language Proficiency Assessment; Considerations and Resources*. Phoenix.
Belgrade, W. L. (June 1992). History of American Indian Community Colleges. In *American Indian Higher Education in Oklahoma*. Oklahoma City: Oklahoma Indian Affairs Commission.
Berry, B. (1969). *The Education of American Indians: A Survey of the Literature*. Special Subcommittee on Indian Education, Committee on Labor and Public Welfare, United States Senate, 91st Congress, First Session. Washington, D.C.: U. S. Government Printing Office.
Cohen, F. S. (1945). *Handbook of Federal Indian Law*. Washington, DC: Government Printing Office.
Commissioner of Indian Affairs, 73rd Annual Report. (October 17, 1904). *Annual Reports of the Secretary of the Interior, Commissioner of Indian Affairs, and Secretary of War Relating to Indian Affairs (1904)*. Indian Archives Division, Oklahoma Historical Society, Oklahoma City.
Constitution of the United States. ([1787] 1987). San Francisco, CA: Library of Congress/Arion Press.
Course of study for the Indian schools of the United States. (1901). Washington, DC: Government Printing Office.
Creek National Council. Minutes of the House of Warriors. (October 29, 1881). Indian Archives Division, Oklahoma Historical Society, Oklahoma City.
Equity in Educational Land Grant Status Act of 1993. November 18, 1993. Hearings on S. 1345, Commissioner of Indian Affairs, United States Senate, 103rd Congress, First Session. Congress of the United States, Senate Committee on Indian Affairs. Washington, DC
Fries, J. E. (1987). *The American Indian in Higher Education, 1975–6 to 1984–5*. Center for Educational Statistics, Office of Educational Research and Improvement, U. S. Department of Education. Washington, DC: U. S. Government Printing Office.
Hill, S. T. (1985). *The Traditionally Black Institutions of Higher Education 1860 to 1982*. National Center for Education Statistics. Washington, DC: U. S. Government Printing Office.
Houser, S. (1991). Underfunded Miracles: Tribal Colleges. In *Indian Nations At Risk*

Task Force Commissioned Papers. Indian Nations At Risk Task Force, U. S. Department of Education, Washington, DC.

Morgan, T. J. (1887). Supplemental Report on Indian Education. In Prucha, F. P. (ed.), *Americanizing the American Indian (Writings by the "Friends of the Indian" 1880–1900).*

Rainy Mountain School Files, vol. 1. Indian Archives Division, Oklahoma Historical Society, Oklahoma City.

Report of the Board of Indian Commissioners. (1877). *Report of the Secretary of the Interior.* House Executive Document no. 1.

Tentative Course of Study for United States Indian School. (1915). Washington, DC: U. S. Government Printing Office.

The Problem of Indian Administration (Summary of findings and recommendations). (1928). Washington, DC: Institute for Government Research.

Thompson, T. (ed.). (1978). *The Schooling of Native America.* Washington, DC: American Association of Colleges for Teacher Education/The Teacher Corps, U. S. Office of Education.

Treaty of Dancing Rabbit Creek. (1830). Reprinted as Appendix B in DeRosier, A. H., Jr. (1970). *The Removal of the Choctaw Indians.* Knoxville: University of Tennessee Press.

U. S. Commission on Civil Rights. (1973). *Constitutional Status of American Indians.* Staff Memorandum, Washington, DC

U. S. Department of Commerce. (June 1991). *1990 Census Profile.* Bureau of the Census. Washington, DC

U. S. Department of Commerce, Bureau of the Census. (November 18, 1992). Cherokee, Navajo, Chippewa, Sioux Top Census Bureau's '90 Tribe List. *U. S. Department of Commerce News.* Washington, DC.

U. S. Senate Select Committee on Indian Affairs. (March 14, 28, 1978). *Indian Self-Determination and Education Assistance Act.* Hearings on S. 2460, Congress of the United States, Washington, DC.

Use of English in Indian Schools. (September 21, 1887). House Executive Document no. 1, 50th Congress, First Session.

White House Conference on Indian Education. (January 24, 1992). Summary of resolutions. Washington, DC.

Wright, B. (1991). American Indian and Alaska Native Higher Education—Toward a New Century of Academic Achievement and Cultural Integrity. In *Indian Nations at Risk: Solutions for the 1990s Commissioned Papers.* Washington, DC: Indian Nations at Risk Task Force, Department of Education.

Court Decisions

Cherokee Nation versus Georgia. U. S. Reports, 5 Peters, p. 16. (1831).
Worcester versus Georgia. U. S. Reports, 6 Peters, p. 559. (1832).

Newspapers

A guide to Oklahoma's colleges and universities. (November 11, 1996). *Tulsa World,* p. A15.

Almanac Issue. (September 2, 1996). *Chronicle of Higher Education,* 43 (1).

Chilocco's burning fire was "light of prairie." (June 15, 1997). *Tulsa World,* p. A25.

Commemorate end of Cherokee Nation. (June 30, 1914). *Tulsa World,* p. 1.

Ellinger, K. (January 25,1997). History cooks the books on Indian tribes. *Oklahoma Observer,* pp. 14, 19.

Espinosa, R. (January 5, 1997). Suit axed tribal sovereign power. *Tulsa World*, p. A3.

Fink, J. (June 29, 1997). Indian tribes meeting success head-on. *Tulsa World*, p. A1.

Foster, D. (January 27, 1997). Tribes redefining themselves. *Tulsa World*, pp. A1, A3.

Humphrey, K. (April 7, 1997). Tribal colleges training leaders. *Indian Country Today*, p. 1.

Nicklin, J. L. (September 8, 1995). New Leadership. *Chronicle of Higher Education*, p. A53–A54.

Report urges significant increase in federal support of tribal colleges. (May 30, 1997). *Chronicle of Higher Education*, p. A40.

Roach, J. (April 7, 1997). AIHEC celebrates 25th anniversary in Rapid City. *Indian Country Today*, p. 1.

University of Arizona creates the first Ph. D. program in American Indian studies, (December 20, 1996). *Chronicle of Higher Education*.

Will, G. F. (February 23, 1997). The grinding of axes. *Tulsa World*, p. G6.

Organizational Reports

Carnegie Council on Policy Studies in Higher Education. (1975). *Making Affirmative Action Work in Higher Education*. San Francisco, CA: Jossey-Bass Publishers.

Carnegie Foundation for the Advancement of Teaching. (1997). *Native American colleges: Programs and prospects*. San Francisco, CA: Jossey-Bass Publishers.

Historical review of federal Indian policy. (1992). Fairfax, VA: The Falmouth Institute.

Lake Mohonk Conference. *Proceedings of the 6th Annual Meeting of the Lake Mohonk Conference of Friends of the Indian*. (1888). Powers, L. D., Secretary. Lake Mohonk, NY: The Lake Mohonk Conference.

Lake Mohonk Conference. *Proceedings of the 7th Annual Meeting of the Lake Mohonk Conference of Friends of the Indian*. (1889). Powers, L. D., Secretary. Lake Mohonk, NY: The Lake Mohonk Conference.

McIntosh, B. J. (1987). *Special needs of American Indian college students*. Mesa, AZ: Mesa Community College, office of research and development.

Planning grant proposal to develop an all-Indian university and cultural complex on Indian land, Alcatraz. Tribes of all nations. (1973). In Moguin, W. (ed.), *Great documents in American Indian history*, (pp. 374–379). New York: Praeger Publishers.

Wheelock, E. (1775). *A continuation of the narrative of the Indian Charity school, begun in Lebanon, in Connecticut, now incorporated with Dartmouth College, in Hanover, in the province of New Hampshire. With a dedication to the honorable Trust in London. To which is added an account of missions the last year, in an abstract from the journal of the Reverend Mr. Frisbie, missionary by Eleazar Wheelock*. Hartford, CT: E. Watson.

Wheelock, E. (1765). *A continuation of the narrative of the state, etc., of the Indian Charity school, at Lebanon, in Connecticut, from November 27, 1762, to September 3, 1765, by Eleazar Wheelock, A. M.* Boston: Richard and Samuel Draper.

College Catalogs

American Indian College catalog 1996–1998. (1996). Phoenix, AZ: American Indian College.

Bacone College 1995–1997 catalog. (1995). Muskogee, OK: Bacone College.

Bay Mills Community College 1995–1997 catalog. (1995). Brimley, MI: Bay Mills Community College.

Blackfeet Community College 1996–1998 catalog. (1996). Blackfeet Indian Reservation, MT: Blackfeet Community College.

Cankdeska Cikana Community College 1996–1997 catalog. (1996). Fort Totten (Spirit Lake Sioux Indian Reservation), ND: Cankdeska Cikana Community College.

College of the Menominee Nation Catalog 1996–1997. (1996). Kehena, WI: College of the Menominee Nation.

Crownpoint Institute of Technology catalog 1995–1997. (1995). Crownpoint, NM: Crownpoint Institute of Technology.

Student information. (1997). Davis, CA: D. Q. University.

Dull Knife Memorial College 1996–1997 catalog. (1996). Lame Deer (Northern Cheyenne Indian Reservation), MT: Dull Knife Memorial College.

First annual catalogue of the officers and teachers of the Indian University 1880–1881. (1881). New Bedford, MA: Knight and Howland Printers.

Fond du Lac Tribal and Community College 1995–1997 catalog. (1995). Cloquet, MN: Fond du Lac Tribal and Community College.

Fort Belknap College 1996–1997 catalog. (1996). Harlem (Fort Belknap Indian Reservation), MT: Fort Belknap College.

Fort Peck Community College course schedule 1995–1997. (1995). Popular (Fort Peck Indian Reservation), MT: Fort Peck Community College.

Haskell Indian Nations University catalog 1996–1998. (1996). Lawrence, KS: Haskell Indian Nations University.

Institute of American Indian Arts 1995–1997 catalog. (1995). Santa Fe, NM: Institute of American Indian Arts.

Leech Lake Tribal College catalog of course and degree requirements 1995–1997. (1995). Cass Lake, MN: Leech Lake Tribal College.

Little Big Horn College catalog 1997–1999. (1997). Crow Agency, MT: Little Big Horn College.

Nazarene Indian Bible College 1995–1997 catalog. (1995). Albuquerque, NM: Nazarene Indian Bible College.

Northeastern State University 1997 catalog. (1997). Tahlequah, OK: Northeastern State University.

Northwest Indian College 1996–1998 catalog. (1996). Bellingham, WA: Northwest Indian College.

Oglala Lakota College 1996–1997 catalog. (1996). Kyle (Pine Ridge Indian Reservation), SD: Oglala Lakota College.

Ottawa University academic catalog 1995–1997. (1995). Ottawa, KS: Ottawa University.

Salish Kootenai College 1997–1999 catalog. (1997). Pablo, MT: Salish Kootenai College.

Sinte Gleska University 1995–1997 catalog. (1995). Rosebud (Rosebud Sioux Reservation), SD: Sinte Gleska University.

Southwestern Indian Polytechnic Institute catalog 1996–1997. (1996). Albuquerque, NM: Southwestern Indian Polytechnic Institute.

Stone Child College general catalog 1996–1998. (1996). Box Elder (Rocky Boy Reservation, Rocky Boy Agency), MT: Stone Child College.

The University of North Carolina at Pembroke 1997–1999 catalog. (1997). Pembroke, NC: The University of North Carolina at Pembroke.

Turtle Mountain Community College 1996–1997 catalog. (1996). Belcourt, ND: Turtle Mountain Community College.

United Tribes Technical College general catalog 1996–1997. (1996). Bismarck, SD: United Tribes Technical College.

University of Tulsa 1994–1996 undergraduate bulletin. (1994). Tulsa, OK: University of Tulsa.

University of Tulsa 1994–1996 graduate/law school bulletin. (1994). Tulsa, OK: University of Tulsa.

Miscellaneous Documents

Dunn, O., and Kelley, J. E., Jr., (eds. and trans.). (1989). *The diario of Christopher Columbus's first voyage of America 1492–1493*. (Abstracted by Fray Bartolome´ de las Casas). Norman: University of Oklahoma Press.

Franklin, B. ([1744] 1938). Proceedings, treaty conference between Pennsylvania, Virginia, and Maryland with Indians of the Six Nations, Lancaster, Penn. Courthouse, July 4, 1744. In Van Doren (ed.), *Indian treaties printed by Benjamin Franklin 1736–1762*. Philadelphia: Historical Society of Pennsylvania.

Fuson, R. H. (ed. and trans.). (1987). *The log of Christopher Columbus*. Camden, ME: International Marine Publishing Company.

Jefferson, T. (1904). (Lipscomb, A. A., ed.). *The writings of Thomas Jefferson*, 20 volumes, vol. 10, correspondence; vol. 11, Notes on the State of Virginia. Washington, DC: The Thomas Jefferson Memorial Association.

Ross, W. D. (ed.). ([1928] 1955). *The works of Aristotle* (vol. 7, Ethica Nicomachea, book VIII, [12], 1116a35–b5; book X [6], 117a7–8). London: Oxford University Press.

De Victoria, Francisco. ([1696] 1917). The first relectio on the Indians lately discovered. (Bate, J. B., Trans.). In Nys, E. (ed.), *De Indis et de Ivre Belli Relectiones*; In Scott, J. B., (ed.), *The classics of international law*. Washington, DC: Carnegie Institute.

Wheelock, E. ([1811] 1972). *Memoirs of the Reverend Eleazar Wheelock, D. D.* (McClure, D., and Parish, E., eds.). New York: Arno Press.

Wheelock, E. 1728–1779. *The papers of Eleazar Wheelock*. Hanover, NH: Dartmouth College Library.

Secondary Sources

Articles

Ackley, R. (Summer 1972). Discussion: Pembroke State University. *The Indian Historian, 5* (2), 43–45.

Adams, D. W. (February 1988). Fundamental considerations: The deep meaning of Native American schooling, 1880–1900. *Harvard Educational Review, 58* (1), 1–25.

Beck, D. R. M. (1995). American Indian higher education before 1974: From colonization to self-determination. In *Critical issues in American Indian higher education*. Chicago: NAES College.

Bennett, S. K. (1990). The American Indian: A psychological overview. In W. J. Lonner and R. Malpass (eds.), *Psychology and culture*, 35–39. Boston: Allyn and Bacon.

Clark, B. (1960). The "cooling-out" function in higher education. *American Journal of Sociology, 65*, 569–576.

Crazy Bull, C. (July-August 1994). Who shall pass judgment? *Academe, 80* (4), 20–25.

Deloria, P. J. (1993). The twentieth century and beyond. In B. Ballantine and I. Ballantine (eds.), *The Native American*. Atlanta, GA: Turner Publishing Company.

Deloria, V., Jr. (Winter 1991). Higher education and self determination. *Winds of Change, 6* (1), 18–25.

Dial, A, and Elisades, D. K. (Winter 1971). The Lumbee Indians of North Carolina and Pembroke State University. *The Indian Historian, 4* (4), 20–24.

Dougherty, K. (1987). The effects of community colleges: Aid or hinderance to socioeconomic attainment? *Sociology of Education, 60*, 86–103.

Duchene, M. (August 1988). Giant law, giant education, and ant: A story about racism and Native Americans. *Harvard Educational Review, 58* (3), 354–362.

Foreman, C. T. (December 1928). The Choctaw Academy. *Chronicles of Oklahoma, 6* (4). Oklahoma City: Oklahoma Historical Society.

Gaillard, F. (Fall 1971). Desegregation denies justice to Lumbee Indians. *The Indian Historian, 4* (3), 17–22.

Greer, S. (Spring 1993). The noble savage. *Winds of Change, 8* (2), 89–92.

Gustafson, C., and Knowlton, L. (Autumn 1993). Exchanging education and culture. *Winds of Change, 8* (4), 180–185.

Hanke, L. (1969). Indians and Spaniards in the New World: A personal view. In H. Peckham and C. Gibson (eds.), *Attitudes of colonial powers toward the American Indian*. Salt Lake City: University of Utah Press.

Havighurst, R. J. (January 1981). Indian education: Accomplishments of the last decade. *Phi Delta Kappan, 62*, 329–331.

Hirschkind, L. (March-April 1983). The native American as noble savage. *Humanist, 43* (2), 16–18, 38.

Jacobs, W. R. (1969). British-colonial attitudes and policies toward the Indian in the American colonies. In H. Peckham and C. Gibson (eds.), *Attitudes of colonial powers toward the American Indian*. Salt Lake City: University of Utah Press.

Key, S. (March-April 1996). Economics or education: The establishment of American land-grant universities. *Journal of Higher Education, 67* (2), 196–220.

Kirkness, V. J., and Barnhardt, R. (May 1991). First nations and higher education: The 4 R's—respect, relevance, reciprocity, responsibility. *Journal of American Indian Education, 30* (3), 1–15.

La Counte, D. W. (Summer 1987). American Indian students in college. In D. J. Wright (ed.), Responding to the needs of today's minority students, *New directions for student services, 38*, 65–79. San Francisco: Jossey-Bass.

McNickle, D. (Summer 1970). American Indians who never were. *The Indian Historian, 3* (3), 4–9.

Morgan, T. J. (December 1902). Indian education. *Journal of Social Science, 40*, 165–176.

Myers, S. L., Sr. (1989). "Black colleges: From prohibition, encouragement, and segregation to desegregation, enhancement, and integration." In S. L. Myers, Sr. (ed.), *Desegregation in Higher Education*. New York: University Press of America.

Nabokov, P. (1993). Long threads. In B. Ballantine and I. Ballantine (eds.), *The Native American*. Atlanta, GA: Turner Publishing Company.

Otis, M. (Fall 1971). Indian education: A cultural dilemma. *The Indian Historian, 4* (3), 23–26.

Potts, D. B. (February 1977). "College enthusiasm" as public response, 1800–1860. *Harvard Educational Review, 47* (1), 28–42.

Snyder, W. H. (1930). The real function of the junior college. *The Junior College Journal, 1* (2), 76–81.

Stein, W. J. (Summer 1990). Founding of the American Indian Higher Education Consortium. *Tribal College. Journal of American Indian Higher Education, 2* (1), 18–22.

Sugden, J. (Fall 1986). Early pan-Indianism: Tecumseh's tour of the Indian country, 1811–1812. *American Indian Quarterly, 10* (4), 273–304.

Szasz, M. C., and Ryan, C. (1988). American Indian education. In W. E. Washburn (ed.), *Handbook of North American Indians. Volume IV, History of Indian-white relations*. Washington, DC: Smithsonian Institute.

Thompson, G. E. (1990). Access versus success: The Native American Indian community college student. *Community/Junior College Quarterly, 14*, 239–250.

Wenglinsky, H. H. (1996). The educational justification of historically Black colleges and universities: A policy response to the U. S. Supreme Court." *Educational Evaluation and Policy Analysis, 18* (1), 91–103.

Wescott, S. M. (March-April 1991). Educate to Americanize. *Change, 23* (2), 47–48.

Wright, B. (1988). "For the children of the infidels?": American Indian education in the colonial colleges. *American Indian Culture and Research Journal, 12* (3), 1–14.

Wright, B. (1989). Tribally controlled community colleges: An assessment of student satisfaction. *Community/Junior College Quarterly, 13*, 119–128.

Wright, B., and Tierney, W. G. (March-April 1991). American Indians in higher education: A history of cultural conflict. *Change, 23* (2), 11–18.

Books

Adams, D. W. (1995). *Education for extinction: American Indians and the boarding school experience 1875–1928*. Lawrence: University of Kansas Press.

Astin, A. W. (1982). *Minorities in American higher education*. San Francisco, CA: Jossey-Bass.

Axtell, J. (1981). *The Europeans and the Indians*. New York: Oxford University Press.

Birnbaum, R. (1983). *Maintaining diversity in higher education*. San Francisco, CA: Jossey-Bass Publishers.

Brown, A. ([1898] 1969). *The first republic in America*. New York: Russell and Russell.

Brown, D. (1970). *Bury my heart at Wounded Knee*. New York: Holt, Rinehart, and Winston.

Burnette, R. (1971). *The tortured Americans*. Englewood Cliffs, NJ: Prentice-Hall.

Butler, A. L. J. (1977). *The distinctive black college: Talladega, Tuskegee, and Morehouse*. Metuchan, NJ: Scare Crow Press.

Byrd, W. ([1728] 1967). *Histories of the dividing line betwixt Virginia and North Carolina*. New York: Dover Publications.

Chase, F. (1891). *A history of Dartmouth College and the town of Hanover*. Cambridge, MA: John Wilson and Sons.

Churchill, W. (ed.). (1983). *Marxism and Native Americans*. Boston: South End Press.

Clark, B. R. ([1970] 1992). *The distinctive college*. New Brunswick, NJ: Transaction Publishers.

Colden, C. ([1727] 1958). *The history of the five Indian nations depending on the Province of New York in America*. Ithaca, NY: Great Seal Books.

Debo, A. ([1940] 1968). *And still the waters run: The betrayal of the five civilized tribes*. Princeton, NJ: Princeton University Press.

Debo, A. ([1934] 1961). *The rise and fall of the Choctaw republic*: Norman: University of Oklahoma Press.

DeJong, D. H. (1993). *Promises of the past: A history of Indian education in the United States*. Golden, CO: Native American Press.

Deloria, V., Jr., and Lytle, C. M. (1984). *The nations within. The past and future of American Indian sovereignty*. New York: Pantheon Books.

DeRosier, A. H., Jr. (1970). *The removal of the Choctaw Indians*. Knoxville: University of Tennessee Press.

Dickason, O. P. (1984). *The myth of the savage (and the beginnings of French colonization in the Americas*. Edmonton: The University of Alberta Press.

Dippie, B. W. (1982). *The vanishing American. White attitudes and U.S. Indian Policy*. Middletown, CT: Wesleyan University Press.

Dor-Ner, Z., and Scheller, W. G. (1991). *Columbus and the Age of Discovery*. New York: William Morrow and Company.

Dougherty, K. J. (1994). *The contradictory college.* Albany: State University of New York Press.

Drake, S. G. (1832). *Biographies and histories of the Indians of North America.* Boston: Perkins and Hillard, Gray and Company.

Ellis, C. (1996). *To change them forever (Indian education at the Rainy Mountain boarding school, 1893–1920).* Norman: University of Oklahoma Press.

Fischer, L. H. (ed.). (1974). *The Civil War era in Indian Territory.* Los Angeles: Lorrin L. Morrison.

Fixico, D. L. (1986). *Termination and relocation: Federal Indian policy 1945–1960.* Albuquerque: University of New Mexico Press.

Grotius, Hugo. (1901). (A. C. Campbell, trans.). *The rights of war and peace—including the law of nature and of nations.* London: M. Walter Dunne, Publisher.

Hanke, L. (1959). *Aristotle and the American Indians: A study in race prejudice in the modern world.* London: Hollis and Carter.

Haring, C. H. (1947). *The Spanish empire in America.* New York: Oxford University Press.

Hertzberg, H. W. (1971). *The search for an American Indian identity: Modern pan-Indian movements.* New York: Syracuse University Press.

Hoxie, F. E. ([1984] 1992). *A final promise: The campaign to assimilate the Indians, 1880–1920.* Cambridge: Cambridge University Press.

Jackson, C. E., and Galli, M. J. (1977). *A history of the Bureau of Indian Affairs and its activities among Indians.* San Francisco, CA: R. And E. Research Associates.

Johnson, C. S. (1938). *The Negro college graduate.* Chapel Hill: University of North Carolina Press.

Kerr, C. ([1963] 1995). *The uses of the university,* 4th ed. Cambridge, MA: Harvard University Press.

Langer, H. J. (ed.). (1996). *American Indian quotations.* Westport, CT: Greenwood Press.

Leap, T. L., and Crino, M. D. (1993). *Personnel/human resource management.* New York: Macmillan Publishing Company.

Leupp, F. E. (1910). *The Indian and his problem.* New York: Charles Scribner's Sons.

Lord, J. K. (1913). *A history of Dartmouth College 1815–1909.* Concord, NH: The Rumford Press.

Love, W. D. (1899). *Samson Occum and the Christian Indians of New England.* Boston: Pilgrim Press.

Mardock, R. W. (1971). *The reformers and the American Indian.* Columbia, MO: University of Missouri Press.

McCallum, J. D. (1969). *Eleazar Wheelock.* New York: Arno Press and The New York Times.

McDonnell, J. A. (1991). *The dispossession of the American Indian 1887–1934.* Bloomington: Indiana University Press.

Morison, S. E. (1936). *Harvard in the 17th Century.* Cambridge, MA: Harvard University Press.

Morison, S. E. (1935). *The founding of Harvard College.* Cambridge, MA: Harvard University Press.

O'Brien, S. (1989). *American Indian tribal governments.* Norman: University of Oklahoma Press.

Olivas, M. A. (1979). *Dilemma of access: Minorities in two-year colleges.* Washington, DC: Howard University Press.

Oppelt, N. T. (1990). *The tribally controlled Indian college: The beginnings of self determination in American Indian education.* Tsaile, AZ: Navajo Community College Press.

Parkes, H. B. (1938). *A history of Mexico*. Boston: Houghton Mifflin Company.

Pascarella, E. T., and Terenzini, P. T. (1991). *How college affects students*. San Francisco, CA: Jossey-Bass.

Pratt, R. H. ([1923] 1964). (R. M. Utley, ed.). *Battlefield and classroom*. New Haven, CT: Yale University Press.

Prucha, F. P. (1973). *Americanizing the American Indian*. Cambridge, MA: Harvard University Press.

Prucha, F. P. (1984). *The great father: The United States government and the American Indian*, 2 volumes. Lincoln: University of Nebraska Press.

Richardson, R. C., Jr., and Skinner, E. F. (1991). *Achieving quality and diversity*. New York: American Council on Education and Macmillan Publishing Company.

Rudolph, F. (1977). *Curriculum: A history of the American undergraduate course of study since 1636*. San Francisco, CA: Jossey-Bass.

Rudolph, F. ([1962] 1990). *The American college and university: A history*. Athens: University of Georgia Press.

Schraff, A. (1979). *Tecumseh: The story of an American Indian*. Minneapolis, MN: Dillon Press.

Stein, W. J. (1992). *Tribally controlled colleges: Making good medicine*. New York: Peter Lang.

Szasz, M. C. (1994). *Between Indian and white worlds. The cultural broker*. Norman: University of Oklahoma Press.

Szasz, M. C. (1974). *Education and the American Indian*. Albuquerque: University of New Mexico Press.

Szasz, M. C. (1988). *Indian education in the American colonies 1607–1783*. Albuquerque: University of New Mexico Press.

Thornbrough, E. L. (ed.). (1969). *Booker T. Washington*. Englewood Cliffs, NJ: Prentice-Hall.

Thornton, R. (1987). *American Indian holocaust and survival: A population history since 1492*. Norman: University of Oklahoma Press.

Tierney, W. G. (1992). *Official encouragement, institutional discouragement: Minorities in Academe—the Native American experience*. Norwood, NJ: Ablex Publishing Company.

Trennert, R. A., Jr. (1988). *The Phoenix Indian School: Forced assimilation in Arizona 1891–1935*. Norman: University of Oklahoma Press.

Unrau, W. E., and Miner, H. C. (1985). *Tribal dispossession and the Ottawa Indian University Fraud*. Norman: University of Oklahoma Press.

VanderWaerdt, L. (1982). *Affirmative action and higher education: A sourcebook*. New York: Garland Publishing.

Washington, B. T. (1937). *Up from slavery: An autobiography*. New York: Dodd, Mead, and Company.

Weeks, P. (1990). *Farewell, my nation: The American Indian and the United States, 1820–1890*. Arlington Heights, IL: Harlan Davidson.

Weinberg, M. (1977). *A chance to learn: The history of race and education in the United States*. London: Cambridge University Press.

White, R. H. (1990). *Tribal assets: The rebirth of Native America*. New York: Henry Holt and Company.

Williams, J. L., and Meredith, H. L. (1980). *Bacone Indian University: A history*. Oklahoma City: Oklahoma Heritage Association, Western Heritage Books.

Wolters, R. (1975). *The new Negro on campus*. Princeton, NJ: Princeton University Press.

Zwerling, S. L. (1976). *Second best: The crisis of the community college*. New York: McGraw-Hill.

Dissertations/Theses

Badwound, E. (1990). *Leadership and American Indian values: The tribal college dilemma.* (Doctoral dissertation, Pennsylvania State University, State College, PA, 1990). *Dissertation Abstracts International,* A 51/09.

Bode, C. (1957). *The origin and development of Bacone College.* Unpublished master's thesis, University of Tulsa, OK.

Horse, P. G. (1982). *Tribal cultural educational concepts in American Indian community college curricula.* (Doctoral dissertation, University of Arizona, Tucson, 1982). *Dissertation Abstracts International,* A 48/06 (University Microfilms no. 8217422).

Layman, M. E. (1942). *A history of Indian education in the United States.* Unpublished doctoral dissertation, University of Minnesota, Minneapolis.

Pease-Windy Boy, J. (1994). The Tribally Controlled Community College Act of 1978—An expansion of federal Indian trust responsibility. (Doctoral dissertation, Montana State University, Billings, 1994). *Dissertation Abstracts International,* A 55/06.

Ramirez-Shkwegnaabi, B. (1987). *Roles of tribally controlled community college trustees: A comparison of trustees' and presidents' perceptions of trustee roles.* (Doctoral dissertation, University of Wisconsin, Madison, 1987). *Dissertation Abstracts International,* A49/03.

Rosh, D. S. (1986). *The Navajo way: Acculturation and Native American higher education.* (Doctoral dissertation, University of Pittsburgh, PA, 1986). *Dissertation Abstracts International,* A 47/10.

Smith, M. H. (1950). *Higher education for the Indians in the American colonies.* Unpublished master's thesis, New York University.

Papers

Buffalohead, W. R. (1970). Native American studies programs. In *Indian Voices: The First Convocation of American Indian Scholars.* San Francisco, CA: The Indian Historian Press.

Chavers, D. (1979). *The feasibility of an Indian university at Bacone College: A report to the board of trustees, Bacone College, September 25, 1979.* Muskogee, OK: Bacone College. (From *ERIC,* 1966–1981, Abstract No. ED196470).

Deloria, V., Jr. (1970). Implications of the 1968 Civil Rights Act in tribal autonomy. In *Indian Voices: The First Convocation of American Indian Scholars.* San Francisco, CA: The Indian Historian Press.

Deyhle, D., and Swisher, K. (1997). Research in American Indian and Alaska native education: From assimilation to self determination. In M. W. Apple (ed.), *Review of Research in Education, 22.* Washington, DC: American Educational Research Association.

Guyette, S., and Heth, C. (1983). *American Indian higher education: Need and projections.* Presented at annual meeting, American Educational Research Association, Montreal, April 11–15, 1983.

Henry, J. (1970). The American Indian in American History. In *Indian Voices: The First Convocation of American Indian Scholars.* San Francisco, CA: The Indian Historian Press.

Jojola, T. S., and Agoyo, H. (1992). One generation of self determination: Native American economic self-reliance in New Mexico. *Proceedings, National Rural Studies Commission Meeting.* Las Vegas, NM, May 14–16, 1992. (From *ERIC,* 1992–1996, Abstract No. ED354130).

Pavel, D. M., and Colby, A. Y. (September 1992). American Indians in higher education. The community college experience. *ERIC Digest*. Los Angeles: ERIC Clearinghouse for Junior Colleges, U. S. Department of Education.

Raymond, J. H. III. (1986). American Indian education and the reservation community college. *University of Florida Graduate Seminar Opinion Papers*. Gainesville: University of Florida. (From ERIC, 1982–1991, Abstract no. ED276489).

Robbins, W. (1974). *The educational needs of Native American Indians*. In W. Beggs (ed.), The educational needs of minority groups, 81–104. Lincoln, NE: Professional Educators Publications.

Tippeconnic, J. W. III. (1988). *Attitudes toward the education of American Indians*. Center for Indian Education, Arizona State University, Tempe.

Tribal colleges. Shaping the future of Native America. (1989). Special report, the Carnegie Foundation for the Advancement of Teaching. Princeton, NJ: Princeton University Press.

Warner, L. S., and Hastings, J. D. (1991). American Indian education: Culture and diversity in the 21st century. *Proceedings, "Culture and diversity: Teaching, learning, and the curriculum for the 21st century" Conference*, Phoenix, AZ, April 7–9, 1991.

Dictionaries, Directories

Dictionary of Indian tribes of the Americas, 2. (1980). Newport Beach, CA: American Indian Publishers.

Straughn, C. T. II, and Straughn, B. L. (eds.). *Lovejoy's College Guide, 23rd ed*. (1995). New York: Macmillan.

Minority student enrollments in higher education: A guide to institutions with highest percents of Asian, Black, Hispanic, and Native American students. (1987). Garrett Park, MD: Garrett Park Press.

Post-secondary institutions and related organizations. (1993). *Native Education Directory (Organizations and resources for educators of Native Peoples of the United States and Territories)*, 57–66. Charleston, WV: ERIC Clearinghouse on Rural Education and Small Schools.

Stoutenburgh, J. L., Jr. (1960). *Dictionary of the American Indian*. New York: Philosophical Library.

Index